NEW STUDIES IN BIBLICAL THEOLOGY 14

From every people and nation

Titles in this series:

NEW STUDIES IN BIBLICAL THEOLOGY 14

Series editor: D. A. Carson

From every people and nation

A BIBLICAL THEOLOGY OF RACE

J. Daniel Hays

APOLLOS

INTERVARSITY PRESS
DOWNERS GROVE, ILLINOIS 60515

APOLLOS (an imprint of Inter-Varsity Press),
38 De Montfort Street, Leicester LE1 7GP, England
World Wide Web: www.ivpbooks.com
Email: ivp@uccf.org.uk

INTERVARSITY PRESS
PO Box 1400, Downers Grove, Illinois 60515, USA
World Wide Web: www.ivpress.com
Email: mail@ivpress.com

First published 2003

British Library Cataloguing in Publication Data
A catalogue record for this book is available from the British Library.

UK ISBN 0–85111–290–0

Library of Congress Cataloging-in-Publication Data
These data have been requested.

US ISBN 0–8308–2616–5

Set in Monotype Times New Roman
Typeset in Great Britain by Servis Filmsetting Ltd
Printed in Great Britain by Creative Print and Design (Wales), Ebbw Vale

Contents

CONTENTS

To my parents, Jim and Carolyn Hays, who taught me from an early age that all people are created equal;

To the Black and Hispanic students of Central Junior High, Alamogordo, NM, 1966–69, who taught me the basics – not only the problems but also possible solutions – of the race issue in North America;

And to my students at Ouachita Baptist University. May their generation be the one that truly overcomes racial division in the North American Church.

Series preface

New Studies in Biblical Theology is a series of monographs that address key issues in the discipline of biblical theology. Contributions to the series focus on one or more of three areas: 1. the nature and status of biblical theology, including its relations with other disciplines (e.g. historical theology, exegesis, systematic theology, historical criticism, narrative theology); 2. the articulation and exposition of the structure of thought of a particular biblical writer or corpus; and 3. the delineation of a biblical theme across all or part of the biblical corpora.

Above all, these monographs are creative attempts to help thinking Christians understand their Bibles better. The series aims simultaneously to instruct and to edify, to interact with the current literature, and to point the way ahead. In God's universe, mind and heart should not be divorced: in this series we will try not to separate what God has joined together. While the notes interact with the best of the scholarly literature, the text is uncluttered with untransliterated Greek and Hebrew, and tries to avoid too much technical jargon. The volumes are written within the framework of confessional evangelicalism, but there is always an attempt at thoughtful engagement with the sweep of the relevant literature.

This volume combines fine technical scholarship on complex matters of history and race with a prophetic call to Christians to abjure racism. On the one hand, it traces out much of what the Bible says about the diversity of races and cultures, against the background of Ancient Near Eastern social history (its treatment of the 'curse of Ham' is particularly penetrating and convincing); on the other, it exposes some of the glib, unbiblical, and frankly immoral stances that not only characterize a fair bit of Western scholarship, but continue to surface in our attitudes and relationships. Dr J. Daniel Hays is able simultaneously to make us long for the new heaven and the new earth, when men and women from every tongue and tribe and people and nation will gather around the One who sits on the throne and around the Lamb, and to cause us to blush with shame when we recognize afresh that the church of Jesus Christ is to be already an outpost of that consummated kingdom in this fallen world. This book deserves the widest circulation and the most thoughtful reading, for it corrects erroneous scholarship while calling Christians to reform sinful attitudes. If the book is sometimes intense, it is because the problems it addresses are not trivial.

D. A. Carson
Trinity Evangelical Divinity School

Author's preface

My pilgrimage along the road of racial strife and racial reconciliation has been an interesting and educational one. My father was an Air Force Chaplain, so I grew up on numerous military bases around the country. In the 1960s, military bases were the most integrated communities in all of America. Air Force families were segregated, but we were segregated by the rank of our fathers, and not by race. We did not have a swimming pool for Blacks and a pool for Whites, as most of the South had at that time (if they had a pool for Blacks at all). Rather, we had a pool for officers and a pool for enlisted men. Blacks and Whites swam together. Blacks and Whites also went to the same school, to the same church, to the same commissary (supermarket), to the same bowling alley, to the same movie theatre, and so on. We played on the same Little League teams, camped with the same Boy Scout Troop, and lived in the same neighbourhoods. All Majors, White or Black, lived in houses of exactly the same size and with exactly the same floor plans. The Colonels lived in larger houses and the Captains lived in smaller ones. As a child and as an adolescent, I was always stunned at the different world that existed off the base, where often a railroad track or a certain highway segregated American towns into Black towns and White towns, with their own Black Churches and White Churches.

In Junior High we were living in New Mexico, and I went to the regular publicly funded school in town. At that time there were two Junior High Schools in town. One was made up of White kids only. The composition of the other one, where I went to school, was approximately 33% Black, 33% Hispanic, and 33% Military kids ('Base Brats', as we were called). During my senior year of High School, Dad transferred to South Carolina, and I entered a school there that was in its very first year of integration. Later I attended State Universities (Auburn and NMSU), went to seminary, and married a wonderful girl from Dallas.

My wife and I followed the Lord's call into missions and from 1982

11

until 1987 we lived in southern Ethiopia in a town called Dilla. Within a fifty-mile radius of Dilla there were probably 500,000 people, of which perhaps fifteen were White. We worked closely with the local Ethiopian Kale Heywet Church and made close friends with our Ethiopian counterparts.

In 1988 we were back in the USA, where I entered a PhD programme. In addition to my standard Old Testament seminars, I took two Ethics seminars under Dr Bill Tillman, who introduced me to the race relations history – or lack thereof – in our own denomination (Southern Baptist). He also introduced me to the legacy of ethicist T. B. Maston, who had spent much of his academic life fighting against racism and prejudice within the Southern Baptist Convention. In 1959 Maston wrote *The Bible and Race*, and said many of the same things that I say in this book. However, he wrote to a Church that simply was not listening to him. Maston's experience brings to my mind the haunting final line in the old Don MacLean song 'Vincent': 'They would not listen; they're not listening still. Perhaps they never will.'

After we came to Ouachita Baptist University, I was given a nudge by one of its alumni – a Black pastor from Arlington, Texas, named Dwight McKissic – to study the Cushites, the Black Africans that appear frequently in the Bible. During my study of the Cushites I was startled to notice how much the Bible does actually say about race, and how little White-dominated theological scholarship has acknowledged this, or even attempted to address the issue. Thus the idea for this book began to form in my head.

In addition to Bill Tillman and Dwight McKissic, I have many others to thank. I thank D. A. Carson, the editor of the *New Studies in Biblical Theology* series, for accepting this proposal and giving valuable editorial input on this project. Likewise my thanks go to Philip Duce at IVP in Leicester, UK, for all his editorial assistance. I am thankful to Ouachita Baptist University (OBU) for giving me sabbatical leave during the spring semester of 2002 to work on this book. I also want to express my sincere appreciation to OBU's Research Librarian, Janice Ford, for her invaluable help. Several OBU undergraduate student workers – Aaron Lemay, Ryan Owsley, and Julie Bradley – assisted me during the summers of 2001 and 2002, and I thank them as well. I have an outstanding group of colleagues here at OBU, and many of them have helped me on this project in some manner or other, especially through their encouragement and supportive friendship. Thus my deep appreciation goes out to Scott Duvall, Preben Vang, Randy Richards, Marvin Pate, Terry Carter, Dennis Tucker, Isaac Mwase, Byron Eubanks, Barbara Pemberton, and Bill Viser. In addition, my parents, Jim and Carolyn Hays, have been a constant source of encouragement throughout this project; Dad even helped proofread several chapters. Finally, I want to thank my wife, Donna, for all of her patience and unwavering support. The writing effort required to produce this book equates to a large number of needed household projects that I have never completed.

Danny Hays

Abbreviations

AB	Anchor Bible
ABD	*Anchor Bible Dictionary*
AJA	*American Journal of Archaeology*
AnBib	*Analecta Biblica*
ANE	Ancient Near East
ATJ	*African Theology Journal*
BA	*Biblical Archaeologist*
BAR	*Biblical Archaeology Review*
BASOR	*Bulletin of the American Schools of Oriental Research*
BBC	Broadman Bible Commentary
BBR	*Bulletin for Biblical Research*
BES	*Bulletin of the Egyptian Seminar*
BECNT	Baker Exegetical Commentary on the New Testament
Bib	*Biblica*
BibSac	*Bibliotheca Sacra*
BkNTC	Black's New Testament Commentary
BNTC	Baker New Testament Commentary
BR	*Bible Review*
BST	*The Bible Speaks Today*
BZ	*Biblische Zeitschrift*
CAH	*Cambridge Ancient History*
CB	The Cambridge Bible
CBQ	*Catholic Biblical Quarterly*
CTM	*Concordia Theological Monthly*
EncJud	*Encyclopedia Judaica*
FOTL	Forms of the Old Testament Literature
Gk	Greek
HAR	*Harvard Annual Review*
Heb	Hebrew
HTKNT	Herders Theologische Kommentar zum Neuen Testament

HTR	*Harvard Theological Review*
ICC	International Critical Commentary
IDB	*Interpreter's Dictionary of the Bible*
ITC	International Theological Commentary
IVPNTC	InterVarsity Press New Testament Commentary Series
JARCE	*Journal of the American Research Center in Egypt*
JBL	*Journal of Biblical Literature*
JEA	*Journal of Egyptian Archaeology*
JETS	*Journal of the Evangelical Theological Society*
JNES	*Journal of Near Eastern Studies*
JRS	*Journal of Roman Studies*
JRT	*Journal of Religious Thought*
JSJPHRP	*Journal for the Study of Judaism in the Persian, Hellenistic, and Roman Period*
JSNTSS	Journal for the Study of the New Testament Supplement Series
JSOT	*Journal for the Study of the Old Testament*
JSOTSS	Journal for the Study of the Old Testament Supplement Series
JTS	*Journal of Theological Studies*
KJV	King James (Authorized) Version
LXX	Septuagint
MT	Masoretic Text
MTZ	*Münchener Theologische Zeitschrift*
NAC	New American Commentary
NASB	New American Standard Bible
NCB	New Century Bible Commentary
NIBC	New International Biblical Commentary
NICNT	New International Commentary on the New Testament
NICOT	New International Commentary on the Old Testament
NIDOTTE	*New International Dictionary of Old Testament Theology and Exegesis*
NIGTC	New International Greek Testament Commentary
NIV	New International Version
NIVAC	NIV Application Commentary
NLB	New Living Bible
NRSV	New Revised Standard Version
NSBT	New Studies in Biblical Theology

OTL	Old Testament Library
PNTC	Pillar New Testament Commentary
SBLSCS	Society of Biblical Literature Septuagint and Cognate Studies
TDNT	*Theological Dictionary of the New Testament*
TDOT	*Theological Dictionary of the Old Testament*
TNTC	Tyndale New Testament Commentary
VT	*Vetus Testamentum*
WBC	Word Biblical Commentary
WEC	Wycliffe Exegetical Commentary
WstBC	Westminster Bible Companion
WUNT	Wissenschaftliche Untersuchungen zum Neuen Testament
ZAW	*Zeitschrift für die alttestamentliche Wissenschaft*

Chapter One

Introduction

Not long ago, in a conversation with my colleague Dr Isaac Mwase, a Black professor and pastor of a local Black congregation, I mentioned that the race problem was *an* important issue for the Church today. Isaac quickly corrected me by stating emphatically that it is *the* most important issue for the Church today. This conversation illustrates to some degree a phenomenon that I encountered regularly as I read through some of the recent literature dealing with the race problem in the Church today.[1] Black scholars identify the racial division in the Church as one of the most central problems for contemporary Christianity, while many White scholars are saying, 'What problem?'

Likewise, even among those who acknowledge the problem, there is a wide difference of opinion concerning just how bad the problem is and whether the situation is improving or deteriorating. On the one hand, in recent years tremendous progress appears to have been achieved. Carson, for example, documents evangelical churches on the east coast and the west coast of North America that are doing a remarkable job of integrating (2002: 95–96). Particularly among many White Christians, there is the perception that in these regions things have improved; even in the south and the mid-west many feel that, although lagging behind the rest of the country, the race problem is not nearly as pronounced as it was a mere generation ago.

On the other hand, some have observed that the evidence for this perception is often anecdotal, and actual statistical survey data appear to suggest otherwise. Emerson and Smith in *Divided by Faith: Evangelical Religion and the Problem of Race in America* (2000) study the problem through statistical data based on actual nationwide surveys and interviews. They point out that there is a tremendous disparity between the way that White evangelicals view the problem and

---

[1] See the excellent bibliography in Sharp (2002: 304–314), and especially the works he cites in his footnote on pages 236–237.

the way that Black evangelicals view the problem. They also note that this phenomenon cuts across regional lines. Their studies indicate that two-thirds of White Christians believe that the situation for Blacks is improving, while two-thirds of Black Christians believe that the situation for Blacks is deteriorating (88). The survey data have led Emerson and Smith to pessimistic conclusions. They write:

> Despite the often very best intentions of most white American evangelicals, the complex web of factors explored in this book produce a rather dismal portrait of the realities of and prospects for positive race relations among American Christians in the United States. Most white evangelicals, directed by their cultural tools, fail to recognize the institutionalization of racialization – in economic, political, educational, social, and religious systems . . . Is the situation hopeless? If white evangelicals continue to travel the same road they have travelled thus far, the future does indeed look bleak (170).

Emerson and Smith (2000: 171) also suggest that one of the underlying factors hindering evangelicalism's ability to address the race issue adequately is that evangelicals have a tendency to define problems in simple terms and to look for simple solutions. The race issue, on the other hand, is extremely complex, involving history, tradition, culture, religion, economics, politics, and a host of other factors.[2] Emerson and Smith state: 'With a few exceptions, evangelicals lack serious thinking on this issue.' Black theologian Ronald Potter makes the same point, writing that 'there exists little if any theological reflection' on this problem (1997: 32).[3]

---

[2] For discussion on the complexity of the racial issue, see Carson (2002: 87–108) and Sharp (2002). This complexity likewise surfaces in Emerson and Smith's conclusions. Their study indicates that Whites tend to see the race problem in individual terms (how does one person feel about another person of a different race?). On the other hand, Blacks usually see the problem as extending beyond the individual to societal structures, a much more complicated situation (2000: 88–91; 170–173). Fields (2001: 67–69) identifies the same problem, labelling it as 'systemic sin'. Both Fields and Emerson/Smith suggest that limited success in dealing with the race problem in the Evangelical Church will occur unless Evangelicals engage with the societal structural problem as well as with the individual attitude problem.

[3] The history of how White Christianity, and in particular American evangelicalism, has dealt with the race issue throughout the twentieth century is beyond the scope of this book. However, in summary one can say that the actions of evangelicalism toward racial issues for much of the twentieth century were highly questionable, to say the least. See, for example, the discussion of how *Christianity Today* opposed the Civil Rights movement in the 1960s (Dorrien 1998: 154). Dorrien also quotes Moberg (1972:

Although there are some significant exceptions, in general there is silence in White evangelical congregations concerning the biblical teaching on this issue. Within these congregations, the current attitude of many Whites often falls into one of three categories. First, some people are still entrenched in their inherited racism. They are interested in the Bible if it reinforces their prejudiced views; otherwise they do not care what the Bible says about race. Second, many people assume that the Bible simply does not speak to the race issue, and particularly to the Black–White issue. Third, many others are simply indifferent to the problem, assuming that the status quo is acceptable and that the Bible supports their current practices.

These views appear to carry over into academia as well. Indeed, evangelical biblical and theological scholarship has continued to remain nearly silent on this issue, even though the indications of the scope of the problem are obvious. Few of our theological training institutions address the race issue, which is rather strange, considering the scale of the problem. Indeed, the traditional Systematic Theologies used for most of the twentieth century did not address the race issue at all. Often these volumes had entire chapters devoted to philosophical and biblical discussions of 'Anthropology' (the study of the nature of humankind), but they failed to address one of the central anthropological problems within the Church today. Likewise they contained entire chapters on 'Ecclesiology' (the study of the Church), but did not address the major division in Church life today. A few of the more recent volumes, however, have at least begun to address the issue. Millard Erickson, for example, in *Christian Theology* (1985: 542–545), presents a good discussion of the race issue. Wayne Grudem, in *Systematic Theology* (1994: 450, 459) while not discussing race as an issue, does at least mention racial equality as an implication of being created in the image of God and also as the practical outworking of Galatians 3:27–28. Yet other influential theologies, such as Alister McGrath's *Christian Theology: An Introduction* (1997), are silent on race. Even Stanley Grenz's *Theology for the Community of God* with its emphasis on 'the community of God', fails to address the race problem.[4] Meanwhile, over twenty-three

---

42–43) as stating that 'evangelicalism had become synonymous with the defense of racial privilege'.

[4] Grenz (2000: 466) comes close, touching on the issue in his discussion of 'the Nation of God'. He writes, 'No longer is status as God's nation based on membership within a specific ethnic group. Now people from the entire world are called together to belong to God; the church is an international fellowship comprising persons "from

million Black American Christians, most of them extremely conservative in theology, feel excluded from the White evangelical 'community of God' that is teaching and studying these theologies. We clearly have a problem that needs addressing; yet much of evangelical theology has, in general, ignored it.[5]

On the positive side, however, it should be noted that several helpful books addressing 'racial reconciliation' have been published recently, containing articles written by both Black and White authors. Two significant examples are *The Gospel in Black and White: Theological Resources for Racial Reconciliation*, edited by D. Okholm at Wheaton College (1997); and *A Mighty Long Journey: Reflections on Racial Reconciliation*, edited by T. George and R. Smith at Beeson Divinity School (2000). E. Yamauchi is producing helpful background studies dealing with Blacks in the Ancient Near East.[6] Also, G. Usry (a Black pastor) and C. Keener (a White professor of New Testament) have together written several important works, focusing primarily on Black audiences.[7] In addition, several other Black scholars and pastors have produced helpful works related to the race issue (Felder, McKissic, Fields, A. T. Evans, and Adamo, to name a few).[8]

In the field of biblical studies the response of scholars has been mixed. As discussed later in the book, many commentators continue to make the same incorrect and prejudiced assumptions that their predecessors made, thus repeating the same errors concerning race as those made by earlier generations. However, in contrast, several commentators, especially those writing in series that are concerned with applicational theology, have confronted the race problem seriously and honestly. Good examples include J. Stott, *The Message of Ephesians*, The Bible Speaks Today (1979); K. Snodgrass, *Ephesians*,

---

every tribe and language and people and nation" (Rev. 5:9)'. Yet when writing about the Church as community, Grenz (2000: 482) states: 'It is a community of shared commitment to Christ transcending spatial, temporal, social, and gender boundaries'. Conspicuously missing from this list is the ethnic or racial boundary.

[5] One of the few contemporary White theologians to address the race issue in a serious theological work is Sharp (2002).

[6] Edwin Yamauchi, ed., *Africa and Africans in Antiquity* (2001b); Edwin Yamauchi, *Africa and the Bible* (forthcoming).

[7] Glenn Usry and Craig S. Keener, *Black Man's Religion: Can Christianity be Afrocentric?* (1996); Keener and Usry, *Defending Black Faith: Answers to Tough Questions about African-American Christianity* (1997).

[8] Cain Hope Felder, *Troubling Biblical Waters: Race, Class, and Family* (1989); William Dwight McKissic, *Beyond Roots* (1990); Bruce L. Fields, *Introducing Black Theology* (2001); Anthony T. Evans, *Let's Get to Know Each Other* (1995); David Tuesday Adamo, *Africa and Africans in the Old Testament* (1998).

NIVAC (1996); and S. McKnight, *Galatians*, NIVAC (1995). Also, one of the few works that deals with the biblical text on the race issue is the brief work by S. L. McKenzie, *All God's Children: A Biblical Critique of Racism* (1997).

The silence on the race issue among evangelical scholars, therefore, is gradually being broken, although it is still present in many of the major theological textbooks that our universities and seminaries are using to train tomorrow's leaders. In addition, although helpful articles on reconciliation are being produced, very little serious biblically based exegetical work is being conducted on passages that are relevant to the race issue.

This book, which is far from exhaustive, is an attempt to help fill the need for a serious exegetically based study of passages that relate to the race issue. It is subtitled *A Biblical Theology of Race* because I am also trying to build upon this exegetical work a relevant biblical theology.

In this book I am not seeking to employ some new 'agenda-driven' hermeneutic. My approach to studying Scripture and developing theology follows standard historical-critical method, based on evangelical presuppositions regarding the nature of the Bible. Part of this method, however, is to identify the cultural baggage or culturally tainted lenses through which we tend to read Scripture. Thorough historical study and careful exegesis can help all of us to mute the influence of the culturally slanted or 'ethnocentric' context from which we read. Likewise, listening to other perspectives from other contexts can help us to critique our own understanding. Obviously we will never be completely free of our contextual location in a culture, but a serious study of Scripture will demand that we at least attempt to set our cultural baggage aside in order to let Scripture speak to us clearly.[9]

In this book we will first explore the ethnic historical context of the Old Testament (Chapter 2) and then examine those texts that relate to race in the rest of the Old Testament (Chapters 3–6). Next we will examine the ethnic world of the New Testament (Chapter 7), followed by a study of relevant texts throughout the New Testament (Chapters 8–9). Thus we will begin in Genesis and end in Revelation.

---

[9] My hermeneutical approach is explained in detail in Duvall and Hays (2001). See especially the introductory chapter ('The Interpretive Journey', 19–27) and the chapter on ethnocentric reading ('What Do We Bring to the Text?', 85–94). Taking a similar approach to the problem of ethnocentric interpretation is Craffert (1996: 449–468).

In Chapter 10 I will present a concluding synthesis and offer a final applicational challenge.

We will explore two types of texts. First, we will examine those texts that have a *general* bearing on the theology of race: that is, texts that speak to the universal aspects of race. Second, because I am particularly concerned with the relationship between Black and White Christians in the Church today, we will explore those texts that make *specific* reference to Black Africans. Taken together, these passages will provide the biblical basis for a strong, clear theology of race.

As mentioned earlier, because the Black–White race issue is so gigantic in the American Church, this work will focus on that particular problem. However, I have spent enough of my life overseas to know that racial problems are endemic to most parts of the world, and are not limited to black and white skin colour. Serious ethnic tensions are not limited to North America, but also exist in the Church all across Africa, Asia, Latin America, and Europe. The recent influx of Eastern Europeans into Western Europe has created racial tensions in many European Churches. In Asia, serious cultural tensions, which can often flare up into racism, exist between Japanese, Koreans, and Chinese. The two-million-strong Myanmar (formerly Burma) Baptist Convention is made up of dozens of ethnic groups, many with completely different languages. Many African national church organizations, such as the 4,000-plus congregations of the evangelical Ethiopian Kale Heywet Church, comprise numerous different ethnic groups that traditionally and historically have felt animosity toward each other. In some regions of the world, Christians of different ethnic groups have recently opposed each other in open war. Often such warfare was fought along ethnic lines, thus creating deep animosity and prejudices.

Thus throughout the world Christian communities are struggling to overcome the historical and cultural prejudices that they have inherited and are striving to use the gospel to forge Christian unity in the midst of their cultural diversity. So while I have attempted to apply the theology developed in this book to the Black–White issue in the United States, the biblical principles that emerge have equal applicability in any Church setting where fellow believers in Christ are being pressured culturally to divide along ethnic lines and to embrace prejudiced views toward other ethnic groups.

Related to this is the observation that Christianity is currently multiplying rapidly in Africa, Asia, and Latin America, but not in the West. Woodward (2001: 48) points out that in 1900 over 80% of the

Christians in the world were in Europe or North America. Today that percentage has dropped to 40%, highlighting the fact that the majority of Christians in the world today are not in Europe or North America. Furthermore, in many of these areas, especially Africa, Christianity is growing at a phenomenal rate, while in the West growth has stagnated. The forecast for the next century is for this trend to continue or even to accelerate. As the twenty-first century progresses, a greater and greater majority of Christians of all denominations in the world will be non-Western. As the world continues to shrink, and as Christians from hundreds of different ethnic groups from around the world come into contact with each other, it will be imperative that we have a proper biblical foundation for dealing with such a world.

Chapter Two

The ethnic make-up of the Old Testament world

Introduction

One of the more difficult hurdles for us to overcome in developing and applying biblical theology from the Scriptures is the ever-constant intrusion of 'cultural pre-understanding' into our interpretative and applicational process. 'Cultural pre-understanding' is the tendency for us to interpret the biblical material through the lenses of our own personal cultural context. Not only do we fill in all the literary 'gaps' in the biblical story with material from our culture, but also we tend to project much of our culture into the setting and into our understanding of the characters.[1] Not all of this projection is bad, for it can often help us to relate better to the text. However, frequently such 'cultural pre-understanding' leads us to skew the text to fit our particular ethnocentric cultural outlook.

For centuries, in art as well as in other media, the people of Western Europe and North America have portrayed the individuals in the Bible as Europeans or North Americans. Thus not only does Michelangelo paint twelve Europeans sitting down at a European table for the Last Supper, but the fair-haired American Charlton Heston portrays Moses in *The Ten Commandments* and the blue-eyed Briton Richard Harris plays the title role in TNT's television movie *Abraham*. Even though most scholars know that few, if any, characters in the Old Testament looked much like Charlton Heston or Richard Harris,[2] the average church member – indeed, probably the average pastor – consciously or subconsciously assumes as much. Such images play powerful roles in shaping popular perceptions about the Bible, and these popular perceptions in turn have a serious impact on the theology of the Church.

---

[1] See the discussion in Duvall and Hays (2001: 85–94) and Brett (1996: 3–22).
[2] Perhaps Uriah the Hittite or Goliath the Philistine had Caucasian features, but probably none of the Israelites did. See the discussion below.

Furthermore, not only are North American or European images projected back on the people of the Bible, but also clear portrayals of Black Africans in the Bible are all but ignored. This 'marginalization' of Black African presence is perpetrated, consciously or subconsciously, not only by the popularizers of Christianity, but also by serious scholars. 'Cultural pre-understanding' apparently influences many of us in the academic guild even though we often piously claim to be historically objective.

A good example of this subtle – and probably subconscious – bias can be found in scholarly discussions about the people of the biblical world.[3] For example, the kingdom of Cush, discussed below, was a Black African kingdom along the Nile River just south of Egypt. The terms *Cush* or *Cushite* appear 54 times in the Hebrew text of the Old Testament, indicating that the Cushites, an African people, played a fairly significant role in the Old Testament story. The term *Hittite* or *Hittites* (an Indo-European group) is similar in frequency, occurring 61 times (although ten of the occurrences refer to the same person, Uriah the Hittite). The terms *Arab*, *Arabs*, or *Arabia* appear less than 20 times. Neither the Sumerians nor the Hurrians are mentioned directly in undisputed biblical texts. However, scholarly discussions practically always devote much more time to discussing the Hittites, Hurrians, Sumerians, and Arabs than they do the Cushites, if they discuss the Cushites at all. For example, in D. J. Wiseman's classic work *Peoples of Old Testament Times* (1973) there are thirteen chapters, each dealing with one of the various peoples of the Old Testament (Hebrews, Canaanites, Philistines, etc.). There is a substantial chapter on the Hittites and the Hurrians, but nothing on the Cushites. There is a chapter entitled 'The Arabs and the Ethiopians', but the discussion on 'Ethiopia' is limited to merely one

---

[3] Many European and American scholars of the nineteenth and early twentieth centuries were blatantly racist. This is particularly true concerning early European Egyptologists, who attempted to appropriate Egyptian culture as 'Western' and to distance the Egyptian cultural advances as far as possible from any African connections. Scholars today in general are much more ethnically sensitive and 'politically correct', but much of the early bias has crept into general, accepted approaches of Old Testament scholarship, and scholars today, somewhat subconsciously, continue to think ethnocentrically, carrying out their scholarship from a clear Anglo-European perspective. Black American scholars such as Felder have tried to point this out, but with only mixed success. See the introductions to his works *Troubling Biblical Waters* (1989) and *Stony the Road We Trod* (1991). Scholars writing from other ethnic viewpoints are likewise joining this chorus in calling on White, male scholars, who dominate biblical scholarship, to reconsider how much their Anglo-American viewpoint might affect their approach to Scripture. See, for example, Carroll R. (1992).

brief apologetic page at the end of the article, and only one sentence mentions the biblical land of 'Cush'. *Peoples of the Old Testament World* (Hoerth, Mattingly, and Yamauchi, 1994), a newer work that updates Wiseman's book, has thirteen similar chapters. This work drops the chapter on 'Arabs and Ethiopians' altogether and adds one on the Sumerians. Furthermore, the map of the Ancient Near East presented at the beginning of the book extends only to Lower Egypt and does not even show Cush! Both of these books address the people of the Old Testament world, but neither addresses the Black African Cushites, even though the Cushites play a significant role in the Old Testament, and a greater role than some of the other groups discussed. The prestigious *Anchor Bible Dictionary* follows a similar orientation. Two and a half pages are devoted to 'Kush'[4] while fourteen pages are devoted to the Hittites.[5] The Hurrians, who are not even mentioned in the Bible, receive three pages: more than the Cushites, who are mentioned 54 times.

Therefore the perception conveyed to the Church, both through the popular media and through serious scholarly work, is that there was a significant Caucasian involvement in the biblical story but no Black African involvement. This perception is erroneous, and it has fostered disastrous theology within today's White Church that has contributed to the continued, almost total, division of the North American Church into Black and White.

In order to tackle biblical texts that relate to ethnic issues it is critical that scholars, pastors, and parishioners open their eyes to the fact

---

[4] Underlining the minimal importance assigned to the Cushites is the somewhat haphazard manner in which *The Anchor Bible Dictionary* addresses them. The country and history are discussed in the article mentioned above under 'Kush'. The *people* with the proper name 'Cush', spelled the same in Hebrew as the nation, are inexplicably discussed under 'Cush' rather than 'Kush', as if they were unconnected. No explanation for the shift in transliteration is provided. Equally puzzling is the article on 'Ethiopia', a one-and-a-half-page discussion of biblical 'Cush' which covers exactly the same material as the article on 'Kush' but adds a paragraph on the relevance of modern Ethiopia (a completely different place). This article does not cite any bibliographic sources on 'Cush' but cites only references relating to post-biblical Axum and modern Ethiopia (i.e. Ullendorff's works on Ethiopia and a book on the Ethiopian folk legend *Kebra Negast*).

[5] This discrepancy cannot be explained by a lack of material regarding the Cushites. Cush appears hundreds of times in the Egyptian literature. Besides the numerous references in the Hebrew Bible, Cush/Ethiopia also appears in Assyrian and Greek literature. Several significant books have been written on the history and culture of the Cushites (although the histories often use the term Nubia rather than Cush – see the discussion on terminology below). See, for example, Trigger (1965 and 1976); Shinnie (1967); Adams (1970); O'Connor (1993); and Török (1997).

that the people of the biblical world did not look like the people of rural Minnesota. This chapter attempts to present a broad picture of the major racial or ethnic groups that play significant roles in the biblical world. A better understanding of this particular aspect of the historical context will help us as we attempt to formulate a theology relating to race.

Ethnicity

Defining and determining 'ethnicity' is complex and controversial, even among contemporary groups where mounds of sociological data exist and live interviews are possible. This problem is illustrated by an argument I overheard years ago between two of my international friends in college. A Palestinian student had remarked to a Somali student that they were Arab brothers. The Somali man objected, stating: 'We Somalis are not Arabs.' 'Yes you are,' the Palestinian argued. 'You are part of the Arab League. You must be Arabs.' 'You cannot tell me what I am,' the Somali countered. 'I know what I am and I am not an Arab.' The Palestinian was not convinced; he concluded, 'Like it or not, you are an Arab and my brother.' Thus, even determining exactly what constitutes the boundaries of the term 'Arab' in today's world can be challenging.

Developing precise definitions and distinctions of ethnic groups in the Ancient Near East or even within the Hellenistic world can be an even more difficult task, one that falls more properly within the realm of cultural anthropology or sociology than that of biblical theology. In recent years numerous helpful works have appeared that apply the methods and experience of anthropology and sociology to the study of the biblical world.[6] These studies have emphasized the complexity of the issue. Because ethnic identity is 'socially constructed and subjectively perceived' it is impossible to find an objective set of criteria that defines the ethnic group in every situation (J. M. Hall 1997: 19). Traditionally, ethnic identity has been understood as connected to either genetics (physical appearance), language, and/or religion.[7] However, since 'ethnicity involves the creation and maintenance of social boundaries,' other factors such as geographical location,

---

[6] For example, see Clements (1989); Chalcraft (1997); Carter and Meyers (1996); McNutt (1999); and Carroll R. (ed.) (2000).

[7] This definition goes back at least as far as Herodotus, *History* 8:144. See the discussion and critique of this definition by Lemche (1998: 8–21).

ancestry (real or mythic), dress, diet, or numerous combinations can also play critical roles (McNutt 1999: 33).[8]

This book makes no pretence of undertaking a thorough anthropological study of ethnicity in the Ancient Near East, a subject well beyond the scope of this project. My intention is to describe very broadly the main ethnic groups that appear in the Scriptures, so that we might better understand the context from which biblical ethnic references are made. Undeniably these descriptions are overly simplistic and narrow, but they serve only as an introduction into the study. As mentioned above, entire books are devoted to describing the specific peoples of the Ancient Near East, and those descriptions do not need repeating here. Also, I am concerned here with only the largest ethnic groupings. In addition, since the focus of this book is on racial issues, I have attempted to discuss the ethnic groups along broad racial lines: that is, focusing on the issue of physical appearance, hazardous as this may be. However, territory, religion, language, and common descent are also important criteria.[9] My goal is to create a proper sociological background context from which to interpret biblical texts and to develop biblical theology regarding race.

One of the few places in the records of the Ancient Near East where distinctions in ethnicity seem to be clearly presented is in ancient Egyptian literature and art. These distinctions appear to be fairly consistent throughout most of the Old Testament time period. Although these distinctions can be seen in much of Egyptian art, perhaps the clearest representation is a scene of humanity painted on the tomb of Seti I (1291–1279 BC). In this scene four main groups are depicted: Egyptians; the Cushites to the south; the Libyans to the west; and the Asiatics to the northeast. Numerous glazed tile 'portraits' from the palace of Rameses III (1180 BC) present a similar breakdown, but include the Hittites as a fifth group. Most of Egyptian art portrays these groups fairly consistently. Almost certainly this representation

---

[8] J. Hall (1997: 19–26) provides a good discussion illustrating how physical appearance, language, or religion may serve as the determining factor in the ethnic identity of one particular group, but not play a significant role at all in the identity of other groups. He suggests that the basic common denominator of ethnic identity, that which shows up most frequently, is that of territory and common myth of descent.

[9] For example, a major distinguishing factor between Cushites and Israelites was physical (skin colour, facial features, hair), but the strong, equally clear differences in territory, religion, language, and dress were no doubt also important. However, it is probable that the differences between an Israelite and an Ammonite or a Canaanite were probably not nearly so clear in any of the categories.

is stereotyped, but the breakdown into these basic groups does seem to be a reflection of how the ancient Egyptians, at least, perceived 'ethnic' groupings.[10]

This division also parallels a similar distinction of language grouping in the region: Semitic, Egyptian, Indo-European, and Meroitic. The Semitic and Egyptian languages comprise two of the six major branches of a larger family of languages called Afro-Asiatic.[11] The Indo-European family of languages consists of several branches, including Anatolian, to which the Hittite language belongs, and Hellenic, to which the Greek and probably also the Philistine language belong.[12] Although many of the Cushites no doubt spoke Egyptian, they also had their own particular language, the descendant of which is called Meroitic. However, at the present time this language has not been completely deciphered.[13]

For lack of better broad-based categories, I will discuss the ethnic world of the Old Testament within these same four categories: Asiatics or Semites (including the Israelites), Cushites, Egyptians, and Indo-Europeans (Hittites, Philistines). Because the fifth group (Libyans) plays a minor role in the Old Testament, it is not discussed.

The 'Asiatics': Israel and her 'Semitic' cousins

The actual origin of the Israelites continues to be a debated topic. One of the central problems in the study of Israelite origins, as mentioned above, is the difficulty in defining such terms as 'nation', 'race', 'ethnic group', or 'country'. Most Western readers of the Bible will tend to project modern concepts of the nation and state into the Old Testament. However, the ethnic or national consciousness of people in Palestine during the formative period of Israel is far from clear. What distinguished Canaanites from Amorites or from Israelites? If a descendant of Abraham living in Canaan picked up the Canaanite

---

[10] See the discussion by Leahy (2000: 226–227).

[11] The Afro-Asiatic languages include Semitic, Egyptian, Berber (North Africa in regions west of Egypt), Cushitic (a group of about 40 languages in Ethiopia, Kenya, and Somalia, unrelated to the country of Cush), Omotic (Western Ethiopia), and Chadic (West Africa). See Huehnergard (1992: 155) and Hodge (2001: 15–27).

[12] Examples of Philistine language and writing are rare, but the few seals that are extant appear to be related to the Cypro-Minoan language used in the Aegean during the Late Bronze Age. This language is likewise part of the Hellenic language family. See Dothan (1992: 332).

[13] As yet, Meroitic is unclassified as a language (Huehnergard 1992: 166). See the overview of issues and the discussion of progress on the language in Török (1997: 62–67).

dialect, married a Canaanite woman and worshipped Baal (as many Israelites apparently did), was he an Israelite or a Canaanite? What about his children and grandchildren? The 'ethnic' situation in Canaan throughout the second millennium (2000–1000 BC) was extremely complex.[14] However, it is probably safe to conclude that the Israelites of the Old Testament had numerous 'ethnic' affinities with their neighbours in and around Palestine and that the lines of ethnic demarcation were not hard and fast.[15]

Another important factor in the discussion of Israel's origins is the view one holds regarding the date and composition of the Pentateuch.[16] I will draw heavily from the biblical tradition in the discussion of Israel's origins, but I suggest that my conclusions regarding the ethnic relationship between Israel and her Semitic-speaking neighbours will not differ substantially from that developed by those who are sceptical of the biblical sources and who lean primarily on non-biblical material.[17]

One important aspect of ethnic identity is language. Hebrew, the language of the Israelites, is a Semitic language. The Semitic language family is split into two main groups. East Semitic is represented by Akkadian, the language of the Assyrians and the Babylonians. The West Semitic branch includes Northwest Semitic, Arabic, and South Semitic (Ethiopic, Amharic, Tigrinya). Hebrew falls within the Northwest Semitic group. Also included in this group are the languages of almost all of Israel's neighbours: Canaanite, Moabite,

---

[14] Even the biblical tradition regarding the people in the region is complicated. For example, 1 Samuel 14:21 employs the term 'Hebrews' in reference to a separate group from the 'Israelites' (lit. 'sons of Israel'). In addition numerous different biblical lists of the groups inhabiting the Promised Land appear. Sometimes the list has five entities (Exod. 13:5), sometimes six (Exod. 34:11), and sometimes seven (Josh. 3:10). Non-biblical sources only add to the confusion: for example, what was the ethnicity of the Habiru in Canaan mentioned in the Amarna Letters (mid-fourteenth century BC)? See Greenberg (1961) and Na'aman (1986: 271–288).

[15] See the helpful monograph by Lemche (1991). Some of Lemche's approach has been seriously challenged, but his point regarding the very thin ethnic line between Israelites and Canaanites is convincing.

[16] See the discussion by Rogerson (1989: 31).

[17] For a discussion of Israel's origins based primarily on archaeology, while showing scepticism toward the biblical account, see Ahlström (1986). Ahlström argues that the term 'Israel' first referred to a territory, regardless of ethnicity. During the monarchial period the name became a political term designating the state in the central hill country north of Jerusalem, and then finally, in the post-exilic period, the term became an ideological term referring to the party of returned exiles who followed Ezra's law. Thus, concludes Ahlström, the term Israel became the ideological term for Judaism. Likewise arguing for a distinction between the biblical picture and the historical picture of Israel is P. Davies (1992).

Edomite, Ammonite, Ugaritic, Phoenician, Aramaic,[18] and Amorite.[19] The Philistines, however, are not in this group, and neither are the Egyptians. Those within the Northwest Semitic group would have had a close linguistic affinity: that is, linguistically speaking, those who spoke Northwest Semitic dialects were cousins. Furthermore, Hebrew, Moabite, Edomite, Ammonite, and Phoenician all probably developed from Canaanite. Thus these groups had an even stronger linguistic affinity.

Examining the biblical tradition for the origin of the Israelites leads to a conclusion that fits well with the linguistic data. Israel is not mentioned in Genesis 10 as one of the ancient peoples of the world. As will be discussed in Chapter 3, it is important to note that Adam, Eve, Noah, and even Abraham cannot be called 'Israelites', and it is highly unlikely that their language would be recognizable as Hebrew. Initially, Abraham is apparently a resident of Mesopotamia, and his family appears to have originated in western Mesopotamia. Based on the names of the family and a northern location of 'Ur of the Chaldees', many scholars have concluded that Abraham is actually an Amorite, part of the many waves of Amorites that migrated into Mesopotamia before and during the patriarchal period (Wenham 1987: 272–273).[20] However, in Genesis 24:4 and 28:5 Abraham is associated with the Arameans. The use of Aramean in connection with Abraham probably refers to those 'scattered tribes of people in upper Mesopotamia who had not yet coalesced into the nation of Aram that appears in later texts' (Walton, Matthews, and Chavalas 2000: 60, 200).[21] The creed-like statement of Deuteronomy 26:5, 'My father was a wandering Aramean,' certainly remembers an Aramean ancestry. The text probably refers to Jacob and not Abraham (von Rad 1966: 158; Cragie 1976: 321), but the distinction is mute for our purposes. Jacob's mother and his two wives are identified as Arameans in Genesis 28:5. No doubt the patriarchs spoke one of the

[18] See Huehnergard (1992: 155–161); and Waltke and O'Connor (1990: 1.2).

[19] Amorite as a written language has only survived through names. However, thousands of Amorite names and probable loan words appear in Mesopotamian (East Semitic) documents. The form of the names provides strong evidence that the language of the Amorites is a branch of the Northwest Semitic family. See Mendenhall (1992: 199), and Gelb (1980).

[20] Ezekiel 16:3 states, 'your father was an Amorite and your mother a Hittite.' However, as Block (1997: 474–475) notes, this text refers to Jerusalem and not Abraham, and is also highly figurative/symbolic.

[21] Hamilton (1990: 364) concurs and notes that the Chaldeans were ethnically related to the Arameans.

Northwest Semitic dialects and looked very similar to numerous other groups originating from western Mesopotamia.

According to Genesis, in response to God's command, Abraham moves his family to Canaan, where the family resides for the rest of his life and the next two generations. Although both Isaac and Jacob return to Mesopotamia to marry Aramean women (Gen. 28:5), Jacob's sons apparently do not follow this tradition. Judah marries a Canaanite woman (Gen. 38:2) and then also fathers twins, Perez and Zerah, by his daughter-in-law Tamar, who is probably also a Canaanite.[22] Genesis 46:10 indicates that Simeon likewise had a Canaanite wife. Joseph, after becoming the adviser of Pharaoh, married an Egyptian woman named Asenath (Gen. 41:50) who bore him two sons: Manasseh and Ephraim. Thus the biblical tradition presents the ancestors of the tribes of Israel as a mix of western Mesopotamian (Aramean and/or Amorite), Canaanite, and Egyptian.

Indeed, throughout much of the Old Testament period the Israelites were probably very similar to their neighbours in appearance. In the post-exilic period, when Judaism as a cultural way of life began to emerge, the Jews began to define their ethnic boundaries very precisely, and Judaism became quite distinctive. But for much of their history the ethnic boundary between Israel and her neighbours was fuzzy and fluid.

What did the ancient Israelites actually look like? Most probably they looked very similar to other Semitic-speaking people of the area in and around Canaan. The best estimation of the actual appearance of the ancient Israelites would perhaps combine the look of the current inhabitants of the Middle East with the representations of the Israelites and other 'Asiatic' peoples in the paintings and monument carvings of the Egyptians and the Assyrians. As mentioned above, numerous 'Asiatics' are depicted in Egyptian art from the Old Testament period. Likewise, numerous Israelites are portrayed in Assyrian sculpture. Jehu, king of Israel, along with several other Israelites, is depicted in the Black Obelisk of Shalmaneser III (about 825 BC). Numerous scenes portraying Israelites are included in the sculptured wall-panels from Sennacherib's palace (701 BC) portraying the siege of the Israelite city of Lachish.[23] The people in these

---

[22] Tamar's Canaanite origin is suggested by Westermann (1986: 51); Fretheim (1994: 605); and Wenham (1994: 366).
[23] See the excellent pictures and discussion in Reade (1983: 44–52).

artistic portrayals are, in general, similar in appearance to the Israelis and Arabs living in and around Israel/Palestine today. Of course, ethnic groups always reflect variety in appearance, and this description is certainly an over-generalization; yet it is important to attempt a description of an average Old Testament Israelite. For Anglo-European Christian readers, it is critical to come to grips with the fact that these people were not blue-eyed, blond-haired Caucasians; they did not look like White Americans or White Britons. They looked more like modern Arabs.

The Cushites

One of the confusing aspects of studying the Cushites is that several different terms are used by scholars to refer to the same continuous civilization that stretched along the banks of the Nile, south of Egypt, upstream of the Nile's cataracts, in what is now the modern country of Sudan. This area is referred to by various scholars as Nubia, Wawat, Cush, Meroe, and Ethiopia. All of these terms are correct in some sense and in certain stages of history.[24] Apparently the Egyptians originally referred to this area as *Ta-sety*, 'Land of the Bow', a reference either to the great bend in the Nile that defined the area or to the Cushite fame with the weapon (Taylor 1991: 5).[25] Within this domain there were two regions, or perhaps two tribes or groups. The northernmost area (between the first and fourth cataracts of the Nile) was called Wawat and the southernmost area (above the fourth cataract) was called Cush (R. J. Williams 1973: 79). During the Eighteenth Dynasty in Egypt (1570–1305 BC) these terms represented two distinct provinces (W. C. Hayes 1973: 349), but soon afterwards the terms became interchangeable. The southern area became more powerful and dominant, and thus the name Cush became the common word used in Egyptian texts for the entire region (Quirke and Spencer 1992: 210).[26]

By the fourth century BC the Cushites had moved their capital

---

[24] For recent discussions of the history of Cush, see Török (1997); Welsby (1998); Yurco (2001); Burstein (1997); and O'Connor (1993).

[25] Numerous Egyptologists, however, translate *Ta-sety* as 'Nubia' in English translations. Breasted (1906) used this term, and much of the scholarly work on this subject has followed his terminology. See also James (1973: 296). Taylor (1991: 5) points out, however, that the term *Nubia* does not occur in the ancient documents until the Roman period. O'Connor (1993: xii) likewise identifies *Nubia* as a late term, but he states the term first appears in the third century BC.

[26] See also the good discussion on terminology by Török (1997: 1–5).

upstream to a city called Meroe. Some recent writers, therefore, refer to the Cush of this period as the Meroitic Empire, or sometimes they simply call the region Meroe.

The greatest confusion was introduced by the Greeks, who indiscriminately called all Black people south of Egypt by the term *Ethiopian* ('the burnt faces').[27] Most of the Greeks' encounters with Black people were with the Cushites, from their connection with Egypt; so most of the Greek literature that mentions Ethiopians is referring to those people along the Nile, above the fourth cataract, whom this book refers to as Cushites. This is a different region and a different people from those of modern Ethiopia, which lies to the east and to the south of the Cushites.[28]

In the Akkadian literature the term 'Kus' is used to refer to this same civilization along the Nile, south of Egypt. The Hebrew Bible follows the Egyptian and Akkadian terminology, likewise using the term 'Cush'. The Septuagint, the Greek translation of the Old Testament, rendered the term as 'Ethiopia', in keeping with the Greek geographical understanding of the day.

Scholars continue to use different terms for this same region and civilization. Classical Greek scholars and New Testament scholars tend to follow the Greek rendering and use the term 'Ethiopia'. Most Egyptologists and some historians still use the Roman-era term 'Nubia'. One of the major archaeologists of Cush, George Reisner, used the term 'Ethiopia' because of the classical Greek usage. His student Dows Dunham, however, who finished the publication of Reisner's excavation data, argued in 1946 that Egyptologists should use the more precise term 'Cush' (1946: 380).

The Hebrew Bible consistently uses the term *Cush* (*kûš*) both for the region and for the inhabitants of the region. English translations of the Bible, however, are incredibly inconsistent in their translation of the Hebrew term *Cush* or *Cushite*. The King James Version, for example, translates the term as 'Cush' about one-third of the time and as 'Ethiopia' the rest of the time. The New Revised Standard Version likewise translates 'Cush' in some passages and 'Ethiopia' in

---

[27] For an overview of the usage of the term *Aithiopia* in Greek and Roman literature see Burstein (1995: 29ff., 97ff.).

[28] The area of modern Ethiopia in East Africa was the homeland of Axum, an ancient empire also inhabited by dark-skinned peoples. However, Axum did not emerge as an entity until well after the New Testament era had ended. Although the Axumites converted to Christianity during the fourth century AD and thus play an important role in Church history, they play no role in the Bible.

others. When 'Ethiopia' is used, the marginal notes add 'or Nubia, Heb. Cush.' The New American Standard Translation, the New Living Bible, and the New English Bible are similar, sometimes translating as 'Cush' and sometimes translating as 'Ethiopia', without any apparent rhyme or reason for the change (other than probable individual translator preference). The New International Version usually translates the Hebrew word *kûš* as 'Cush', except in Jeremiah 13:23, where for some reason 'Ethiopia' is used, and in Daniel 11:43, where 'Nubia' is used. The New Jerusalem Bible is similar, normally translating as 'Cush' but using 'Ethiopia' in a handful of instances. The 1988 Jewish Publication Society's English translation of the Tanakh (the Hebrew Bible) uses all three terms – Ethiopia, Cush, and Nubia – without any apparent reason for the shift. The translation strategy for this important term in the English translations of the Bible makes no apparent sense. The use of the term 'Ethiopia' is misleading, because modern Ethiopia is a different place from ancient Cush. Likewise, the use of several different English terms to translate the one Hebrew term *kûš* tends to diffuse the significance that the Cushites play in the Scriptures. This phenomenon may also reflect an attitude of indifference on the part of the White translation editors toward the significance of this term.

Of course the terminology is not the critical issue. What is critical is to recognize that these different terms refer to the same continuous civilization: a civilization that stood as one of the major powers in the Ancient Near East for over 2,000 years; a civilization that appears again and again in the biblical text.

The Cushites are particularly important to this study because they were clearly Black African people with classic 'Negroid' features.[29] There are two lines of evidence for this conclusion. First, the Cushites are presented this way in the ancient art of the Egyptians, and, later in history, in that of the Greeks and Romans. Second, numerous ancient literary texts refer, directly and indirectly, to the black skin colour and other 'Negroid' features of the Cushites.

First, the argument from art: W. Hayes writes in the *Cambridge Ancient History* that the art of Egypt clearly identified the Nubian/ Cushite group as 'Negro'. It was this connection, Hayes continues, that put the Mediterranean world into contact with the black peoples (1973: 352–353). Strouhal, in his work *Life of the Ancient Egyptians* (1992: 202), using the term 'Nubian' rather than 'Cushite', states that

---

[29] See the helpful discussion by Trigger (1978: 26–35).

from very early in the historical record 'we meet with captured enemies whose features, hair or beard, and clothing identify them as Nubian or black Africans infiltrating from the south . . .' The Cushites were famous as archers, and Strouhal refers to several Egyptian paintings that show black troops (1992: 203, 207). The most spectacular artwork on this subject is a painting in the Egyptian Museum in Cairo depicting a battle between Pharaoh Tut-ankh-amon (1352–1344 BC) and the Cushites. The Cushite warriors are not merely dark-skinned or tanned; they are clearly black. This painting can be seen in the volume by Strouhal (1992: plate 213) mentioned above or in a double-page foldout in the German publication by Eggebrecht (1984: 190–191).

A quick perusal through most books on Egyptian art will reveal portrayals of people, usually Cushites, who have very black skin colour. Aldred's *New Kingdom Art in Ancient Egypt During the Eighteenth Dynasty* identifies a black dancer as 'Nubian' (1951: plates 54 and 60). In James's book *Ancient Egypt: The Land and its Legacy* (1988: plates 137 and 147) there is a scene of Cushites bringing to the Pharaoh products of tropical Africa: gold, ebony, leopard skins, giraffe tails, monkeys, and baboons. James also presents a good picture of a sculptured granite sphinx with the head of Taharqa, the Cushite king who ruled Egypt as Pharaoh during the Twenty-fifth Dynasty. Taharqa is not depicted in the same art style as Egyptian pharaohs, for his features are Negroid – thick lips, broad nose, and tight curly hair.[30]

Snowden has researched extensively the depiction of Blacks in Greek and Roman art. In his two books he presents numerous pictures of paintings and sculptures that are clearly representations of Black people. Snowden (1983: 5, 10–11) comments that Blacks were apparently popular subjects for art in the Greek and Roman world, and he presents sixty-two photographs of Greek and Roman art depicting people of the Negroid race. Since most of the Greek and Roman contact with Blacks was with the Cushites via Egypt, it is probably safe to conclude that most of the Blacks depicted are Cushites or their descendants.[31]

---

[30] See also H. Hall's discussion of ethnicity in Egypt and among the royal families of Cush (Ethiopia) and Egypt. He states that there is clear evidence of 'Negroid' features, frequently from intermarriages, at all levels of Egyptian society (1969: 160).

[31] Snowden (1970: 113), although using the classical term 'Ethiopians' instead of 'Cushites', writes, 'The Ethiopians inhabiting the regions south of Egypt, however, have a special relevance for this book and, hence, merit a fuller treatment. In the first

The most extensive collection of artistic portrayals of the Cushites is the significant work *The Image of the Black in Western Art*, Volume I, entitled *From the Pharaohs to the Fall of the Roman Empire*. This volume contains hundreds of pictures of ancient Egyptian, Greek, and Roman art, which portray Black people with clear Negroid features. Most of the examples mentioned above in the various volumes on Egypt are also included in this volume (Bugner 1976).[32]

The other line of evidence identifying the Cushites as Blacks or Negroes is that of ancient literature. Although the Egyptians depicted Cushites frequently in their art, literary references to skin colour or other ethnic features are rare. Snowden suggests that this is because the Egyptians were very familiar with the Cushites, having lived with them as neighbours, and having seen them regularly in Egypt. The Cushites, therefore, were not a curiosity to the Egyptians. When foreigners outside of Egypt encountered the Cushites, however, they were frequently struck by the obvious physical differences between the Cushites and themselves (Snowden 1983: 7). Skin colour was the most distinguishing difference, and Greco-Roman literature frequently mentions the black skin colour of the Cushites. Indeed, the dark colour of the Cushites (or Ethiopians, as the Greeks called them) became the yardstick by which antiquity measured people of colour. Thus when the Greeks described the colour of the inhabitants of India it was said that their skin was dark, but not as dark as the Cushites (Gk. 'Ethiopians') (Snowden 1983: 7;

---

place, it was the Ethiopians south of Egypt with whom Greeks and Romans had contacts extending over the longest period of time. Secondly, it is certain that Greco-Roman experience with these Ethiopians and the records thereof, providing more details than of any other Ethiopian peoples, molded to a great extent the classical image of Ethiopia and Ethiopians and influenced attitudes toward dark or black Africans, regardless of the part of Africa from which they came. Furthermore, it was to the kingdoms of Napata and Meroe (frequently mentioned by classical authors) that a large portion of Greco-Roman observations on Ethiopia referred.' For a similar, yet more complex, conclusion regarding the Roman perception of the Latin term *Aethiopes*, see L. Thompson (1989: 57–85).

[32] Note especially the following articles: 'The Iconography of the Black in Ancient Egypt: From the Beginnings to the Twenty-fifth Dynasty', by Jean Vercoutter; 'Kushites and Meroïtes: Iconography of the African Rulers in Ancient Upper Egypt', by Jean Leclant; and 'Iconographic Evidence on the Black Populations in Greco-Roman Antiquity', by Frank M. Snowden. Although this is an outstanding work with fine articles, one wonders how Egyptian art can be included under the rubric of 'Western Art'. Perhaps during the Hellenistic period Egyptian art and culture became sufficiently interconnected with that of the Greco-Roman world to be classified as 'Western,' but prior to that, especially during the second millennium BC, Egyptian art and culture was hardly 'Western'.

1970: 2–3).[33] The colour of the Cushites' skin even became prover-bial: in Jerusalem Jeremiah wrote, 'Can the Cushite change his skin?' (Jer. 13:23). The Greeks and Romans used a similar proverb: 'to wash an Ethiopian white' became a common expression used to convey the futility of trying to change nature (Snowden 1983: 7).[34]

Other physical features are discussed in the ancient sources as well: the Cushites were described as having not only black skin, but also flat noses, thick lips, and woolly hair (Snowden 1983: 10).

The descriptions given by the ancient authors combine with the portrayals painted by the ancient Egyptian artists to present a very convincing case that the Cushites were, as Snowden (1983: 5) defines them, of the 'pure' or 'pronounced' Negroid type. Even today, the northern Sudan is populated with people having some of the darkest skin colour in all of Africa.

The Egyptians

The ethnicity of the ancient Egyptians has been a source of consid-erable controversy in recent years. Early European archaeologists and anthropologists tried to connect Egypt culturally and ethnically with the forerunners of Western civilization. They tended to deny any input into the advancements of Egyptian civilization from Black Africa (which they viewed as too primitive and backward to have been the force behind the development of Egypt).[35] Indeed, the

---

[33] Snowden cites numerous ancient Greek and Roman sources.

[34] Snowden cites six primary sources and argues that the proverbs carried no nega-tive connotations. Thompson (1989: 45–48), however, deals with numerous Roman sources and maintains that Snowden has oversimplified the data. Thompson suggests that several of the sources imply a mocking attitude toward the black-skinned 'Ethiopians'. However, Thompson is quick to point out that the Romans also mocked others who differed from them, including the Germanic tribes who had 'blond and grease-knotted hair'.

[35] Budge (1902: vii), for example, acknowledges an African element in the early origins of 'primitive' Egypt. However, he then assumes that some type of advanced outside civilization must have invaded in order to produce the early dynasties of Egypt. He writes, 'The facts related in it [the following chapter] illustrate the manner in which the civilization of the dynastic Egyptians developed out of the primitive culture of the indigenous predynastic peoples of Egypt, after it had been modified and improved by the superior intelligence of a race of men, presumably of Asiatic origin, who invaded and conquered Egypt.' Note that while Budge's works are dated, they remain in print and they are on the shelves of most large bookstores today. H. Hall (1969: 160), in the prestigious *Cambridge Ancient History*, in discussing intermarriage that occurred later in Egyptian history after the development of this 'superior race', writes, 'This cannot have been any but a degenerate component in the new Egyptian race, to which the Ethiopian and the Negro elements contributed nothing good except a certain amount

prevailing theory throughout the latter half of the nineteenth century and up to the middle of the twentieth was that *all* significant cultural achievement in *all* African empires was brought about by a small group of White elite rulers. These writers argued that the Africans were utterly unable to achieve anything significant in the area of culture or government. Obviously, many of these early archaeologists reflect a blatantly racist interpretation of the data.[36] In recent years some writers have fallen into the error of the other extreme, arguing that *everything* in Egyptian culture was the product of Black African input or that the Egyptian people and culture were synonymous with Black African culture.[37] Both of these extreme positions have tended to distort and manipulate the data in order to claim the Egyptian civilization as either 'White' or 'Black'.

However, a fairly strong consensus is emerging among scholars today that the early Egyptians were probably a mixture of both Black African elements and Asiatic elements. Although the early origins cannot be known with certainty, von Soden has suggested that the study of language and comparative linguistics offers the best means for drawing conclusions about prehistoric migrations. The presence of both Semitic and Hamitic (African) elements in the ancient Egyptian language, according to von Soden (1994: 14), suggests a mixing of the two peoples in Egypt at a very early date. The archaeological evidence appears to point to the same conclusion, suggesting tentatively that during the thousand years or so before the rise of dynastic Egypt (i.e. prior to 3100 BC) the ancient inhabitants of the Nile Valley were joined in the north by desert tribes from the east and the west, while those in the south were joined by groups migrating up from what would later become Cush.[38] Although the details are uncertain, it does appear that the Egyptians emerged out of an indigenous group that contained both African and Asiatic elements, and benefited from the unique environmental situation of the Nile Valley (J. A. Wilson 1951: 16–17).

---

of energy.' Hall continues by describing the results of this intermarriage as a 'particularly villainous cast of countenance', and as a 'contamination'. Although Hall wrote this back in 1927 it continues to be reprinted as part of the *Cambridge Ancient History*.

[36] See the discussion of this theory and its impact on Western thinking in Howe (1998: 115–121).

[37] See the thorough discussion and critique in Howe (1998: 122–137).

[38] This synthesis, however, is an oversimplification. For a detailed discussion see Hoffman (1979); Wilson (1951); Hassan (2000: 665–678); and B. Williams (1992: 331–342).

Although the actual origin of the Egyptians is uncertain, without doubt there was a constant influx of different ethnic groups into Egypt throughout the pharaonic period, and thus throughout most of the Old Testament period. Especially from around 2000 BC onward, Egypt reflected a wide range of ethnic diversity (Leahy 2000: 225–234; Bresciani 1997: 221–253). Foreign conquest by Egyptian armies brought to Egypt a steady stream of foreign slaves. In addition, a large portion of Egypt's army was composed of foreign elements: especially Cushites, but including Libyans and Asiatics, and later, Greeks and even Jews. Upon completing their military service, these troops often came to Egypt without wives, and they married native Egyptian women and settled down, becoming part of the Egyptian social fabric (Leahy 2000: 228, 232; Bresciani 1997: 224–225, 230–231). However, numerous other non-military foreigners, especially Cushites, became 'Egyptians' and advanced in Egyptian society (Bresciani 1997: 231).

Furthermore, when the Egyptians conquered a territory, they often brought many of the children from the royal families back to Egypt and educated them alongside the children of Egyptian nobility in a school referred to as the *Kap*. This was a prestigious school, and graduates carried the name of the school as part of their title. The foreigners who graduated from this institution often then advanced into the 'civil service' within the palace, the administration of the empire, or the army. Bresciani (1997: 231–232) notes: 'The existence of the *Kap* reveals both a basic absence in ancient Egypt of racial prejudice and a policy of cultural assimilation of the "defeated" by the victors.' Numerous Cushites entered the *Kap* and served throughout Egypt in a wide range of administrative positions.[39] In addition, Cushites often show up in Egyptian records as court magicians (Bresciani 1997: 232). Finally, foreigners also entered Egypt as conquerors and rulers. Egypt was ruled at one time or another in its history by pharaohs and ruling classes who were Hyksos (Semites), Libyans, and Cushites (Leahy 2000: 230–231).

There is also evidence throughout much of Egyptian history of intermarriage between the local residents and the incoming groups. Thus it is difficult to define with any precision the 'race' or 'ethnicity' of the ancient Egyptians. Obviously they were not Caucasians; the art of the Egyptians portrays them as having light brown skin. Furthermore, the art shows that the Egyptians distinguished themselves graphically from both their Asiatic neighbours to the north and

---

[39] See also the discussion of the *Kap* in Bryan (1991: 261); and Leahy (2000: 229).

their Black African neighbours to the south. However, these portrayals are probably somewhat generalized and they may reflect the thinking of the ruling class only. Without doubt there was wide diversity in the physical appearance of the ancient Egyptians. Trigger (1978: 27) suggests that ancient Egypt and Cush probably reflected a similar physical appearance to that found today in the Nile Valley. There is a continuum, Trigger writes, from north to south. He explains:

> On an average, between the Delta in northern Egypt and the Sudd of the Upper Nile, skin color tends to darken from light brown to what appears to the eye as bluish black, hair changes from wavy-straight to curly or kinky, noses become flatter and broader, lips become thicker and more everted, teeth enlarge in size from small to medium, height and linearity of body build increase to culminate in the extremely tall and thin 'Nilotic' populations of the south, and bodies become less hirsute. All of these people are Africans.

The situation in Ancient Egypt was probably similar. In the Delta, the northern part of Egypt, the majority of Egyptians probably appeared as they are portrayed in Egyptian art: with straight black hair and light brown skin. Undoubtedly, however, there were other people in the society, both Asiatics and Cushites, who looked different but were, nonetheless, Egyptians.

Thus the term 'Egyptian' probably did not define a strict physical appearance. Indeed, Leahy states that from the second millennium BC onward Egypt reflected a wide diversity in physical appearance, and thus Egyptians defined themselves not by physical appearance but by 'residence in the Nile Valley, by language, by religion, and by general culture' (Leahy 2000: 232).

The Indo-Europeans (Philistines, Hittites)

The ethnic world of the Old Testament also included two major non-Semitic-speaking peoples, the Philistines and the Hittites. While the Israelites would have shared numerous cultural aspects with the Canaanites and other Semites of the region, it is probable that they had very little cultural affinity with either of these two groups. That is, stark cultural contrasts in language, religion, dress, and myths of origins would have existed between these 'Indo-European' groups and the Semitic Israelites.

Like the Israelites, the Philistines are a group who migrated into Palestine. Indeed the English name 'Palestine' comes from the term 'Philistine', via the Greek transliteration of Herodotus and then the Latin usage by the Romans. The origin of the Philistines is not known with certainty, but most scholars place their origin in the Aegean Sea region – the coastal areas and islands between eastern Greece and western Anatolia (modern Turkey). Toward the end of the thirteenth century BC the Mycenaean civilization in this region underwent serious turmoil, and this upheaval apparently produced numerous migrations into the Eastern Mediterranean (Dothan 2000: 1267). This group spread down the eastern coastline of the Mediterranean Sea along the coastal plain of Palestine and even threatened to penetrate into Egypt. The Egyptian pharaoh Rameses III (1184–1153 BC) defeated them in a series of land and sea battles. The Egyptian annals of this conflict refer to these people generically as 'the Sea Peoples'. One of the groups within the Sea Peoples was called *Peleset*, which most scholars identify with the biblical Hebrew term 'Philistine' (Dothan 2000: 1267–1269). Kitchen (1973a: 53–60) notes that in Egyptian literature the Philistines are never mentioned alone; he concludes that the term 'Philistine' probably includes several groups involved in this aggressive migration. The Bible tends to associate the Philistines with the island of Crete (Deut. 2:23; Amos 9:7; Jer. 47:4), which implies that Crete was either the home of some of the Philistine groups or else a 'stepping-stone' in their migratory path to the Eastern Mediterranean (Dothan 2000: 1269; Kitchen 1973a: 56).[40] The Philistines settled along the coastal plain of Israel and at several points in history challenged Israel for domination of Palestine. After the Assyrian and Babylonian invasions, however, the Philistines faded from history. Through war, assimilation, deportation, and incursion of foreign settlers the Philistine cities in Palestine lost all ethnic or national distinction (Dothan 2000: 1271).

One of the major differences between the Philistines and the Israelites that the biblical texts mention repeatedly is that the Philistines were uncircumcised (Judg. 14:3, 15:18; 1 Sam. 14:6, 17:26, 36; 31:4; 2 Sam. 1:20). This was a significant difference because most of the Northwest Semitic groups (Israel's Semitic cousins) practised

---

[40] Howard (1994: 237–238) suggests that the origin of the Philistines may be much more complex, even including Canaanite elements. He notes the difficult text in Genesis 10:14 that connects the Philistines with the Egyptians, and suggests that this may be a reference to a totally separate group.

circumcision, as did some classes of Egyptians (priests, for example). The Philistines were one of the few groups in the region that did not practise this rite (R. Hall 1992: 1025–1026; V. Matthews 1991: 84–85).

Another major Indo-European group that appears in the Old Testament is the Hittites.[41] The origin of the Hittites is not known, but they apparently migrated into Anatolia (modern Turkey) around 2000 BC and assimilated the Hatti people who inhabited the area at the time. By 1700 BC they had established a powerful state; they continued as a major player in the geopolitical scene of the Ancient Near East until 1190 BC, when the Hittite empire collapsed, probably because of pressure from northern tribes and also the migrating Sea Peoples (Hoffner 1973: 198–199; 1994: 128–130; Macqueen 2000: 1085–1105). However, during the end of the thirteenth century BC and the beginning of the twelfth century BC the Hittites migrated down into Syria, probably continuing as far as Canaan (Hoffner 1994: 153). They established firm control of Syria, where they continued to dwell and rule even after the collapse of their civilization in Anatolia (Macqueen 2000: 1099). In Syria they came into direct conflict with the expanding Egyptian influence of the Nineteenth Dynasty (1305–1200 BC), and numerous battles were fought between the two (Macqueen 2000: 1094; Hoffner 1994: 130). Hittite prisoners appear in Egyptian monumental art from this period. Bresciani notes that they are depicted with 'beardless faces, double chins, and long ringleted hair' (Bresciani 1997: 238). Because of their presence in Syria and their probable migrations into Canaan, Israel also comes into frequent contact with them, especially during the early years of the monarchy.[42]

Thus, if today's readers of the Bible want to find people of 'Caucasian' appearance in the Old Testament, the Indo-European Philistines and Hittites are probably the closest. However, even the individuals from these ancient Indo-European groups probably resembled the people of modern Greece or Turkey more than they may have resembled the people of modern England or mid-western America.

---

[41] For an excellent discussion of Hittite history see Bryce (1998).

[42] However, numerous references are also made to the Hittites in the biblical books that cover the early years of Israel's history (Genesis–Joshua). Hoffner (1973: 214) doubts whether this term, especially during the patriarchal period, refers to the same Hittites that dominated Anatolia. Hamilton (1995: 126–129), on the other hand, in addressing the presence of Hittites in Genesis 23, presents numerous arguments in favour of identifying the references to 'Hittite' in Genesis with the Hittites of Anatolia.

Conclusions

The people in the Old Testament reflected a wide range of ethnic diversity. However, contrary to popular perceptions, few of these characters, if any, looked like modern northern Europeans or mid-western Americans. Although the concept of 'ethnicity' is difficult to delineate precisely, it is possible to determine distinctions between four major ethnic groups that appear in the Old Testament. The group appearing most frequently, of course, is the Northwest Semitic group, composed of Israel and many of her neighbours (Canaanites, Moabites, Edomites, Ammonites, etc.). Also playing a role in the Old Testament are the Cushites (Black Africans), the Egyptians (probably a mix of Asiatic and Black African), and the Indo-Europeans (Philistines and Hittites). Thus the Old Testament world was completely multi-ethnic.

It is important that today's readers of the Old Testament, particularly readers within the White Church, realize this multi-ethnic background. White North American Christianity has a strong historical tendency to be ethnocentric, and part of this distortion is to project Caucasian people back into all aspects of the biblical story. Coming to grips with the multi-ethnic, non-Caucasian cultural context of the Old Testament is a critical foundational step in developing a truly biblical theology of race.

Chapter Three

Creation, blessing, and race (Genesis 1 – 12)

Introduction

The first twelve chapters of Genesis are critical – indeed, founda-tional – to biblical theology. Genesis 1 – 11 contrasts the wonderful creation of God with the terrible, sinful tendency of his creatures. These chapters describe who we are and what our problem is. Genesis 12:1–3, however, presents the great redemptive plan of God – the solution to the human problem described in the first eleven chapters.[1] These chapters provide a theological framework for how we as Christians understand the rest of the Bible. Several texts within these important chapters have direct implications for our theology of race. We will explore being created in the image of God (Gen. 1:26–31), the scattering and description of people into families, languages, lands, and nations (Genesis 10 – 11), and the promise of blessing on all the peoples of the earth (Gen. 12:1–3). Because the 'curse on Canaan' (Gen. 9:18–27) has been so badly misinterpreted and abused in Christian history, we will also examine that text, but, as we shall show, it is not actually related to the issue of race at all.

Created in the image of God

The Bible does not begin with the creation of a special race of people. When the first human is introduced into the story he is simply called *'āḏām*, which means 'humankind'. As mentioned in Chapter 2, Adam and Eve are not Hebrews or Egyptians or Canaanites. It is incorrect for the White Church to view them as White or for the Black Church to view them as Black. Their 'race' is not identifiable; they are neither

---

[1] There may be an adumbration of the redemptive plan suggested in Gen. 3:15 ('he will crush your head') or in Gen. 3:21 ('the LORD God made garments of skin for Adam and his wife'), but these allusions are faint and subtle, and they do not play the central role in the rest of the biblical story that Gen. 12:1–3 plays.

Negroid nor Caucasian, nor even Semitic.[2] They become the mother and father of all peoples. The division of humankind into peoples and races is not even mentioned until Genesis 10. Adam and Eve, as well as Noah, are non-ethnic and non-national. They represent all people, not some people.

Genesis 1 describes the six days of creation. The climax of the creation comes on day six, when humans are created. Indeed, this event is the focus of the creation narrative. Genesis 1:26–27 delineates God's action:

> Then God said, 'Let us make man [*'ādām*] in our image, in our likeness, and let them rule over the fish of the sea and the birds of the air, over the livestock, over all the earth, and over all the creatures that move along the ground.'

> So God created man [*'ādām*]
>   in his own image,
> in the image of God
>   he created him;
> male and female
>   he created them.

What exactly is the 'image of God'? The meaning of this phrase is actually rather ambiguous. Scholars have written extensively about the image of God, but no cross-discipline consensus has emerged.[3] Wenham (1987: 29–32) summarizes the various proposals into five main positions:

(1) 'Image' and 'likeness' are distinct, with image referring to natural qualities (reason, personality, etc.) and likeness referring to the supernatural graces that make the redeemed godlike;
(2) The image refers to the mental and spiritual faculties that people share with their creator;
(3) The image consists of a physical resemblance;

---

[2] McKissic (1990: 17–19) disagrees, raising the issue of genetics, both for Adam and Eve and for Noah and his wife. The genetic pattern for all of the races of humankind, argues McKissic, had to be present in both of these sets of people. Thus they had to carry the genetic pattern for the Negroid race. If they carried these genes then one of them at least, according to McKissic, would have had Negroid features.

[3] See the bibliography and overview of the history of exegesis on these verses in Westermann (1984: 147–155). Westermann begins his discussion with the statement, 'The literature is limitless.'

(4) The image refers to the appointment of humankind as God's representatives on earth; and

(5) The image is a capacity to relate to God.

Few current scholars hold positions 1 (a patristic view) or 3 (physical resemblance). However, the other views appear in numerous forms and combinations.

In addition, Old Testament scholars, both those writing commentaries and those writing biblical theology, tend to discuss and understand this term in a different way from systematic theologians. Typically, systematic theologians, holding views 2 and/or 5, discuss the image in the context of the 'fall' in Genesis 3.[4] They focus on the question: 'How is the image of God in man marred or destroyed by man's sin, and how is it restored in Christ?' One popular answer to this line of inquiry is that part of the image of God was destroyed in the fall to await restoration in Christ, but that some of the image remains even in unregenerate people.

Many Old Testament scholars, however, observe that within the text of Genesis the image of God in Genesis 1 is not connected in any way to the fall in Genesis 3 (Childs 1985: 98; Brueggemann 1997: 452). Leaning on the immediate scriptural context of man's ruling over God's creation, and arguing from Ancient Near Eastern parallels which use statues of the 'image of the king' to function as boundary markers, Old Testament scholars tend to gravitate either to view 4 (God's representative) or to a combination of view 4 and view 5 (capacity to relate to God).[5]

Psalm 8 appears to confirm that something related to the image of God continues to distinguish humans from the rest of creation even after the fall. Numerous points of connection exist between Genesis 1 and Psalm 8. In Psalm 8:3 the Psalmist refers to the heavens, the moon, and the stars. In verse 4 he asks, 'What is man . . . and the son of man that you care for him?' Verse 5 states, 'You made him a little

---

[4] See for example, Berkouwer (1962).

[5] 'While the meaning of "the image of God" is open to much debate, this phrase refers basically to those characteristics of human beings that make communication with God possible and enable them to take up the God-given responsibilities specified in these verses' (Birch 1999: 49). This view is also expressed by House (1998: 60–61). Writing in 1988, Jónsson states that Old Testament scholarship has approached reaching a consensus view of this text, one which understands the image of God as referring to mankind's 'dominion over the animal world, exercised by him as God's representative.' Westermann, following Karl Barth, is the noted exception. See Jónsson (1988: 219–225).

lower than the heavenly beings (*'elōhîm*).' Verses 6–8, similar to Genesis 1:28, refer to humankind's role as God-appointed ruler over flocks, herds, birds, fish, etc. The Psalmist marvels at the special status that God has given to humans.

Thus, whether or not one believes that the image was marred or blurred in the fall, it seems clear that humankind was created in the image of God and that remnants of that image, at the very least, still remain, distinguishing humans from animals and the rest of creation. Furthermore, the racially generic Adam represents all of humankind.[6] All people of all races are thus created in the image of God. Blacks, Whites, and peoples of all other races are all created in the image of God. Therefore, the quality that distinguishes humankind from the animals and from the rest of creation is shared by all the races of the earth.

This conclusion has far-reaching implications for theology and ethics.[7] Stott writes, 'Both the dignity and the equality of human beings are traced in Scripture to our creation' (Stott 1999: 174–175). Racism or the presupposition that one's own race is superior or better than another is a denial that all people have been created in the image of God. H. P. Smith (1972: viii) places this connection at the heart of his definition of *racism*, writing: 'In short, racism from the Christian standpoint is a response that violates the equalitarian principle implied in the biblical doctrine of the *imago Dei* [the image of God].'

Proverbs 14:31 and 17:5 likewise connect the implications of God's creation of people with one's ethical behaviour toward other people. Proverbs 14:31a states: 'He who oppresses the poor shows contempt for their Maker.' Proverbs 17:5a is similar: 'He who mocks the poor shows contempt for their Maker.' Ross (1991: 991) notes the implied connection to the image of God, writing, 'Here is the doctrine of the Creation in its practical outworking. Anyone who oppresses the "poor" shows contempt for his Maker, for that poor person also is the image of God.' These verses are pointing out that the superior attitude taken by one in a wealthy socio-economic setting toward another in a poor setting is an affront to the God who created them both. The same principle would apply to race and racial attitudes. Not only is the 'oppression' of another race an affront to God, but

---

[6] Crüsemann (1996: 66) cites an appropriate comment from the Mishnah (Sanh. 10.5): 'Why did God create only one human being? So that no one can say to a fellow human being: my father was better than yours.'

[7] Maston (1959: 1–15) builds much of his theology of race relations upon this central tenet.

the 'mocking' of that race is likewise offensive, underscoring the fact that racial jokes are a direct insult to God. That is, the telling of racial jokes is similar to mocking the poor in Proverbs 17:5. To ridicule someone created in the image of God is to ridicule God.

So the creation of humans in the image of God has far-reaching implications for how we view each other and how we treat each other. All people of all races are created in God's image and therefore deserve to be treated with dignity and respect.

The so-called 'curse of Ham' (Genesis 9:18–27)

Throughout this book we will primarily focus on what the Scriptures say or imply regarding race and our attitude towards racial differences. However, in this section it is necessary to cover what the Bible *doesn't* say: that is, it is necessary to correct one of the most serious and most damaging misinterpretations of Scripture on this subject. Indeed, as early as 1808, David Burrow, writing against slavery, bemoans, 'I am persuaded that no passage in the sacred volume of revelation has suffered more abuse than "Noah's curse or malediction"' (1808: 28n).[8]

At the end of Genesis 9, Noah and his family are settling down after the flood. Noah plants a vineyard, drinks wine from the vineyard, becomes naked, and then lies uncovered in his tent (9:20–21). His son Ham, explicitly identified as 'the father of Canaan' (9:22), sees his father's nakedness and then tells his two brothers Shem and Japheth. The two brothers take a garment (lit. 'the' garment) back into the tent, and cover Noah without looking at him. When Noah awakes and finds out what his youngest son Ham had done to him (9:24), he pronounces a curse on Canaan, the youngest son of Ham (9:25), stating:

> Cursed be Canaan!
> The lowest of slaves
> will he be to his brothers.

He then proceeds to bless Shem and Japheth, saying:

> Blessed be the LORD, the God of Shem!
> May Canaan be the slave of Shem.

---

[8] Cited by H. Smith (1972: 131).

May God extend the territory of Japheth;
may Japheth live in the tents of Shem,
and may Canaan be his slave.

(9:26–27)

Throughout the last twenty centuries, numerous Christian, Jewish, and Muslim writers connected this curse to Ham and then to Black Africa in various ways, sometimes derogatorily and sometimes not.[9] However, in the antebellum South of the United States, this text became a standard, central Scripture for the defence of slavery. Put on the defensive by the scriptural arguments of the northern abolitionists during the first half of the nineteenth century, southern writers – often clergy – appropriated this text as one of their foundational biblical arguments justifying slavery. They argued that, first, the curse was really intended for all of the descendants of Ham rather than just for Canaan, because Ham was not blessed in 9:26–27 and because Ham was the one who committed the offence. Second, 'Ham' means 'black' or 'burnt', thus explicitly referring to the Black race; and third, God commanded that these descendants be slaves to Japheth, who represents the White races. Thus, they argued, God commanded the slavery of Black Africans (H. S. Smith 1972: 130–131; Bradley 1971: 100–110). Josiah Priest, one of the more powerful proponents of this view, writes:

The servitude of the race of Ham, to the latest era of mankind, is necessary to the veracity of God Himself, as by it is fulfilled one of the oldest of the decrees of the Scriptures, namely, that of Noah, which placed the race as servants under other races.

(Priest 1853: 393)[10]

Bradley (1971: 103) notes the logic of Priest's appeal, stating:

What Priest was really saying was that the truthfulness or infallibility of God's prophetic statements, as contained in

---

[9] See J. Lewis (1968) and Copher (1989: 105–128). Yamauchi notes that the employment of this 'curse' to justify the enslavement of Black Africans was apparently first made by Muslims as they began trafficking in Black slaves in the eighth century AD (Yamauchi forthcoming, Chapter 1). Also documenting this point of view is B. Lewis (1990: 55, 125).

[10] Cited by Bradley (1971: 103).

Scripture, hinged upon the acceptance of Negro slavery as the necessary fulfillment of the curse of Ham. This had the effect of placing the truthfulness of God's self-revelation on the same level as acceptance of Negro slavery and white supremacy.

After the American Civil War, the 'curse of Ham' was used by white clergymen to fight the notion of racial equality and the rights that would accompany such equality (voting, education, etc.). Richard Rivers, for example, editor of the Louisville *Central Methodist*, argued in an 1889 editorial for the popular view that, so long as the two races must live together on American soil, the Black man 'must occupy the position of inferiority', and that 'Ham must be subservient to Japheth.'[11]

Although Old Testament scholarship today views this position as exegetically ridiculous, the connection between this curse and the slavery of Africans continues to be taught to the church via commentaries that are reprinted and for sale even today. For example, Pink, in *Gleanings in Genesis* (reprinted by Moody Press, 1950), writes:

> The whole of Africa was peopled by the descendants of Ham, and for many centuries the greater part of that continent lay under the dominion of the Romans, Saracens, and Turks. And, as is well known, the Negroes who were for so long the slaves of Europeans and Americans also claim Ham as their progenitor.
>
> (1950: 126)[12]

The view that the slavery of Africans was a fulfilment of this curse was not limited to American writers. Keil and Delitzsch, in their popular *Commentary on the Old Testament* (reprinted by Eerdmans, 1986), write:

> In the sin of Ham there lies the great stain of the whole Hamitic race, whose chief characteristic is sexual sin; and the curse which Noah pronounced upon this sin still rests upon the race . . . the remainder of the Hamitic tribes either shared

---

[11] Cited by H. S. Smith (1972: 271).
[12] Cited by Bradley (1971: 104).

the same fate, or sigh still, like the Negroes, for example, and other African tribes, beneath the yoke of the most crushing slavery.

(1986: 157–158)[13]

Likewise, the *Preacher's Complete Homiletic Commentary* (reprinted by Baker as the *Preacher's Homiletic Commentary*, 1980), in illustrating the fulfilment of the curse of slavery on the descendants of Ham, states, 'it is well known that most of the nations of Europe traded in African slaves' (Exell and Leale 1892: 186).

Although all three of these works espouse a rather racist interpretation of this text, a view that has been consistently rejected by Old Testament scholarship for over fifty years, nonetheless they are in print and for sale through popular distributors such as Christian Book Distributors (CBD) and Amazon.com. Indeed, during the time I wrote this chapter, I discovered Pink's *Gleanings in Genesis* displayed on the shelf and for sale in a Lifeway Christian Bookstore (Southern Baptist). Thus this view continues to be disseminated among Christians in the Church today.

Keep in mind that this position was popularized in the United States primarily to justify slavery of Africans. Even now, as it is stated by the three works above, this view implies very clearly the theological view that the imposition of slavery on Black Africans by White Europeans and Americans was in fulfilment of a prophecy by God and was, therefore, justified. This is a very dangerous and damaging theological heresy that tends to cover up or 'whitewash' a very serious sin.[14]

How *should* this text be interpreted?[15] First of all, note that it is Canaan, and not Ham, that is cursed (Gen. 9:25).[16] Thus to extend

---

[13] Keil and Delitzsch's statement is puzzling, because they should be quite familiar with the general history of the region. If Ham's descendants are determined by Genesis 10, as most who hold this position maintain, then these descendants include the Egyptians, Cushites, Philistines, Hittites, and even the Assyrians. These groups *dominated* the Ancient Near East throughout the second millennium and well into the first millennium BC. Centuries and centuries of geopolitical domination are not likely to be a fulfilment of a curse prophesying slavery.

[14] It should be noted, however, that Jewish and Muslim writers also connected this curse with the slavery of Black Africans, so, unfortunately, Christianity is not the only guilty party. See Isaac (1992: 31–32).

[15] See the good exegetical and theological discussions by Hamilton (1990: 323–327) and Robertson (1998: 177–188).

[16] The Byzantine Lectionaries of the Septuagint read 'Ham' instead of 'Canaan'. However, these manuscripts are minor witnesses to the Septuagint tradition, and

this curse to all of Ham's descendants is to misread the text. The Canaanites are the focus of the curse. Many scholars note that this is a prophetic curse against Israel's classic, but future, enemy – the Canaanites (Hamilton 1990: 324–327; Ross 1988: 217–218; Sailhamer 1990: 96–97). Apparently these Canaanites are aptly cursed in connection with this sexual-related sin because they are also characterized by the same type of sin in other texts within the Pentateuch. See, for example, Leviticus 18:2–23, where sexual sins are identified with the sins of the Canaanites. Note that throughout Leviticus 18 the term 'nakedness' (the same term used of Noah in Genesis 9:22–23) is used consistently as a euphemism for sexual sin ('nakedness', which occurs 24 times in Leviticus 18, is translated by NIV throughout the chapter as 'sexual relations') (Ross 1988: 217).[17] Thus the curse on Canaan does not appear to be pronounced so that Canaan will be punished for Ham's sin. The curse is apparently a prophetic curse against the future enemy of Israel, a descendant of Ham who will be like Ham in this regard.

It may also be pertinent to note that the Canaanites are ethnically very close to the Israelites. As mentioned in Chapter 2, the Canaanite language and culture is similar to that of the Israelites. They were also probably very similar in appearance. The critical difference was in regard to the gods that they worshipped. So, as mentioned above, the curse on Canaan has absolutely nothing to do with Black Africa. Furthermore, because of the close ethnic affinity between the Canaanites and the Israelites, it can be said that this curse has nothing to do with 'race' at all.

How does this curse play out in Israel's history? The fulfilment of this curse begins when the Israelites, descendants of Shem, invade

---

appear to reflect a late attempt at harmonization. All of the major Septuagint manuscript witnesses have 'Canaan' as the one who is cursed. See Wevers (1993: 124). Some of the commentators are somewhat misleading in regard to this weakly attested variant reading. For example, Hamilton (1990: 324) states (incorrectly) that the Septuagint reads 'Ham' instead of 'Canaan'. Westermann (1984: 482) is better, noting that *some* Greek manuscripts replace Canaan with Ham in an obvious attempt to harmonize the text. The older critical text of the Hebrew Old Testament, *Biblia Hebraica* (BHK), is perhaps to blame, listing the variant 'Ham' in some manuscripts of the Septuagint but not specifying which ones. The Byzantine Lectionaries reflect such a weak attestation of this reading that the more recent critical text, *Biblia Hebraica Stuttgartensia* (BHS), does not list *any* variants for this verse. Likewise, the critical edition of the Septuagint by Rahlfs (1979) does not even list any variants within the Septuagint manuscripts for this verse.

[17] Also connecting Leviticus 18 with Genesis 9:25–27 is Brueggemann (1982: 90–91).

Canaan in the conquest, and is eventually completed when Israel totally subjugates the Canaanites during the monarchy. How the descendants of Japheth fulfil this prophecy is not quite as clear. Hamilton (1990: 325–327) suggests that the Philistines, part of the Sea People migration from the Aegean (see Chapter 2), are descendants of Japheth and thus fulfil this prophecy as they also overrun parts of Canaan. In 1 and 2 Samuel, for instance, the Israelites and the Philistines both dominate the land of Canaan. Practically all of the Canaanite inhabitants had been conquered by one of these two powers.[18]

The curse on Canaan, therefore, should be interpreted within the Old Testament context and identified with the victory of the Israelites over the Canaanite inhabitants of the Promised Land. It is incorrect to call this the 'curse of Ham', or to identify it with Black Africa or Africans in any way.

The Table of Nations (Genesis 10)

Genesis 10, often called 'the Table of Nations,' recounts how the peoples of the world descended from the three sons of Noah and spread out over the world. This chapter contains some challenging historical/hermeneutical issues that should not be dismissed lightly. Sarna (1989: 68), for example, writes, 'The Table itself is riddled with difficulties, many of which remain insoluble in the present state of knowledge.'[19] Most Old Testament scholars – evangelical, non-evangelical, and Jewish – approach this chapter cautiously and state their conclusions tentatively. This caution by those who have studied this chapter seriously and extensively should serve perhaps as a warning to those who may approach it casually. We should likewise proceed with caution in this chapter and refrain from simplistic, overly dogmatic conclusions.

Two radically different groups have interpreted the classification of peoples in Genesis 10 along simple racial lines. This view interprets the three sons of Noah as heading three major races of mankind. Thus Japheth represents the White or Caucasian race, Ham the Black race, and Shem the Semitic race. On the one extreme was the old

---

[18] Also identifying the Philistines with the prophecy in Gen. 9:27 is Sarna (1989: 64). However, note that Genesis 10, enigmatic as the chapter may be, connects the Philistines to Egypt, and thus to Ham (10:13–14).

[19] For an overview of the interpretative problems in this chapter see Simons (1994: 236–238).

argument of those who held to White superiority and maintained that the curse of Ham applied to all Black people, especially Africans. They argued: the name 'Ham' means 'black'; Ham is connected to Cush or Africa; therefore all Black Africans are under the curse of Ham. A newer interpretation comes from the other extreme. Using a similar approach to Genesis 10, but reinterpreting, of course, the so-called 'curse of Ham', are several current authors who argue for a widespread presence and influence of 'black peoples' throughout the Ancient Near East. They argue: the name 'Ham' means 'black'; his descendants include Cush, or Africa; therefore all of Ham's descendants were 'black', including the forefathers of the Egyptian and even the Mesopotamian civilizations (through Nimrod) (McKissic 1990: 16–34).

Both of these approaches ignore the complexity of Genesis 10 and both overlook scholarly discussion on the chapter. Also, note that the supposed meaning of 'black' for the name 'Ham' is derived by both approaches by connecting Ham etymologically to the Egyptian word *Keme*, 'the black land', which refers to Egypt itself. However, both of these approaches then proceed to take the genealogy in a very strict, literal 'physical descent' sense. Note that under a literal 'physical descent' interpretation, the Egyptian language would not even have been developed yet (i.e. the Egyptians descended from Ham), so to suppose that the word 'Ham' (the father of Egypt) is based on an Egyptian word for 'black' would be highly unlikely. If there *is* a connection between these two words, the significance is more likely that Ham is symbolic of Egypt itself, a view advocated by Sarna (1989: 64).[20] Yet, as Brenner (1982: 156) points out, it is quite hermeneutically hazardous simply to spot phonetic similarities between names and colours and then to draw conclusions from the similarity. The name 'Laban', for example, the father-in-law of Jacob (Genesis 29 – 31), is the exact same Hebrew word as the word for 'white'. However, it would be quite incorrect to assume that Laban somehow represented the 'White' race.

Associating Ham with the Black race actually requires two questionable steps. First, one has to assume that the name Ham comes from the Egyptian word for 'black'; second, one has to assume that the significance of this relation is that the colour term black refers to

---

[20] Note the parallelism between Ham and Egypt in Psalms 78:51; 105:23, 27; and 106:21–22. However, note that Sarna interprets the chapter in a symbolic sense, and not at all as a literal physical descent genealogy.

a race of people and not something else. Both steps are dubious. There are several other equally compelling options for the possible meaning for Ham. Ham may be related to the Hebrew word for 'warm' (*ḥāmam*) or to the Hebrew word *ḥām*, 'wife's father-in-law'. It is quite likely that the name has absolutely nothing to do with the colour black. Copher (1989: 108–109), a leading Black scholar who writes on this subject, recognizes this and acknowledges that the term 'Ham' had nothing to do with the colour of his descendants. Indeed, the consensus view of Old Testament scholarship is that it is impossible to state with any degree of certainty *what* Ham means – or Japheth and Shem, for that matter (Wenham 1987: 129; Matthews 1996: 319–320; Cassuto 1978: 290).

Genesis 10, in fact, does not appear to organize the world into three simple categories of racial groupings. Sarna (1989: 68), for example, writes, 'Racial characteristics, physical types, or the color of skin play no role in the categorizing.'[21] This is not to say that racial groups are not present in Genesis 10, but to note that the criteria for organizing the world into three main groups connected to Ham, Shem, and Japheth does not appear to be primarily racial or even linguistic.

What is the criterion for the organization of Genesis 10? From his study of other Ancient Near Eastern genealogies, R. Wilson (1994: 213–214) concludes that genealogies function in one or more of three spheres: a domestic sphere, showing kinship relationships based on biological, economic, or geographical ties; a political sphere; and/or a religious sphere. Sarna notes from other Ancient Near Eastern literature that treaty relationships are often expressed with kinship terms, and the phrase 'son of' can refer to a vassal–lord arrangement (1989: 68). Ross proposes a similar view, stating that genealogies in the Ancient Near East were used both to trace lineages and to chart alliances (1988: 228). McNutt (1999: 76–77) argues a similar view, writing, 'The primary function of genealogies, then, is not to produce and transmit accurate lists of biological relationships through time, but to define social, political, and economic relations.'

It cannot be merely assumed, therefore, that all of the names in Genesis 10 refer to individuals. Indeed, the Table includes names of individuals, peoples, tribes, countries, and cities (Ross 1988:

---

[21] See also von Rad (1961: 136); Brueggemann (1982: 91–92); and Crüsemann (1996: 66).

228).[22] The text itself indicates that a range of various criteria has been used. In each summarizing verse for the genealogies of Japheth, Ham, and Shem is a statement indicating that the groupings are based on family/tribe/clan (*mišpāḥāh*), language (*lāšôn*), land/country/territory (*'ereṣ*), and nation (*gôy*) (Gen. 10:5, 20, 31). Thus the basis for the classifications of peoples in this chapter is a combination of anthropological, linguistic, political, and geographical elements. Yet all three genealogies end with nations, perhaps indicating that political and national affiliations are the primary emphasis (Ross 1988: 227–228). For example, Genesis 10:6 groups together Cush, Mizraim (Egypt), Put (Libya), and Canaan. Current scholarship indicates that these four 'countries' were not directly related racially, linguistically, or religiously. Politically, however, all four were under Egyptian control for much of the patriarchal period and even up to the conquest. Thus the majority of Old Testament scholars, while acknowledging that Genesis 10 is quite complex, do nonetheless maintain that the central organizing feature of the breakdown of nations in Genesis 10 is not based on physical descent, but rather related to territorial or geopolitical affiliations (Sarna 1989: 68; Ross 1988: 228; Westermann 1984: 511; Brueggemann 1982: 91; von Rad 1961: 136).

Also, there are undoubtedly some symbolic elements in the chapter, indicated by the fact that there are *seventy* nations mentioned, and several groups of *seven* are included (Sailhamer 1990: 98–101; Sarna 1989: 69; Matthews 1996: 430).[23] However, even though much of this chapter remains enigmatic, one central theological point of the chapter is clear: the stress on the common origin of all nations. This explanation of origins stands in strong contrast to Egyptian mythology, in which the Egyptians saw themselves alone as 'men', and everybody else in the world as having descended from the enemies of the gods (Sarna 1989: 69). Genesis 1 – 10, by contrast, does not elevate the Israelites to a special created status. In fact, the Israelites are not even an identifiable entity until later in Genesis. There are not even any Israelites mentioned in Genesis 10. This is an important distinction and it has strong implications for our theology

---

[22] Sarna (1989: 68) writes, 'Many of the personal names listed here are otherwise known to be those of places or peoples. Ten names have plural endings, nine others take the gentilic adjectival suffix –*i*, which indicates ethnic affiliation, and they also have the definite article, which is inadmissible with personal names in Hebrew.'

[23] Note that at the end of Genesis Abraham has seventy descendants, paralleling the number of nations in Genesis 10. See Waltke (2001: 164).

of race. Hess (1994: 68) writes, 'Finally, whatever else the Table of Nations in Genesis 10 should emphasize, it is clear from its context in Genesis 1 – 11 that it points to the common humanity of all peoples, who share in the failures and hopes of a common ancestry, and ultimately in a common creation in the image of God.' Westermann (1984: 529) draws the same conclusion, citing Dillman: 'All individuals and peoples are of the same race, the same dignity, and the same character.'

As part of our goal in focusing particularly on texts relating to the Black–White tensions in the Church today, it is significant to note that the biblical picture of the common humanity that descended from Noah included the Cushites (10:6–12), a Black African people.[24] Obviously, Black people were not a late addition to the Judeo-Christian story, as the Nation of Islam (Louis Farrakhan and his predecessor Elijah Muhammed) has argued.[25] The Black Cushites are part of the biblical story from the very beginning.

It is also significant to note the relationship between Genesis 10 and Genesis 11. The generation-account (*tôlēḏôt*) section begins in 10:1 ('this is the account of Shem, Ham, and Japheth') and continues to 11:9. This indicates that the Tower of Babel story in 11:1–9 is connected to the Table of Nations in Genesis 10 (Ross 1988: 221; Matthews 1996: 430). The Tower of Babel story explains how and why people spread out and filled the earth with different languages. It explains why the nations are scattered as they are in Genesis 10. Although God gives the command in 9:1 to increase and fill the earth, the Tower of Babel episode in 11:1–9 underlines that the division into different people groups with different languages was a consequence of human disobedience. Taken together the two chapters hold in tension two opposing aspects: 'the unity of the tribes and nations as of one blood under God's blessing and their diversity into many languages under God's wrath' (Waltke 2001: 162). This situation sets the stage for Genesis 12 and the promise to Abraham.

---

[24] The connection between Cush, the enigmatic Nimrod, and the civilizations of Mesopotamia remains puzzling. However, the solution to the difficulty does not lie in assuming that the term Cush is really a reference to the 'Cassites', a Mesopotamian group, instead of the 'Cushites'. Cush is a very common name in the Old Testament and it consistently refers to the nation of Black Africans who lived along the Nile south of Egypt. There is no reason to interpret it any differently in Genesis 10 than in the rest of the Old Testament. See Westermann (1984: 510) and Simons (1994: 239–241).

[25] For a good discussion of the Christian response to the Nation of Islam's charges, see the chapter, 'How Do We Answer the Nation of Islam?' in Keener and Usry (1997: 56–66).

Blessing for all the families of the world (Genesis 12)

God's call of Abraham in Genesis 12 is in direct response to the disastrous human situation described in Genesis 3 – 11. More specifically, Genesis 10 – 11, the Table of Nations and the Tower of Babel, stand as the prologue to Genesis 12:1–3. God calls Abraham out of his concern for those nations described in Genesis 10. Recall that Genesis 10 described the division of the world according to family/tribe/clan (*mišpāḥāh*), language (*lāšôn*), land/country/territory (*'ereṣ*), and nation (*gôy*) (Gen. 10:5, 20, 31). The call of Abraham picks up on three of these terms: 'Go from your country (*'ereṣ*)' (12:1); 'I will make you a great nation (*gôy*)' (12:2); and 'in you all the families (*mišpāḥāh*) of the earth will be blessed' (12:3) (NRSV). The term 'families' (*mišpāḥāh*) in 12:3 provides a very tight connection back to Genesis 10, for this term occurs not only in the summary statements (10:5, 20, 31) but also in 10:18 and 10:32.[26] The NIV is a little misleading, translating this term as 'clans' in Genesis 10 but as 'peoples' in 12:3. The NRSV maintains the semantic connection much better, translating the term as 'families' in both chapters. Thus the promise in 12:3 clearly connects back to Genesis 10. The promise to Abraham is the answer to the sin and the scattering of Genesis 3 – 11.

The call and promise to Abraham in Genesis 12:1–3 introduces God's spectacular redemptive plan, one that culminates in Jesus Christ himself. But from the beginning God has the diverse peoples of the world in mind. God focuses on Abraham not to be exclusive, but to use this individual and his descendants to bless and deliver the entire world. This is a critical aspect of Genesis 12 and the unfolding presentation of God's redemptive plan. Brueggemann (1982: 105) writes, 'The call to Sarah and Abraham has to do not simply with the forming of Israel but with the re-forming of creation, the transforming of the nations.' Westermann (1985: 152) adds, 'God's action proclaimed in the promise to Abraham is not limited to him and his posterity, but reaches its goal only when it includes all of the families of the earth.'

The promise of Genesis 12:1–3 is restated and expanded throughout the Abrahamic narratives. In Genesis 12:3, God promises that through

---

[26] Carroll R. (2000: 20) notes this connection and concludes, 'Whatever else the call of Abram might entail, at the very least one can see that it is designed to reach "all" the peoples descended from the sons of Noah.'

Abraham all the *families* of the earth will be blessed. As mentioned above, *families* are the first element in the fourfold list of Genesis 10. In Genesis 18:18, however, God restates the promise with a slight change. He promises that all the *nations* (*gôy*) of the earth will be blessed through Abraham, referring back to the *fourth* element in the fourfold list of Genesis 10. The two promises, taken together, imply that the totality of the fourfold list is to find blessing through Abraham.

Indeed, the promise of blessing on the *families* or *peoples* of the earth through Abraham emerges as the focal point of the Genesis 12:1–3 promise. Regarding Genesis 12:3, Fretheim (1994: 424) writes:

> This final phrase presents the objective of all previous clauses – God's choice of Abram will lead to blessings for *all* the families of the earth (see 10:32; note the corporate focus). God's choice of Abram serves as an initially exclusive move for the sake of a maximally inclusive end. Election serves mission (in the broadest sense of the word).

The theme introduced here – that sin scatters the peoples of the world but that God's blessing reunites them – runs throughout the Scriptures. Although I will discuss this theme in more detail throughout the book it is important to make the connection here with Genesis 10 – 12. The prophets will frequently paint a future picture of all peoples uniting together to worship God, a direct reversal of Genesis 10 – 11 and a fulfilment of Genesis 12:1–3 (Ross 1988: 234). Luke will present Christ as the fulfilment of the promise to Abraham. Likewise the power of the Spirit seen at Pentecost (Acts 2) to overcome language is a reversal of Genesis 10 – 11. Finally, the ultimate picture in Revelation of 'every tribe and language and people and nation' (Rev. 5:9, 7:9, 11:9, 14:6) united as the people of God saved by Christ is a direct trajectory of the promise made to Abraham here in Genesis 12:1–3.[27]

Conclusions

From Genesis 1 comes the basic foundational premise for a theology of race: *all people are created in the image of God*. This gives every

---

[27] The list in Revelation uses the same exact words and the same order as does the LXX in Genesis 10:20, except that the Revelation texts substitute *laos* (people) for *chōra* (territory). This connection will be explored in more detail in Chapter 9.

individual of every race in the world a remarkable status before God. It demolishes every theory of racial superiority or racial inferiority. Furthermore, as Deddo (1997: 65) writes:

[H]uman identity cannot be grounded ultimately in race. The human being is essentially constituted by its relationship to God as the creature, reconciled sinner and glorified child of God. Who we are is determined in and through this relationship, and on the basis of this identity we are called to relate to others as those who also belong to God in this three-fold way.

The 'curse of Canaan' in Genesis 9:18–27, often mislabelled the 'curse of Ham', has absolutely nothing to do with race. The gross misuse of this text to justify slavery or to defend theories of inferiority has done immense damage to the Church in America. Unfortunately, echoes of this misinterpretation can still be heard in the Church today, a distortion of Scripture that is in clear opposition to God's revelation.

The scattering of the peoples of the world according to their families, languages, lands and nations as delineated in Genesis 10 is a result of the disobedience described in the Tower of Babel episode (Genesis 11). Genesis 10 is not an ethnic map tracing the development of three races, but rather a complex picture of people-group affiliations based primarily on political and geographical associations. It involves ethnic groups – and Black Africans (Cushites) are part of the described world – but the organization of the chapter is not racial. Nonetheless, Genesis 10 – 11 underscores the division and the scattering of people across the earth.

Genesis 12:1–3 introduces God's great redemptive plan, a plan that ultimately culminates in Christ. Part of God's redemptive plan as revealed in Genesis is to save and bless individuals from all peoples of the earth and to reunite them as the people of God. Racialization or racial division in the Church thwarts the plan of God and is in direct disobedience to this central biblical theme. Racial segregation among the people of God is a movement away from following God's redemptive plan. Racial segregation within the Church is a disobedient movement backwards toward Genesis 10 – 11, rather than an obedient movement forward toward the fulfilment of Genesis 12:3 as described in the New Testament.

Chapter Four

Israel, the Torah, foreigners, and intermarriage

Introduction

Chapter 3 discussed theological issues of race emerging from the book of Genesis. Chapter 4 will explore the issue of race throughout the rest of the Torah (Pentateuch). Thus we will be discussing texts from the books of Exodus, Leviticus, Numbers, and Deuteronomy. These books deal with Yahweh's call, deliverance, and formation of the 'nation' Israel. These books contain both narrative and legal material, both of which reflect theology pertinent to us. The Torah lies at the heart of the Old Testament, and any study of Old Testament biblical theology must spend a substantial amount of time discussing the issues in these books. Do these critical books address racial issues either implicitly or explicitly? What about the Black Cushites? Do they play any kind of role in the early formation of Israel? Under the Torah, how was ancient Israel to relate to 'foreigners' such as the Cushites? Was intermarriage permitted? These are the questions that we will seek to answer in this chapter.

The formation of Israel

Exodus 1:1–5 recounts how Jacob (Israel) and his sons moved from Canaan to Egypt. The biblical record tells us that for the next four centuries this family resided in Egypt. It is during this time that Jacob's 'family' transforms into something larger: it becomes an identifiable entity, a tribe, a people, or even a nation.[1]

Recall the family's brief history. Originating in Mesopotamia, it is composed of Aramean or Amorite elements. Its members probably

---

[1] As mentioned in Chapter 2, the definition and applicability of these terms to Israel is currently being debated in Old Testament scholarship. The fine semantic distinctions between terms like 'tribe', 'people', and 'nation', however, are not critical to this aspect of our study.

speak some form of a Northwest Semitic language. After arriving in Canaan, their language probably begins to be influenced heavily by their Canaanite neighbours; they may actually become speakers of Canaanite. A few of them (Judah, Simeon) marry Canaanite women. Joseph, on the other hand, marries an Egyptian. This family, a mixed group with Aramean, Canaanite, and Egyptian elements, then spends 400 years in Egypt, some of this time under the oppression of slavery. It is probably during this time that it begins to develop a sense of 'ethnic' identity. Its Semitic dialect probably develops into the separate language that we know as Hebrew. One of the main unifying and identifying factors is its members' common origin; thus they become known as the 'sons of Israel'.[2] Likewise their tribal identification (Judah, Benjamin, Ephraim, etc.) also remains strong, and throughout their history they will frequently disintegrate into tribal entities and fight along tribal lines. However, the central unifying and identifying feature of this people is the covenant relationship that Yahweh (the LORD) will form with them in the book of Exodus. Thus one of the major boundaries that will delineate this 'ethnic group' called the 'sons of Israel' from other groups is a theological one and not merely a biological one. To be part of the covenant relationship with Yahweh is as critical a factor of identity as any other, at least from the viewpoint of the biblical books in the Torah.

Exodus 1 – 11 narrates the call of Moses, his confrontation with Pharaoh, and the judgmental plagues that Yahweh strikes upon Egypt. Finally, Pharaoh 'orders' the Israelites to leave. Exodus 12 describes the climactic deliverance of the Israelites – the actual departure of the 'sons of Israel' from Egypt. As the Israelites set out to leave Egypt on their trip to the Promised Land, the text comments, 'A *mixed crowd* also went up with them' (Exod. 12:38, NRSV). What are the implications of the term translated 'a mixed crowd'? The clear

---

[2] The term 'sons of Israel' occurs but four times in Genesis and refers to the literal sons of Jacob (Israel). In Exodus, however, the term occurs 125 times and refers to the entire nation. Most modern translations (NIV, NRSV, NLB) translate the phrase as 'Israelites'. The NASB is one of the few to retain the literal 'sons of Israel'. The KJV uses the more gender-inclusive phrase 'children of Israel'. The other term used to designate the descendants of Abraham is 'Hebrew'. This term may reflect more of a sociological 'ethnicity' rather than a political one. Freedman and Willoughby (1999: 431) summarize the usage of this term by stating, 'The expression defines an ethnic group with no negative connotations. In a general sense the term was used by foreigners with reference to proto-Israelites, or by the latter themselves as a self-designation over against foreigners. After the founding of the Israelite state, the term *'ibri* [Hebrew] fell into disuse except in archaic passages.'

stress of the Hebrew term used ('*ēreḇ*) is that these people were non-Israelites.[3] Enns (2000: 251) writes that this term indicates an 'ethnic mixture of peoples'. Propp (1999: 414) also understands the word to refer to foreigners. Fretheim (1991: 143) likewise comments, 'Many non-Israelites were integrated into the community of faith.' Durham (1987: 169) translates the phrase as 'a large and motley group', and states, 'that there were many who became Israelites by theological rather than biological descendancy is many times referred to in the OT.' Brueggemann (1994: 781) concludes, 'the phrase suggests that this is no kinship group, no ethnic community, but a great conglomeration of lower-class folk . . . This term is important for the view that earliest Israel was not an ethnic community.'

Who were these foreigners? Were they Egyptians? Other nationalities? Where did they come from and what were they doing in Egypt? Ancient Egyptian literary records can assist us here, for they are replete with references to foreigners in Egypt during this period.[4] Indeed, during the Eighteenth and Nineteenth Dynasties (1550–1200 BC), the period encompassing the events of the Exodus, the Egyptians had nominal control over both Cush and Syria-Palestine. During this time the Egyptians carried out numerous military campaigns into these regions and brought back thousands of conquered peoples to Egypt as slaves and labourers (Redford 1992: 214–237). It is highly likely that these people constituted the 'mixed crowd' of Exodus 12:38 (Hoffmeier 1996: 112–116). This group would include both Semitic and non-Semitic peoples.

Of particular interest to us is the degree to which the Black Africans of Cush would have been part of this group. The Egyptian literary records of the period frequently mention Cushite slaves or labourers being brought back to Egypt. Breasted's work *Ancient Records of Egypt: Historical Documents* (1906) cites several specific references in Egyptian documents to Cushite (Nubian) slaves during the reigns of Eighteenth-Dynasty Pharaohs (1570–1305 BC): Ahmose I (II:14), Amenhotep I (II:39, 41), and Thutmose III (II:495, 502–503).[5] In fact,

---

[3] Note the usage of this word in clear reference to foreigners in Neh. 13:3; Jer. 25:20, 24; 50:37.

[4] See the chapter entitled 'Ethnic Diversity in Ancient Egypt', by Leahy (1995: 225–234), and the chapter entitled 'Foreigners', by Bresciani (1997: 221–253).

[5] Evidence of Cushite slaves or labourers in Egypt is not limited to historical annals. Cushites appear frequently in Egyptian monumental art as well. Likewise other genres of ancient Egyptian literature mention Cushite slaves. For example, a love poem entitled 'Seven Wishes' from the *Cairo Love Songs* (1305–1150 BC) reads, 'Would that I were her Nubian [Cushite] slave, her servant in secret' (M. Fox 1997: 1.50; Fowler 1994: 39).

although Cushites had been in Egypt for centuries, it is precisely during the time of the Exodus story (Eighteenth or Nineteenth Dynasties) that they arrive in Egypt in great numbers (Bresciani 1997: 230). Not all of these Cushites were slaves; during this period Cushites were also found at other levels of Egyptian society. There is clear documentation that during this time Cushites worked in Egypt, not only as slaves, but also as soldiers, merchants, magicians,[6] civil servants, and nobility (O'Connor 1993: 61–64; Bresciani 1997: 221–253; Leahy 1995: 225–234). Because of the large number of Cushites in Egypt at this time, it is almost certain that 'a mixed multitude' of foreigners in Egypt would include Cushites. Whether this crowd included only former slaves and labourers, or whether it included a broader range of people, there is strong evidence that Cushites were included in the group. Adding to this argument is the fact that Moses marries a Cushite in Numbers 12 (discussed below). Also, as discussed below, the name of Moses' prominent great-nephew and priest, 'Phinehas', means 'the Nubian', or 'the Negro', a clear reference to Cush (see the discussion below).

So there is a strong argument that Cushites were part of the 'mixed crowd' that came out of Egypt as part of Israel. Brueggemann (1994: 781), as already cited above, is quite correct in saying that 'earliest Israel was not an ethnic community.' Included with the biological descendants of Jacob were other Semitic peoples (probably Arameans, Amorites, Canaanites, etc.) as well as Black Africans from Cush.

---

[6] Magicians are of particular interest to us because of the important role they play in Exodus 7–8. Cushite magicians had a special reputation in Egypt; they were famous for their power and there were many of them functioning in Egypt (Bresciani 1997: 232–233). There is a strong possibility that some of the 'magicians' who confronted Moses in Exodus 7 and 8 were Cushites. The phrase translated 'Egyptian magicians' (Exod. 7:11, NIV) literally means 'magicians of the Egyptians'; it gives no indication of nationality. There are two other points of interest regarding these magicians. First, note that they are the first ones to acknowledge that Moses has divine power, declaring to Pharaoh in Exod. 8:19 'This is the finger of God.' It is therefore probable that these magicians are included in the term 'officials' when used in Exod. 9:20, which states 'Those officials of Pharaoh who feared the word of the LORD hurried to bring their slaves and their livestock inside.' Did some of these people join the Israelite exodus as part of the 'mixed crowd' in Exod. 12:38? The other point of interest is that these 'magicians' were also priests. 'Magic' and priestly activity cannot be separated. The Hebrew word used for 'magician' in Exodus derives from an Egyptian word that refers clearly to a class of priests that studied theology and manipulated spiritual powers. See Propp (1999: 322); Pernigotti (1997: 140); Borghouts (2000: 1775–1776); and Ritner (2001: 323). While the connection is purely speculative, it is interesting to note the high probability of a Cushite presence among these priests and then the emergence of a central Israelite priest, Phinehas, whose name means 'the Negro' or 'the Cushite'. See the discussion on Phinehas later in this chapter.

The sojourner and the foreigner

Exodus 12:31–39 describes the actual departure from Egypt (the Exodus) of the newly formed Israel. As mentioned above, participating in the Exodus is also 'the mixed crowd': that is, people of other ethnic groups. To commemorate the Exodus event Yahweh inaugurates the Passover, and Exodus 12:40–49 describes this ritual. The particular focus of this text regarding the Passover meal is the distinction between who can and who cannot participate in it. This text appears to be placed here specifically to address the presence of foreigners within Israel as described a few verses earlier in 12:38 and as discussed above. Exodus 12:40–49 uses two distinctive terms to describe non-Israelites in regard to the Passover. These two terms are used frequently throughout the Torah with the same basic distinctions. The *gērîm*, usually translated as 'sojourners' or 'aliens', are those from other groups who have accepted the worship of Yahweh. The other group, the *nokrîm*, usually translated 'foreigners', are the ones who have not accepted Yahweh (Lang 1998: 426). The other implied distinction is that the *gērîm* (sojourners) have actually settled among the Israelites and are in the process of being assimilated while the *nokrîm* have not (Martin-Archard 1997: 308). The critical issue is circumcision: once the *gērîm* have been circumcised they can participate in the Passover (Exod. 12:48). In fact, Exodus 12:49 reads, 'The same law applies to the native-born and to the alien (*gērîm*) living among you.' The *gērîm* are thus equal to the Israelites in religious aspects (Martin-Archard 1997: 309).[7] This is reflected fairly consistently throughout the Torah.

Theologically, participation in both the Exodus and the Passover meal by people of the 'mixed crowd' is highly significant. The Exodus is the paradigmatic picture of salvation in the Old Testament and the Passover is the central ritual memorializing this critical event (Childs 1974: 212–214). The Exodus and the Passover of the Old Testament are paralleled by the Cross and the Lord's Supper in the New Testament. Thus the Exodus event and the Passover celebration of Exodus 12 are highly significant theologically. The presence of other 'peoples' or 'nationalities' at this juncture of the story has strong implications as to the nature of 'true Israel'. It also suggests a partial

---

[7] Martin-Archard (1997: 309) also points out that the LXX regularly translates this Hebrew term with the Greek word *prosēlytos*, a technical term implying that one has identified himself with Judaism through the initiatory act of circumcision.

fulfilment of Yahweh's promise to Abraham in Genesis 12:3: 'and in you all the families of the earth will be blessed' (NRSV). Finally, Exodus 12:43–49 indicates that participation in the celebration of Yahweh's great redemptive act was not based on birth or ethnicity, but rather on relationship to Yahweh and his covenant.

Moses and intermarriage

The two main characters in the books of Exodus, Leviticus, Numbers, and Deuteronomy are Yahweh (the LORD) and Moses. From the human side, Moses dominates the story. He is Yahweh's appointed leader, the lawgiver, and the great mediator between Israel and their God. As central figures in the Old Testament only Abraham and David can compare to Moses.

Surprisingly, the Torah presents a significant amount of material that deals with Moses' personal life, particularly in regard to the two women that he marries.[8] It is important to remember that narrative texts, whether in the Torah or in other Scripture, convey theology just as powerfully as any other genre.[9] It is not merely the legal material in the Torah that teaches theology. So the marriages of Moses – or perhaps we should say the *intermarriages* of Moses – have something to say to us theologically.

In Exodus 2:15–22 Moses meets and marries a Midianite woman named Zipporah. The Midianites were a Semitic-speaking people, ethnic cousins of the Israelites. What is shocking about the marriage is not the ethnicity of the bride but rather the fact that her father Reuel is a priest of Midian. Numbers 25 indicates that the Midianites worshipped Baal and not Yahweh. Moses apparently marries into a Baal-worshipping priestly family!

It is critical to place this event into the narrative context. In Exodus 2 Moses murders an Egyptian and then flees to Midian, presumably to hide from Pharaoh. At this point Moses has not yet encountered God nor has he received his dramatic call from God. He is running away from Egypt and from his people; his marriage to Zipporah is part of his escape. Placed within this context, this marriage is not necessarily a positive event in his life. There is no indication that God approves of it. Exodus 18:2 indicates that after God calls him and he

---

[8] See the detailed discussion of Moses' two marriages in J. Hays (2000: 16–26, 60–62).
[9] See the development of this view in Wenham (2000: 1–15).

returns to Egypt to free the Israelites, Moses 'sends her (Zipporah) away' back to her family. In Exodus 18, Zipporah's relative Jethro brings her back to Moses in the camp of the Israelites and he apparently accepts her. However, note the shift in context. She now joins Moses and the nation of Israel, who worship Yahweh, rather than Moses joining her and her family, who worship Baal. This theological transition is important.[10]

Ironically, not long after the events of Exodus 18 the Midianites will appear as a deadly and dangerous enemy of Israel. In Numbers 25 Midianite women lure Israelite men into promiscuity and the worship of Baal. This act threatens the very existence of Israel and challenges the heart of their relationship with Yahweh. Only by responding severely to those who posed this threat was total disaster to Israel averted. Indeed, one of the last public acts of Moses is to completely destroy the Midianites (Numbers 31). This is hardly a picture of a blissful relationship with one's in-laws. In summary, Moses' entire relationship with Zipporah and her priestly Midianite family appears somewhat questionable. His marriage to Zipporah does not occur while he is walking closely in obedience to God and thus it does not appear to serve as any type of positive model for us. Indeed, as discussed below, the dangers of marrying outside the faith will be emphasized throughout the Torah and the entire Old Testament.

Another, different wife, however, is introduced in Numbers 12:1, which reads: 'Miriam and Aaron began to talk against Moses because of his Cushite wife, for he had married a Cushite.' Who is this woman? What is the significance of stating that she is a Cushite?

Recall that the term Cush was discussed in some detail back in Chapter 2. Cush is a fairly common term in Egyptian literature. It also appears over fifty times in the Old Testament, and is attested in Assyrian literature as well. It is used regularly to refer to the area south of Egypt, above the cataracts on the Nile, where a Black African civilization flourished for over two thousand years (J. Hays 1996a: 270–280). Thus it is quite clear that Moses marries a Black African woman.

Several older commentators, however, argue that this woman was not a Black Cushite from the country south of Egypt, but rather an Arabic-looking Midianite (Zipporah). Martin Noth, for example,

---

[10] For a detailed discussion on this passage, including an explanation of Zipporah's relationship to Jethro, see J. Hays (2000: 18–26).

presents the standard argument by citing Habakkuk 3:7, where the term 'Cushan' is used in parallel with Midian (1968: 98). From this reference in Habakkuk, Noth (and others) conclude that there was a group in Arabia known as Cushites that were related to or identical to the Midianites. Several writers also conclude that since this is a reference to Midianites, the woman in question must be Zipporah. Noth (1968: 98) criticizes Luther's translation of 'Cushite' as 'negress', stating that this usage of 'Cushite' cannot possibly refer to the region south of Egypt because that area is too far removed from Moses' activity.

However, Noth's arguments are weak and outdated, reflecting a very limited understanding of the situation in Egypt. During the Eighteenth and Nineteenth Dynasties of Egypt, relations between Egypt and Cush were extremely close. Cush was under direct Egyptian control; indeed, it was practically part of Egypt. There were thousands of Cushites in Egypt at all levels of society. If Moses was born and raised in Egypt, it is not only possible, but almost certain, that he would have known numerous Cushites in his youth. Noth's statement that the African Cushites were too far removed from Moses' activity reflects a serious misunderstanding on Noth's part regarding the extent to which Cushites permeated Egyptian society.[11] Furthermore, as discussed earlier in this chapter, Exodus 12:38 states that 'many other people' came out of Egypt with the sons of Israel. The implication is, of course, that these were other nationalities, reflecting the ethnic make-up of Egypt. It is very likely that there were Cushites in this group as well. So, the Cushite woman of Numbers 12:1 could have been either one that Moses knew in his youth or one that he met as the Exodus began.[12]

The argument from Habakkuk 3:7 does nothing to alter the normal meaning of the term 'Cush'. Many commentators, including Noth, begin their discussion by acknowledging that Cush usually refers to the region south of Egypt. But, they claim, Numbers 12 is an exception, as Habakkuk 3:7 supposedly demonstrates. However, the text in Habakkuk 3:7 does not read 'Cush' but rather 'Cushan'.

---

[11] For a discussion on the relationship between Egypt and Cush see J. Hays (1996a: 275–277).

[12] Yamauchi (forthcoming: Chapter 2) writes, 'In the light of the fact that there is ample Egyptian evidence of the presence of many Nubians in Egypt from as early as the Old Kingdom, and of intermarriage between Egyptians and Nubians, we should not identify this woman with Zipporah from Midian and should not doubt the account of Moses' marriage to a Cushite or Nubian woman.'

'Cush' and 'Cushan' are not necessarily the same word. Cush occurs dozens of times in the Old Testament, clearly as a reference to the civilization south of Egypt. 'Cushan' occurs only once, in Habakkuk 3:7, and the reference is somewhat enigmatic.[13] There is little evidence in the literature of the Ancient Near East outside of the supposed connection in Habakkuk 3:7 of any Midianite-related group referred to as Cushites.[14] There should be overwhelming evidence before a common, normal usage of a word is rejected in favour of a poorly attested usage. Furthermore, throughout the Old Testament the term 'Cush' is associated closely with Egypt. In a narrative text of a story relating to the exodus from Egypt, why should one go to the word 'Cushan' in Habakkuk for an understanding of the term 'Cush' in Numbers? Also note that early translations such as the Septuagint and the Vulgate translate the term 'Cushite' in Numbers 12:1 as 'Ethiopian', the term used by the Greeks and Romans to refer to the region south of Egypt inhabited by people with black skin.

Another point to be considered is the observation that Reuel, the father-in-law of Moses from his Midianite wife Zipporah, is mentioned two chapters earlier in Numbers 10:29–32, where he is specifically called a 'Midianite'. Why should the narrator of Numbers change terms between Numbers 10 and Numbers 12? If the reference in 12:1 is to Zipporah, why is her father called a Midianite in Numbers 10, yet she is called a Cushite in Numbers 12?

A modern example might help to put the passage in perspective. Suppose a man was born and raised in Texas. Later in life he was travelling north with a large ethnically 'mixed' group from Texas. While the group was passing through Iowa the man married a Mexican woman. Would any reader of this story today question the meaning of the term 'Mexican'? Would we try to find some vague semantic connection with a locale in Iowa so we could assert that the woman has blond hair and blue eyes? Of course not. Because Mexico borders Texas, and because there are millions of ethnic Mexicans in Texas, the meaning of the term 'Mexican' in regard to this man's wife is obvious. The meaning of 'Cushite' in Numbers 12 is just as obvious, and for the same reasons.

Yet what has become of Zipporah? Perhaps she has died and this

---

[13] The term 'Cushan' does occur in a compound form as the name 'Cushan-Rishathaim' (Judg. 3:7–11). This usage appears to be unrelated to the term in Hab. 3:7. See Baker (1992: 1220).

[14] The best-documented defence for such a group is by Haak (1995), but his evidence is not convincing.

text refers to Moses' second marriage. This is unlikely, however, because only a short time elapses in the story between the appearance of Zipporah in Exodus 18 and the mention of the Cushite wife in Numbers 12. Of course, at this time in the ancient world it would not be unreasonable for Moses to have more than one wife. The Cushite woman may be a second wife. More likely is the possibility that Moses marries the Cushite woman after he sends Zipporah away, but before Jethro brings her back (B. Levine 1993: 328). At any rate, the Numbers text implies that this is a recent marriage, and that this marriage is the reason for the hostility from Miriam and Aaron.[15]

The term 'Cushite' is repeated twice in Numbers 12:1, probably for stress. Throughout the ancient world this term carried strong connotations of Black ethnicity. Ancient readers of this text would visualize a Black woman from the region south of Egypt. Jeremiah, for example, refers to the unique skin of the Cushites without any explanation of who they were or where they lived ('Can the Cushite change his skin?' Jer. 13:23). This implies that Jeremiah's audience was familiar with the term 'Cushite' and the uniqueness of their skin colour. The ethnicity of Moses' new wife is stressed and then opposition arises within his family. The most logical explanation is to associate these two as cause and effect.[16]

There are also numerous non-biblical ancient texts and traditions which connect Moses with Cush (Ethiopia). Josephus, for example, in *Antiquities of the Jews* 10:1–2, relates an incredible, non-biblical story in which Moses leads an army of Egyptians and Hebrews against the Cushites to deliver Egypt from a Cushite invasion. While Moses is defeating the Cushites, Tharbis, the daughter of the Cushite king, falls in love with him and proposes marriage. Moses accepts and marries Tharbis, a marriage that concludes the successful campaign and seals a treaty with the Cushites. This is one of the most extensive

[15] See the good discussion on this text by Adamo (1989: 230–237).

[16] Snowden (1970: 192–193), however, argues that interracial marriage between Blacks and other ethnic groups, especially Egyptians, was not all that unusual. He cites Herodotus *History* 2.30 and Plutarch *De exilio* 601, who refer to an event in the reign of the Egyptian king Psamtek I when 240,000 rebellious Egyptian men moved south, settled, and intermarried with the Cushites (called 'Ethiopians' by these Greek writers). In a later work Snowden (1983: 95) states that there was an unknown prince of a royal family in Egypt with a Negro wife. Snowden cites Haycock (1972: 230, 237). Citing Wenig (1969: 50), Snowden also argues that the physical features of queen Tiy, the wife of Amenophis III, indicate that she was a Cushite (Snowden calls her 'Nubian'). Runnalls (1983: 135–156) states that the Egyptian pharaohs frequently took Cushite (Nubian) wives to provide legitimacy for ruling Cush (Nubia).

accounts of an 'addition' to the biblical text by Josephus. Runnalls (1983: 148) writes that this episode indicates rather clearly that Josephus understood the Cushite of Numbers 12:1 to be from the Cush south of Egypt.[17]

Earlier than Josephus is Artapanus, probably an Alexandrian Jew writing in the second century BC. Artapanus describes the military expedition by Moses to Cush but he does not mention the marriage.[18] Later Jewish legends continued to expound on Moses' escapades in Cush. In several of these legends Moses marries a Cushite (Ethiopian) princess named Adoniah.[19]

Without the ethnicity issue it is difficult to associate Numbers 12:1 with the rest of the passage. Indeed, many source critics dismiss the verse as a later insertion, thus waving the problem away.[20] This approach, however, merely begs the question. *Someone* associated Moses' marriage to a Cushite with the opposition from Miriam and they constructed the text in this manner. Throughout the entire period suggested for the composition of the Hebrew Bible, the term 'Cush' would have been understood to refer to the Black inhabitants of the civilization south of Egypt. In the Numbers 12 narrative, the result of the conflict over Moses' marriage is that Miriam is judged and Moses is reaffirmed. Apparently his family (Miriam and Aaron) objects to this interracial marriage, but Yahweh approves. In fact, Yahweh's punishment on Miriam is swift and severe. He strikes her with a skin disease and she becomes (white) as snow. Cross (1973: 204) suggests that the punishment of white, leprous skin was an

---

[17] Whiston (1960: 58) notes that Irenæus cites this story from Josephus. Whiston also suggests that this episode might be behind the statement of Stephen in Acts 7:22. Stephen is quoted as referring to Moses as 'powerful in speech and action' *before* God called him to deliver the Israelites. For a discussion of the Jewish literary background for Stephen's statement see Johnson (1992: 125–126). Another interesting observation is that made by Montet (1968: 92), who notes that the Cushites (Ethiopians) are mentioned in Egyptian texts recounting stories of magic power, especially in competition with the Egyptian magicians. The similarities between this and Moses' encounter with the magicians are perhaps suggestive.

[18] This account is cited by Eusebius, *Præparatio Evangelica* 9.27, who copied the story from Alexander Polyhistor, who apparently obtained the account by Artapanus. The differences between Artapanus and Josephus are puzzling. Numerous scholarly discussions on Josephus' probable sources have been written. See Runnalls (1983: 135–156).

[19] This account is presented in the spurious *Book of Jasher*, 23.5–25.5. See also Ginzberg (1956: 299–302) and Beegle (1992: 4:917).

[20] See Gray (1912: 121–122). In his discussion, however, Gray does cite Dillmann, who 'considers that the Cushite offended Miriam not because she was a foreigner, but because she was black.'

intentional, appropriate response to Miriam's prejudice against the Black wife.[21]

However, it is difficult to be certain about Miriam's motives behind her opposition. The text implies that she and Aaron are caught up in some type of power struggle. Perhaps she is merely jealous that Moses would add another person, especially another woman, into their small circle of power. However, there is another, perhaps more plausible, explanation, based on the Egyptian customs of that era. During the Egyptian New Kingdom period, and especially during the Eighteenth Dynasty (1570–1305 BC), the pharaohs of Egypt frequently married foreigners, but they also frequently married their *sisters* (Wilfong 2001: 343; Černý 1954: 23–29). Miriam may well envision the leadership of Moses according to the model provided by the pharaohs of the Eighteenth Dynasty. As such, she may be incensed that Moses has chosen a foreign wife instead of her. Although the biblical commentators on Numbers never discuss this option, the Egyptian custom is clearly documented and this documentation clearly matches this particular era. It should at least be listed as a viable option for the motive behind Miriam's opposition.

More important, and much clearer, is the theological dimension of Miriam's punishment. She was sent outside the camp, a temporary expulsion from the family and the people of God. While the Cushite woman becomes part of Moses' family and the people of Israel through marriage, Miriam, through her opposition to Moses, is separated both from the family and the people of Israel.[22]

---

[21] Cross (1973: 204) is cited by Budd (1984: 137). Also suggesting this view is Felder (1989: 42). Note also the narrative context of Numbers 11, where the nation is grumbling against Moses. Perhaps Moses turned to this Cushite woman for support and consolation in the midst of this difficult time for him. It is noteworthy, however, that at a time when the nation as a whole is hostile to the man of God it is a Cushite that appears to be sympathetic. This theme will recur several times.

[22] This underlines the fact that the critical element in both of Moses' marriages appears to be how the marriage affects the relationship between Moses and Israel, the people of Yahweh. The Midianite marriage pulls Moses away from Yahweh and from the people of Israel and into the family of a Midianite priest. Moses is forced to annul (he sends her away) this marriage until Jethro acknowledges Yahweh and brings Zipporah into the camp of the Israelites. In essence, she becomes one of them. The destruction of the Midianites at the end of Numbers highlights the fact that Moses no longer has a valid marriage/treaty relationship with them. The Cushite woman, on the other hand, appears to be already in the Israelite camp, in essence already part of Israel. She is probably part of the 'mixed multitude' that came out of Egypt with Israel. Moses does not become a pagan Cushite by marrying her. Rather she becomes a Yahweh-fearing Israelite by marrying him. To Yahweh this makes all the difference.

Therefore, the case is extremely strong that Moses married a Black Cushite woman from the Cushite civilization south of Egypt. This understanding not only fits with the details of the biblical text; it also fits the historical picture of Cushites in Egypt at that time and the way in which the text was translated and understood by the ancient writers.[23]

Yet what of the biblical injunctions *against* intermarriage? Has Moses violated these injunctions? Does the biblical text suggest two different approaches to intermarriage between the sons of Israel and foreigners? Not at all. First observe that in the Torah the prohibition against intermarriage is always strictly in regard to the inhabitants of Canaan and not to foreigners in general. Second, the reason given for this prohibition is always theological: the inhabitants worship other gods and intermarrying with them would inevitably lead to the apostasy of God's people. The central text is Deuteronomy 7:1–4, which reads:

When the LORD your God brings you into the land you are entering to possess and drives out before you many nations – the Hittites, Girgashites, Amorites, Canaanites, Perizzites, Hivites and Jebusites, seven nations larger and stronger than you – and when the LORD your God has delivered them over to you and you have defeated them, then you must destroy them totally. Make no treaty with them, and show them no mercy. Do not intermarry with them. Do not give your daughters to their sons or take their daughters for your sons, for they will turn your sons away from following me to serve other gods, and the LORD's anger will burn against you and will quickly destroy you.

The command is for the Israelites to drive out and destroy the current inhabitants of the land and to refrain from intermarrying with them. The reason: if you marry them 'they will turn your sons away from following me to serve other gods.' The same warning with the same reasons is stated in Exodus 34:15–16 and in Joshua 23:12.

Underscoring this distinction is Deuteronomy 21:10–14. In Deuteronomy 20 God told the Israelites that they must completely destroy all of the cities and all of the people in the land they were invading. However, cities and people outside of the land fell into a

---

[23] This is also the conclusion of B. Levine (1993: 328).

different category. Deuteronomy 20 explains that the Israelites were to make an offer of peace to these people, and that, even if peace was refused, they were not to kill the women and children in these foreign cities. Following up on this explanation, Deuteronomy 21:10–14 explains the procedure for taking these *foreign* captured women as wives. Thus in this case, i.e. in conquests outside the Promised Land, intermarriage with foreigners was clearly permitted (C. Hayes 1999: 36).

The limitation of the ban on intermarriage to apply only to the inhabitants of Canaan is consistent for early Israel. Furthermore, the reason – a theological one – is always clearly stated. This reason has absolutely nothing to do with race or physical appearance. Note that Israel is specifically forbidden to intermarry with the Canaanites and other inhabitants of Canaan, who are the very people most closely related to them ethnically. They are allowed to intermarry with other foreigners, as Deuteronomy 21:10–14 and Numbers 12:1 illustrate. The foreigners that they are allowed to marry are much more racially different than those whom they are prohibited from marrying. Obviously racial difference is not the issue; faith and theology are.

Judges 3:5–6 chronicles the sad reality that after the Israelites settle in the land they forget this prohibition, intermarry with the original inhabitants, and promptly begin to worship the gods of the other people. The story of Ruth bucks the trend, demonstrating that foreigners who profess faith in Yahweh can intermarry with Israel and be blessed.[24] Solomon, however, dramatically illustrates the danger of foreign intermarriage when the foreign partners are not worshippers of Yahweh. 1 Kings 11:4–6 stresses the connection between his faithlessness to Yahweh and his marriage to foreign, pagan women. Ultimately, as the texts in Deuteronomy and Joshua predict, this phenomenon will bring Yahweh's judgment and will send Israel out of the land and into exile.[25]

Thus after the judgmental exile, when Israel returns to the land during the post-exilic era, it is no surprise that Ezra and Nehemiah both react vigorously when they discover that the Jews of the return are marrying foreigners (and non-foreigners?) who are not faithful

---

[24] Rahab probably also falls in this category, even though she is apparently a Canaanite. Both Ruth and Rahab, obvious foreigners, are included in the genealogy of David.

[25] Knoppers (1994: 132) writes, 'According to the Deuteronomist, mixed marriages were the means by which the Israelites forgot their god and began worshipping other gods.'

worshippers of Yahweh. They both connect their current situation with the disaster that resulted from earlier violations of this prohibition. Thus the situation in Ezra 9:1 is cast against the prohibitions of Deuteronomy and Joshua while the issue in Nehemiah 13:23–27 is presented in light of the disaster that resulted from Solomon's marital experience. Both Ezra and Nehemiah seem to be saying that earlier intermarriages in Israel's history led to the apostasy that resulted in the exile (Knoppers 1994: 137). They are horrified that Israel is falling into the same pattern again. But both Ezra and Nehemiah cast the danger of intermarriage with foreigners as one of apostasy driven by the pagan beliefs of the foreign spouse.[26] Ethnic or racial issues, other than religion, are not at all related to the prohibition.[27]

Thus Moses' marriage to a Black woman from Cush did not violate any biblical prohibition. Consistently throughout the Scripture, both in the Old and the New Testaments, the prohibition is against marrying outside the faith, not against marrying someone of another race. Furthermore, Moses' marriage to a Black Cushite should also probably be viewed as a developing fulfilment of God's promise to Abraham in Genesis 12:3 ('all peoples on earth will be blessed

[26] Malachi 2:10–16 reflects a similar situation. If Malachi's words are to be understood literally (and the majority of commentators seem to lean this way) then the Jews of the return were guilty not only of intermarrying with pagan, foreign women, but also of divorcing their own Jewish wives in order to do so. See the overview and discussion by R. Smith (1984: 318–325), who favours the literal view; and Glazier-McDonald (1987: 603–611), who argues for a combination of a literal view (foreign wives) and a figurative view (apostasy). Puzzling, perhaps, is Malachi's statement of Yahweh's disdain for divorce when placed in the context of Ezra's command ordering the Israelites to divorce the foreign wives.

[27] This point is stressed by numerous commentators. Throntveit (1992: 57) writes, 'It is not their racial or national ties that are at issue but the religious practices that the foreign wives brought to their marriages and the effects those practices would surely have had upon family and community structures.' Klein (1999: 733) states 'marriages outside the community were *prima facie* evidence of faithlessness.' Fensham (1982: 124) argues, 'The influence of a foreign mother, with her connection to another religion, on her children would ruin the pure religion of the Lord and would create a syncretistic religion contrary to everything in the Jewish faith.' See also Williamson (1985: 130–131). G. Davies (1999: 58) suggests that Ezra never intended this as a permanent injunction. However, as Judaism developed in the Second Temple Period the tendency was to play down or ignore the allowable foreign marriage element evident in the Torah and to stress a firm, universal application of Ezra's prohibition. Thus the books of Jubilees and 4QMMT (from Qumran), as well as later rabbinic writings, all stressed a strict prohibition against marriage of any Jew to any Gentile. For a discussion of this development and the socio-theological reasons behind it see Epstein (1942: 145–177) and C. Hayes (1999).

through you'). The promise to Abraham in Genesis drives much of the story in the rest of the Torah and the inclusion of one of the peoples from Genesis 10 (Cush) into the 'sons of Israel' is a move toward fulfilment of that promise.

The theological implications of Numbers 12:1 are significant. Moses is not a minor, backwater biblical character. He is a gigantic character in the biblical story and one of the central servants of God in the Bible. This event occurs, not while he is running away from God or while he is disobeying God, but while he is obviously walking closely with God.[28] In fact, God points this out to Miriam and Aaron very forcefully by stating:

> Listen to my words:
>
> When a prophet of the LORD is among you,
>   I reveal myself to him in visions,
>   I speak to him in dreams.
> But this is not true of my servant Moses;
>   he is faithful in all my house.
> With him I speak face to face,
>   clearly and not in riddles;
>   he sees the form of the LORD.
> Why then were you not afraid
>   to speak against my servant Moses?
>
> (Num. 12:6–8)

Miriam and Aaron had spoken against Moses because of this marriage, and after the lecture above, God's anger burns against them (12:9) and he strikes Miriam with a 'skin disease'. It is due only to the intervention of Moses (12:13) that God cuts the judgment short. Clearly God affirms Moses' marriage to this Black woman.

What theological conclusions should we draw from this text? I would suggest that *interracial intermarriage is strongly affirmed by Scripture*. Marrying unbelievers, on the other hand, is strongly

---

[28] This is an important factor in determining whether a character in the narrative is functioning as a positive model for the readers or as a negative model. Likewise, the commentary by the narrator or by God in the narrative serves to assist us in determining whether the story should serve as paradigmatic. On methodology relating to the development of theology from OT narrative, see Duvall and Hays (2001: 293–315). For further discussion on interpreting narrative theologically (i.e. ethically), see Wenham (2000) and Janzen (1994).

prohibited. The criteria for approving or disapproving of our children's selected spouses should be based on their faith in Christ and not at all on the colour of their skin. This theological affirmation should have profound implications for the Church today. White families frequently rise up in arms when their children want to marry Blacks, regardless of how strong the chosen person's Christian faith is. On the other hand, White Christian young adults can marry other Whites with little opposition even if the faith of their selected mate is virtually non-existent. Such behaviour reflects the Church's weak theological understanding of Scripture on this subject.

Furthermore, the common cultural ban on intermarriage lies at the heart of the Black and White racial division in America. Isichei (1995: 107) writes, 'Inter-ethnic marriage is the litmus test of racial prejudice.' White Christians who say that they are not prejudiced but who vehemently oppose interracial marriages are not being honest. They are still prejudiced, and I would suggest that they are out of line with God's revealed will. This theology applies equally to intermarriages between any two ethnic groups within the Church throughout the world: Japanese, Korean, Chinese, Hausa, Yoruba, Fulani, or any other.

The theology derived from the marriage of Moses to a Black woman corresponds well with the rest of biblical theology. Genesis 1 taught us that all people are created in the image of God and have equal status before God. Paul tells us in the New Testament that in Christ there is neither Jew nor Gentile, but that *all* Christians are brothers and sisters in the family of God. Marrying outside the family is forbidden, but the clear biblical definition of family is based on faith in Christ and not on race or descent. Interracial marriage between Christians is clearly supported by Scripture.

Phinehas the priest

Another interesting connection in the Torah between early Israel and Cush is Phinehas the priest. The name Phinehas is an Egyptian loan word. The Egyptians called the *region* along the Nile and to the south of Egypt by the term 'Cush', but they referred to the *inhabitants* of that region by the ethnic term *nehsiu* (J. Wilson 1951: 136; Budge 1968: 104). In Egyptian the 'ph' prefix on the name Phinehas functions in a fashion similar to a definite article. Thus his name translates as 'the Negro', 'the Nubian', or 'the Cushite': that is, one of the Black people who inhabit the land of Cush (Gardiner 1961: 133;

Montet 1968: 32; Budd 1984: 280; Stern 1971: 466; Mauch 1962: 799). Propp (1999: 280) notes that this was a common New Kingdom Egyptian name which 'connotes either a person with unusually dark skin or a true African.'[29]

Phinehas plays a major role in the pentateuchal story. Exodus 6:16–25 traces the priestly genealogy from Levi to Phinehas. Aaron's son Eleazar married one of the daughters of Putiel (also an Egyptian name)[30] and she became the mother of Phinehas (Exod. 6:24). Thus although Phinehas is the great-nephew of Moses, it is his connection with the priestly line of Levi and Aaron that is stressed. Indeed, it is significant that the priestly genealogy of Exodus 6:16–25 terminates or *culminates* with Phinehas (Propp 1999: 280; Enns 2000: 177). He is certainly a central figure in the story of the priesthood.

Phinehas appears again in Numbers 25 and 31. The text in Numbers 25 is particularly significant. Once again Israel is on the brink of sliding into apostasy, this time being tempted by the women of Moab/Midian to indulge in sexual immorality and Baal worship. In judgment Yahweh sends a plague on Israel. After an Israelite man takes a Midianite woman (as wife?) into his tent, Phinehas, in zeal for Yahweh, kills them both (25:6–9), and the plague ends. It is striking that someone other than Moses intervenes to save Israel from Yahweh's wrath. After Phinehas' intervention, Yahweh then comes to Moses and says,

> Phinehas son of Eleazar, the son of Aaron, the priest, has turned my anger away from the Israelites; for he was as zealous as I am for my honour among them, so that in my zeal I did not put an end to them. Therefore tell him I am making my covenant of peace with him. He and his descendants will have a covenant of a lasting priesthood, because he was zealous for the honour of his God and made atonement for the Israelites.
>
> (Num. 25:11–13)

---

[29] Yurco (2001: 88) translates the name as 'the Kushite'. He points out that a vizier under Merneptah and a viceroy under Rameses XI also have this name. Yurco concludes that the somewhat frequent occurrence of this name (including the biblical Phinehas) indicates that there were large numbers of Cushites (Nubians) in Egypt throughout this time.

[30] The name Putiel is probably an Egyptian loan word with the Hebrew '*ēl* added as a suffix, 'the one whom El has given'. See Hostetter (1992: 5:561) and Propp (1999: 280).

Later, in Numbers 31, Phinehas leads the military battle that completely annihilates the Midianites.[31]

Phinehas also appears in Joshua 22, where he plays a key role in defusing a potentially dangerous misunderstanding between the eastern tribes (Reuben, Gad, Manasseh) and the rest of Israel. Indeed, the nation hovers on the brink of civil war (Josh. 22:12) until Phinehas leads a delegation to discuss and correct the problem. Butler (1983: 246) points out that Phinehas is the only leader other than Joshua that takes the initiative in any action within the book of Joshua.

Spencer (1992: 347) underlines several significant aspects emerging from these texts about Phinehas. First of all he notes that Yahweh bestows the priesthood on Phinehas and his descendants. Thus all priestly factions (Aaronites, Levites, and Zadokites) must be related to Phinehas. Second, Phinehas' zealous defence of Yahweh becomes a model for subsequent generations (Psalm 106:30–31; 1 Maccabees 2:26, 54; Sirach 45:23–24).

In fact, as Psalm 106 reflects back over Israel's stormy history, it places Phinehas (106:30–31) alongside Moses (106:23, 32–33) as the two great intercessors of the wilderness time (Janowski 1983: 244). They are the only two individuals mentioned in the Psalm. This text clearly refers back to the event in Numbers 25, but the assessment of Phinehas is cast in a slightly different, yet still extremely positive, light. The text reads:

> They yoked themselves to the Baal of Peor
>   and ate sacrifices offered to lifeless gods;
> they provoked the LORD to anger by their wicked deeds,
>   and a plague broke out among them.
> But Phinehas stood up and intervened,
>   and the plague was checked.
> This was credited to him as righteousness
>   for endless generations to come.
>
> (Psalm 106:28–31)

---

[31] There is a tremendous amount of literary irony in this story. Remember that Moses first married into a *Midianite* priestly family (Exod. 2:16–22). Later he marries a *Cushite* woman (Num. 12:1). Then *Midianite* women lead Israel into apostasy, resulting in a plague from God. A relative of Moses, with a name that could be translated as 'the *Cushite*', delivers Israel by annihilating the *Midianites*, including the women. Are these events unrelated? For a study exploring the implications of this irony see J. Hays (2000).

Of additional theological interest to us is verse 31: 'This was cred-ited to him as righteousness for endless generations to come.' The phrase referring to the crediting (*ḥāšaḇ*) something to someone as righteousness (*ṣᵉḏāqâ*) only occurs in one other place. In Genesis 15:6 Abraham believes God and God credits it to him as righteousness. In Psalm 106:30–31 Phinehas intercedes on behalf of Israel and God apparently credits this to him as righteousness. This phrase becomes a foundational theological tenet for Paul in the New Testament. In Galatians 3, Paul uses this phrase (from Genesis 15:6) to prove that Gentiles are justified by faith and thus to be accepted into the Church as equal to Jews.[32] It is, therefore, rather interesting that this phrase is also used of Phinehas ('the Negro').

Thus we see that Phinehas plays an important role, not only in the Torah, but in other texts as well. Does the meaning of his name carry significance within the context of the role that he plays? How does the son of Eleazar the high priest end up with a name that means 'the Negro'? Keep in mind that the Egyptian word *nehsiu* (from which 'Phinehas' derives) does not just mean 'dark skinned', but is rather an explicit reference to the ethnic inhabitants of Cush. Therefore, since Numbers 12 states twice that Moses' wife is from Cush, it is sug-gestive at least that another relative with a name that refers to the inhabitants of Cush might be connected in some way. Yamauchi writes that Phinehas' name clearly suggests a connection to the Cushite wife of Moses (Yamauchi forthcoming: Chapter 2). Phinehas is the great-nephew of Moses. The family is also a priestly family. Perhaps Moses' marriage to the Cushite woman also united her family to his, resulting in other intermarriages between the two families. Phinehas might very well have had a Cushite mother and therefore might have looked like a Cushite at birth, thus receiving the name 'the Negro'. This is as plausible an explanation for his name as any other.

Note the significance of this connection. Yahweh makes an eternal covenant of peace with Phinehas ('the Negro'), promising the priest-hood to his descendants. Phinehas becomes a model of piety and faithful zeal for Yahweh. Finally, Yahweh credits this action to him as righteousness, a theological phrase to which the New Testament assigns great significance.

Imagine the different route American Christianity might have trav-elled if the translators of the King James Bible had known Egyptian

---

[32] Noting this connection is Davidson (1998: 350).

and had thus translated 'Phinehas' as 'the Negro'. The early Americans would have read that God made an eternal covenant with 'the Negro', that all legitimate Israelite priests are descended from 'the Negro', and that God credited righteousness to 'the Negro'. With such clear texts available, it would have been extremely difficult to defend slavery or to maintain any type of superiority–inferiority racial views.

While the meaning of Phinehas' name is absolutely clear, the significance of this meaning is admittedly not quite as certain. However, I would propose several theological conclusions. First of all, it is extremely probable that Phinehas was at least half Black. When combined with the 'mixed multitude' of Exodus 12:38 and the Cushite wife of Moses, Phinehas reveals to us that there was a significant presence of Cushites among the early Israelites. These Cushites were clearly Black Africans by the modern definition of the term. The stories of Phinehas show that at least one of these people related to Black Africa was tightly incorporated into the leadership of Israel. Indeed, at its beginning, the highest level of Israelite priesthood apparently had Black ethnic elements within it. Yet all this mix was still 'Israel', the 'assembly', or the 'people of God'. Early Israel, at all levels, was made up of an ethnic mixture of people.

Conclusions

In its early formative stage, Israel was far from being ethnically monolithic. The family of Jacob had Aramean, Amorite, Canaanite, and Egyptian elements within it. During their four-hundred-year sojourn in Egypt this mix evolves into the 'Sons of Israel'. God then forms them into a nation and brings them out of Egypt, binding them to himself through the covenant. During this event, however, numerous people of other ethnicities, including the Black Cushites, participate in the Exodus and the Passover, becoming part of the 'people of God'. Indeed, the trajectory of this Black presence appears in numerous places and plays a significant role in the early story of Israel. Moses marries a Cushite woman and Phinehas (the 'Negro' or the 'Cushite') emerges as the central faithful priest of the next generation.

Thus the Torah, the foundation of the Old Testament story, paints a picture of racial diversity present among the people of God. Black people are an integral part of this diversity. Furthermore, this diversity is present from the early stages of the story. Black people are part of the story from the beginning.[33]

Clearly the perception (conscious or subconscious) among many White Christians that the biblical story is a story about White people is wrong. The biblical story is full of different people of different ethnicities – and none of those in the Torah are Caucasian. As God's promise to Abraham in Genesis 12:3 (blessing to all peoples) unfolds, numerous different ethnicities are melded into the people of God in fulfilment of this promise. In the Torah, part of this melding process occurs through interracial marriage. Moses, the hero of the Torah, marries a Black woman with God's approval. Marriage across theological lines – that is, marrying unbelievers – is prohibited, but marriage to another of God's believing children, regardless of race, is affirmed.

---

[33] This fact directly refutes Louis Farrakhan's preposterous statement that Islam is the true religion of Blacks and that the Judeo-Christian religion was only introduced into Africa in the latter part of the second millennium AD through slavery.

Chapter Five

Israel and Black Africa during the monarchy

Introduction

One of the goals of this book is to explore the involvement of Black Africans in the biblical world of the Ancient Near East (ANE). As discussed in Chapter 2, along the Nile south of Egypt lay the country of Cush, a Black African nation. One of the most interesting facets of Cushite history is the role that Cush played in the geopolitical and military history of the ANE. Reading through the historical annals of the region during the time before Christ, one encounters Black Cushite soldiers serving in the armies of Egypt, Assyria, Israel, Judah, Persia, Greece, and Carthage, as well as in their own forces (J. Hays 1998: 31–33). Furthermore, from 715 BC to 663 BC the Cushites ruled Egypt as the Twenty-fifth Dynasty. As the rulers of Egypt the Cushites became aggressively active in the geopolitical struggle to contain the Assyrians. Thus during the monarchial period of Israelite history (1020–587 BC), as Israel and Judah become enmeshed in the intrigues of international power struggles, it is no surprise that they come into frequent contact with the policies, armies, and soldiers of Cush. In this chapter we will discuss the historical background of Cushite involvement in the armies of the ANE, and then we will focus on their particular points of contact with Israel and Judah, as described in the Scriptures. Much of the material in this chapter focuses on historical aspects, but determining and describing the actual historical situation is an asset in developing theology. If nothing else, establishing the fact that Black soldiers (and others) participate often in the history of Israel should affect the manner in which both Black Christians and White Christians read and interpret many of these OT texts.

Cushite soldiers in the Ancient Near East prior to the Israelite monarchy

As discussed in earlier chapters, the history of Cush is closely inter-twined with the history of Egypt. During the three millennia before Christ, Cush and Egypt were often enemies, and skirmishes between the two were frequent. Cush had tremendous gold mines, and thus its powerful neighbour to the north was frequently trying to add the vast riches of Cush into its coffers. Cush was often under Egyptian control; occasionally it was more or less part of Egypt. Once, how-ever, Cush turned the tables and for a while actually ruled Egypt.

One of the more regular features of this relationship, however, was that, throughout most of ancient Egyptian history, Cushite soldiers and Cushite officers served in the Egyptian army. The Egyptians gen-erally relied heavily on foreign troops to staff their armies. Although other nationalities also served in the Egyptian armies, the Cushites are the most common and the best documented (Leahy 1995: 288).[1] They also served in significant numbers, usually as identifiable and separate ethnic military units.[2] Indeed, Cushite mercenaries served in the Egyptian army as early as the Sixth Dynasty (2350–2170 BC). J. Wilson (1951: 136–138) writes that these Black troops were used for raids on the Asiatics. Throughout most of the second millennium BC, Cush was under Egyptian control, and Cushite soldiers were regularly incorporated into the Egyptian army. This was particularly true during the New Kingdom period (1539–1075 BC) (Leahy 1995: 228; Gordan 2001: 545; Gnirs 2001: 403). During this period the Egyptians relied heavily on their Cushite auxiliaries (Gnirs 2001: 403).

The Amarna Letters, a collection of correspondence letters between the Pharaoh of Egypt and his vassals in Canaan during the mid-fourteenth century BC, mention Cushite troops serving in Egyptian garrisons in Canaan (Pritchard 1969: 488).[3] This particular

---

[1] For discussions of the Egyptian military and the role that foreigners, especially Cushites (Nubians), played, see al-Nubi (1997: 151–184); Leahy (1995: 228); Bresciani (1997: 221–253); and Gnirs (2001: 400–406).

[2] Gnirs (2001: 404) cites the composition of one particular Egyptian military unit as 3,100 mercenaries from Libya, Nubia, and the Mediterranean coast along with 1,900 Egyptian bowmen. Al-Nubi (1997: 173) cites another unit with the following ethnic make-up: 520 Shardan, 1,600 Qehaq (Libyan), 100 Meshwesh (Libyan), and 880 Nubian (Cushite).

[3] For a translation of the entire Amarna collection see Moran (1992). For a discus-sion of the literature and the problems associated with it, see Na'aman (1992: 174–181).

unit, although supposedly under Egyptian control, appears to be at least occasionally hostile to the Canaanite vassals. In one of the Amarna Letters the prince of Jerusalem, 'Abdu-Heba, complained to Pharaoh that Cushite soldiers had broken into his house and nearly killed him. He requested that Egyptian archers be sent to help him restore order. He also called on the Egyptian king to avenge him against the soldiers of Cush (Pritchard 1969: 488). Although it is difficult to determine the true details of the political intrigue behind the correspondence, it is clear that Cushite soldiers were stationed in Canaan during the fourteenth century BC. Although the number of these soldiers appears to be small, the implications of the correspondence are that they may have been in several different locations, manning several different Egyptian garrisons and projecting Egyptian military control on the region.

Most of the Cushite soldiers of this era were probably bowmen. In fact, Cushite soldiers developed a reputation as bowmen throughout the Ancient Near East. The Egyptians, for example, often called the region of Cush by the name *Ta-sety*, 'Land of the Bow', a probable reference to the weapon most closely associated with its people (Taylor 1991: 5).[4] Excavation of a tomb in Kerma (early capital of the Cushite region) revealed a young archer, lying on his side, with his bow and bowstring in his hand (c. 2500–2052 BC). Models of forty Cushite soldiers, all archers carrying bows, were discovered in the tomb of Mesehty at Aissiut from near the same period (c. 2040 BC).[5] Strouhal (1992: 203) suggests that these Cushite archers were the pharaoh's elite bodyguards. The Cushites continued their reputation as bowmen into the New Kingdom period, forming a critical component of Egyptian military power (Gnirs 2001: 403). Welsby, however, notes that although the Cushites were famous as archers throughout much of ancient history, there are also records of Cushite cavalry units (1998: 40). In fact, as mentioned below, Cush developed a further reputation for producing chariot horses.

---

[4] It is also possible, however, that the name 'Land of the Bow' is a reference to the shape of the land. The Nile River is relatively straight in its course through Egypt. In Cush, however, due to the cataracts, the Nile makes a dramatic 180-degree bend, resembling the shape of a bow.

[5] The models are in the Egyptian Museum in Cairo. An excellent picture of the models can be seen in Westendorf (1968: 72).

Soldiers and generals: Cushites in the early monarchy

One aspect of the Davidic monarchy that is often overlooked is the role of foreigners in David's administration and in his army. This foreign element plays a particularly important role during the rebellion of Absalom. As Israel betrays David and rushes to follow the usurper Absalom, numerous foreign troops and administrators remain loyal to David. His loyal personal bodyguard consists of Kerethites (Cretans) and Pelethites (Philistines) (2 Sam. 8:18; 15:18).[6] Ittai the Gittite (a Philistine) leads a contingent of 600 Philistines and insists on staying beside David during his retreat from Jerusalem even though David attempts to talk him out of it (2 Sam. 15:19–22). Later David places Ittai in charge of one-third of his army. Likewise the list of David's mighty men in 2 Samuel 23 includes at least three foreigners (Uriah, Igal, and Zelek) (A. Anderson 1989: 277).

It is within this context that we encounter a Cushite soldier in David's army (2 Sam. 18:19–33). After the death of David's rebellious son Absalom and the defeat of Absalom's army, Joab – David's general and the one who killed Absalom – chooses 'the Cushite' to take the news of Absalom's death to David.[7]

In light of the frequent appearance of Cushites in the various armies of the Ancient Near East, it should come as no surprise that David had Cushites serving in his army. Thus the normal understanding of the passage would be to view this Cushite as a soldier, perhaps a mercenary but perhaps not. Redford notes that later in history (under Taharqa) Cushite soldiers also had a reputation as being good runners and messengers (1992: 305–306).[8] Whether or not this

---

[6] See the discussions by A. Anderson (1989: 137, 244), and Delcor (1978: 409–422).

[7] It is not clear whether the term *kûšî* is to be taken as a proper name ('Cushite') or an ethnic reference ('the Cushite'). In the MT, 2 Samuel 18 uses this term five times (twice in 18:21, once in 18:31, and twice in 18:32). Four times the word has the definite article – implying 'the Cushite'. Once it does not – implying 'Cush' as the man's proper name. A. Anderson (1989: 221) suggests that the omission of the article reflects a scribal mistake. Most modern translations treat it as an ethnic reference and translate it as 'the Cushite'. The LXX, however, translates it as a proper name, and the KJV follows the LXX. There is no evidence to connect this *kûšî* with the *kûšî* in the superscription (verse 1 in Hebrew) of Psalm 7. The Cushite [*kûšî*] of Psalm 7 is a Benjamite and an enemy of David, neither of which characteristics appears to match the man in 2 Samuel 18.

[8] Redford (1992: 305), who regularly challenges (and ridicules) those who assign any historical reliability to the Hebrew Scriptures, argues that this text must be a retrojection, reflecting an understanding of the Cushites that did not develop for another few hundred years.

Cushite is mentioned because of his running skill, his appearance in the story of David's army, taking place immediately after a major battle, indicates that he was a soldier in the army of David, one of numerous foreign troops. This fits with both the text and our understanding of Cushites in the Near East at this time. Furthermore, runners were commonly used in the armies of the Ancient Near East both to direct the movements during a battle and to send announcements of the results. Some of these runners were young men employed because of their stamina and speed, but others held a certain diplomatic rank. They were used to carry messages with diplomatic consequences (Walton, Matthews, and Chavalas 2000: 347–348); thus it was required that they possess a certain poise, presence of mind, and eloquence. The Cushite in 2 Samuel 18 could fall into either category; his articulate verbal message delivered to David (18:31–32) and the fact that Ahimaaz left later but still outran him point to the latter.

There is nothing whatsoever in the text or in the historical background to suggest that this Cushite was a slave. H. P. Smith (1899: 359) thus makes an unwarranted (and prejudiced) statement when he writes, 'Joab then calls a Negro (naturally, a slave) and commands him . . .' In fact, there is a tendency among older commentators to *assume* that all Blacks (Negroes) that appear in Scripture must be slaves. Keil and Delitzsch (1986 reprint: 440), for example, write that the term suggests a 'Moorish slave in the service of Joab'. Kirkpatrick (1890: 174) explains that the Cushite was 'an Ethiopian slave in Joab's service, who would have had little to lose by the king's displeasure'. Even some recent commentators suggest this understanding. Bergen (1996: 423), for example, normally more careful with his exegesis, suggests that the Cushite 'was perhaps Joab's slave.' M. Evans (2000: 216) makes the same identification. Caird (1953: 1142) writes, 'The Cushite was an Ethiopian, probably a slave, and so a more suitable person for the unpleasant task.' At the more popular level, the Ryrie Study Bible states, 'Joab wanted the Cushite slave to report the incident, in case David reacted with violence' (1976). Yet there is no mention whatsoever in the text that this Cushite is a slave, and there is no historical evidence that Cushite slaves were common in Palestine at this time. Cushites were occasionally captured in war (especially by Egypt, as mentioned earlier) and so there were Cushite slaves in the Ancient Near East, but this was true for *all* nationalities of that time. Any invading army could make slaves of the conquered people. However, when people of other nationalities are mentioned in the

Bible, no one declares that they were slaves just because their nationality is given. No one suggests, for example, that Uriah the Hittite was a slave just because of his Hittite nationality. Why, then, have numerous scholars made the assumption that this Cushite was a slave?

The quick jump, without evidence, from the term 'Cush' to the notion of slavery probably reflects an unintentional subconscious connection between Blacks and slaves in the minds of some White scholars.[9] They assume – without doing adequate research – that if a character in the story is a Black African then he must be a slave.[10] Such an assumption in the context of 2 Samuel is totally without historical or textual support. It reflects the kind of subtle prejudicial thinking among Whites that is so frustrating to the Black Christian community because White scholarship is so reluctant to admit it, or even acknowledge it. Methodologically, this error falls in the category of cultural pre-understanding, whereby the interpreter reads his or her own (often biased) cultural understanding into the text instead of letting the text and solid historical and cultural background shape their understanding. Often this is a subconscious step. Subconscious or not, however, this erroneous assumption needs to be challenged and corrected by careful exegesis and careful historical background analysis.

Joab is reluctant to give the job to Ahimaaz, an Israelite and the son of Zadok the priest, perhaps because he is worried about David's response to the death of his son. Apparently Joab decided that it would be more appropriate for a foreigner to deliver the news of Absalom's death than for an Israelite.[11] Note that the text is ambiguous about the reason. It does not say that Joab feared that David would kill the messenger.[12] Perhaps, like Ebed-Melech three hundred years later, this Cushite was one of the few not overawed by the king – one who was not afraid of the king and who could thus speak forthrightly, even to the point of delivering the news of the death of the king's son.[13] The Cushite is neither timid nor tongue-tied, but rather

---

[9] See the discussion by Adamo (1998: 85–86).

[10] For example, in commenting on Amos 9:7, Mays (1969: 157) writes: 'On the evidence one can say no more than that the Cushites were a distant, different folk whom Israelites *knew mostly as slaves*' (italics added).

[11] Conroy (1978: 69) suggests that Joab chose the Cushite, not necessarily because he was Black, but simply because he was a foreigner.

[12] The NIV translation of 18:20 is misleading ('you are not the one to take the news today'). Literally the text reads, 'you are not a man of good tidings today'.

[13] Brueggemann suggests a similar view. He states that the Cushite is 'unlike the cowardly Ahimaaz' (1990: 322).

delivers an articulate oral message (hardly the action of a slave). Peterson points out that Ahimaaz's approach was to break the news gently to the king while the Cushite's was blunt and forthright. Both methods, Peterson argues, were correct, and both were needed (1999: 223–227).

The association of the Cushite with David in this section of the narrative should also be viewed as a positive association. The Cushite is on the side of David, the one chosen by Yahweh. The strong positive support that David receives from his foreign soldiers, especially when most of Israel turns against him, is a suggestive theological link to the unfolding promise of Yahweh to bless the peoples of the earth. Illustrated more clearly by Ittai the Gittite (2 Sam. 15:19–22)[14] is the theme of foreigners supporting God's plan or God's person in the context of national rejection.[15] While the Cushite's statements are not as clear as Ittai's, when placed in context they form a strong suggestive contrast to the words of Ahimaaz.

The passage is rich in irony and contrast. When David sees Ahimaaz coming, he notes that he is a good man who comes with 'good tidings' (*bᵉśōrâ*). This term will be used five times in this story (18:20, 22, 25, 27, 31). Ahimaaz, however, says nothing of having *bᵉśōrâ* (good news), while the Cushite, by contrast, introduces his announcement with the proclamation of *bᵉśōrâ* ('good news', 18:31). Note the other contrasts in statements. Ahimaaz says, '*Šālôm*! Praise to Yahweh, *your god*, who has delivered [lit. 'hidden, shut up', *siggar*] the men who have raised up their hand against my lord the king.' The Cushite,[16] however, says, 'Hear the good news [*bᵉśōrâ*; the verbal form of the word is different here, but the root is the same, indicating a continued word play]. Yahweh has vindicated [*šāpaṭ*] you today from the hand of all those who rose up against you.' The Cushite uses the name Yahweh without tying it exclusively to David as David's god, as Ahimaaz does. This usage may imply an acknowledgment of

---

[14] In 15:20 David declares figuratively that Ittai came only 'yesterday'. David then pronounces a blessing on him: 'May the LORD show steadfast love [*ḥesed*] and faithfulness [*ᵉemet*] to you' (NRSV, following the LXX). Thus Ittai's action is intertwined with strong covenantal terminology.

[15] This theme will recur in the stories of Ebed-Melech (Jeremiah 38 – 39) and of the Ethiopian eunuch (Acts 8). The context of both stories is that of national rejection and open hostility against God's chosen person and plan. Both stories will be explored later.

[16] In the Hebrew text there is an unnecessary repetition of the term 'Cushite' in 18:31, apparently for stress. The NRSV picks this up, rendering it as: 'Then the Cushite came; and the Cushite said . . .'

Yahweh as God by the Cushite. Also, the Cushite uses the theologically pregnant term 'vindicated' (lit. 'to judge', šāp̄aṭ) to interpret the events, instead of the vague term Ahimaaz uses ('to hide, cover up'). Schultz (1997: 217) notes that when šāp̄aṭ is used of Yahweh along with the phrase 'from the hand of', the term implies the establishment of justice through deliverance. Likewise the Cushite states that Yahweh has delivered David from *all* those who rose up against the king. When pressed for details about Absalom,[17] the Cushite invokes a wish that all of David's enemies who seek to do him evil (rā'â) may be like that young man. Perhaps Ahimaaz is more sympathetic to David's feelings, but the Cushite is much more accurate theologically. The rebellion against Yahweh's anointed was a bad or evil (rā'â) thing and Yahweh has judged (šāp̄aṭ) it.

Not long after the time of David, Cushites appear again in the history of Israel, but this time as enemies. Shishak (931–910 BC), King of Egypt and founder of the Twenty-second Dynasty, plays an active role in breaking up Solomon's kingdom, harbouring and apparently supporting the fugitive Jeroboam. After Solomon's death and the split of the kingdom into the two competing countries of Israel and Judah, Shishak invades Palestine and plunders Jerusalem (1 Kings 14:25–28).[18] Rehoboam, the new king of Judah, apparently quickly capitulates. A parallel account of this invasion is presented in 2 Chronicles 12:1–11. The account in 2 Chronicles adds the detail that Cushite units were part of Shishak's army. Thus during the late tenth century BC there were Cushite soldiers involved in the attack and sack of Jerusalem.

The next event occurs a few years later and is recounted in 2 Chronicles 14:9–15. This text describes an expedition by Zerah the Cushite against Judah during the reign of Asa (913–873 BC). Zerah attacks with a vast army (Heb. lit. 'a thousand thousands') and three hundred chariots. Asa, unlike the disobedient Rehoboam, calls to Yahweh for help and Yahweh gives Asa a great victory over Zerah the Cushite.

Because this episode is not included in 2 Kings, several scholars doubt its historicity. Knauf (1992: 1080–1081), for example, maintains

---

[17] Note the irony of David's question in light of Absalom's name. Literally, the king's question in 18:29 reads, 'šālôm to the boy, to 'aḇšālôm?' Absalom's name means 'father of peace'.

[18] In the Egyptian literature this king is known as Sheshonq I. See the discussion by Kitchen (1973b: 287–302; 2001: 280–281); Redford (1992: 312–315); and Currid (1997: 174–189).

that this event as recorded is not historical. He argues that Zerah could not have been a ruler from Cush (although he cites no evidence for this). Knauf states that Zerah also could not have been an Egyptian because no Egyptians have names starting with 'z'. He suggests that the story may be a reference to a later skirmish with Bedouins, especially since the text mentions camels.[19]

Myers (1965: 85) and Bright (1981: 234–235), however, argue for the historicity of the text. They state that Zerah was either a Cushite mercenary in the Egyptian army or perhaps an Arab. Their evidence for the Arab possibility, however, is Habakkuk 3:7 and Numbers 12:1, both of which, as discussed above, are dubious passages in regard to establishing an Arab connection to the term 'Cush'. Dillard (1987: 119) points out that Zerah is not called a king. He suggests that Zerah was a Cushite general sent by Osorkon I, who was the pharaoh in Egypt at that time. This accords well with the earlier invasion by the Egyptian pharaoh Shishak in 2 Chronicles 12, where Cushites are also listed as part of the Egyptian army (12:3). Note that in 2 Chronicles 16:8 the make-up of Zerah's army is described as consisting of Cushites and Libyans. Osorkon I was a Libyan, and no doubt Libyans composed much of his army. As discussed above, Cushites also regularly served in the Egyptian army. The Libyan and Cushite composition of the army mentioned in 16:8 accords well with the historical situation as we know it. The most logical explanation of Zerah is that he is a Cushite general serving under Osorkon I.

The argument that Zerah is an Arab (or Bedouin) is weak. As discussed in Chapter 4, Habakkuk 3:7 is hardly proof that 'Cush' can refer to Arabia. The overwhelming majority of usages of Cush in the Old Testament clearly refer to the area south of Egypt. Also the context includes Egyptians (Shishak in chapter 12), and this Egyptian association further cements the normal identification of Cush. The mentioning of Libyans as part of this alliance (16:8) should be the final conclusive piece of evidence.

The argument from the mention of camels is likewise weak. The camels are not mentioned as part of the army, as they are in the case

---

[19] Tuell (2001: 168–169) cites the reference to 'Cushan' in Hab. 3:7 and concludes that Cush can also refer to people in northern Arabia. Thus, like Knauf, he suggests that Zerah was an Arab raider. He likewise notes the presence of camels to support this suggestion. However, as discussed in Chapter 3, Cush is a clear reference to the kingdom south of Egypt. There is nothing fuzzy about the identification. The 'Cushan' connection is incredibly weak, although commentators continue to reproduce it without any substantial evidence.

of the Midianites in Judges 6:5, but rather with the sheep and goats of the captured booty (2 Chron. 14:14–15). The implication is that Zerah captured these herds during his advance, and then Asa captured them again when he defeated Zerah. The Bedouin or Arab argument is further weakened by the mention of chariots in 14:9 and 16:8. The army of Zerah did not come on camels like Arabs, but rather on chariots, like Egyptians, Libyans, and Cushites. Nowhere in the Hebrew Bible are chariots associated with Arabs, Bedouins, Midianites, or any other Arabian Peninsula peoples. Nomadic peoples did not construct chariots. On the other hand, chariots are frequently associated with Egypt and Cush.[20] Likewise chariots were listed as part of Shishak's army in 2 Chronicles 12:3.

In conclusion, therefore, Zerah the Cushite should be viewed as a Cushite general or noble either working directly for Osorkon I, or invading under a treaty provision with him. The significance of the story to this study is to note another example of Cushites playing important military or geopolitical roles in the Ancient Near East in general, and in Israel/Judah in particular.

Enemies and allies: Cush, Assyria, and Judah

With the rise of the Neo-Assyrian Empire during the ninth century BC, Judah and Israel found themselves located between two competing world powers, Egypt and Assyria. From the ninth century until the collapse of Assyria at the end of the seventh century, the affairs of the small states of Judah and Israel were tightly intertwined into the geopolitics of these two powers.

In the years that followed the reigns of the Egyptian kings Shishak and Osorkon I, Egyptian power waned as Assyrian power grew. In 853 BC the Assyrian King Shalmaneser III, attempting to invade Syria and Israel, was held in check at the battle of Qarqar by an alliance of Israel and her neighbours. The Egyptian king Osorkon II also supported this alliance, but the meagre number of troops that Egypt supplied to the endeavour (only 1,000) suggests perhaps that he was hedging his bets. It is not known whether or not any Cushites participated in this battle. Shortly afterwards, as Egypt declined in power, she appeared to try appeasement instead of confrontation, and we

---

[20] Dalley (1985: 31–38) presents evidence that Cush was integrally involved in the chariot trade of the Ancient Near East, particularly in the development of specially bred chariot horses.

read of Egyptian (and Cushite – see below) envoys residing in Assyria within two generations after Osorkon II (Redford 1992: 339).

In 728 BC the Cushite king Piye (in earlier scholarship referred to as Pi-ankhi) conquered Egypt and by 715 BC there was a Cushite dynasty (the Twenty-fifth) established in Egypt. The Cushites ruled Egypt from 715 BC to 663 BC, and they were continually involved in the affairs of Judah and her neighbours.[21] Redford (1992: 356) notes that during this time there was a marked increase in commercial and political relations between Judah and Cushite-ruled Egypt. This is an important fact to establish clearly, because this active political, military and commercial involvement provides a helpful historical background for several OT passages. There would have been numerous Cushite soldiers, diplomats and merchants in Judah at this time, as well as Judahite merchants and diplomats in Cushite-ruled Egypt.

Initially, the Cushites also established cooperative relations with the Assyrians, a relationship that probably began even before Piye conquered Egypt. Cush apparently established a military and economic relationship with Assyria at this time. Dalley (1985: 31, 43–44) notes an interesting reference in a group of Assyrian cuneiform texts from this time, labelled 'Horse Lists'. The Assyrian cavalry horses are called *mesaya*, 'from Mesu', which bordered Urartu, famous for its cavalry. The Assyrian chariot horses, however, are called *kusaya*, 'from Cush'. Dalley writes: 'from the evidence there is a strong possibility that many of the chariot horses used in the Levant during the 9th and 8th centuries were imported from Nubia [Cush] via Egypt'.[22] The Assyrians never controlled Cush directly, so they depended on trade to acquire the specialized Cushite horses. War technology was changing and horses were a critical component. Indeed, Tiglath-Pileser III (745–727 BC) opened a trade station in Egypt, evidently for the primary purpose of acquiring Cushite horses for his chariots (Dalley 1985: 46–47).

Individual Cushites are also mentioned by the name *Kusaya*, 'the Cushite', in the Wine Lists of Tiglath-Pileser III. In one text the man *Kusaya* delivered twenty bales of straw and fifteen homers of barley, presumably for horses. Dalley connects the reference to the Cushite horses in the Horse Lists with the Cushite administrators in the Wine Lists, and concludes that some of the Cushites in the Wine Lists of

---

[21] For a detailed presentation of the history of the Twenty-fifth Dynasty, see Kitchen (1973b: 362–398).

[22] The texts themselves are published in Dalley and Postgate (1984: Nos. 99–118).

Tiglath-Pileser III were employed as equestrian experts in the Assyrian army. This practice, Dalley suggests, continued down into the reign of Ashurbanipal (1985: 46).[23]

Although the Cushites probably had warm relations with the Assyrians during the reigns of Tiglath-Pileser III (745–727 BC) and Shalmaneser V (726–722 BC), by the time of Sargon II (721–705 BC) the Cushites, who now had control of Egypt, began to fight directly against Assyria, who had by now conquered and depopulated the northern kingdom of Israel (722 BC). Thus the Cushites began to form alliances with the enemies of Assyria in this region. Assyrian art of this period implies that Cushites were actively serving alongside the Israelites and their neighbours as they tried to stop the Assyrian juggernaut from moving southward. Reliefs on the walls of Sargon's palace at Khorsabad depict foreign foot-soldiers fighting against the Assyrian army during Sargon's campaign against Palestine in 720 BC.[24] One of these soldiers has the stylistic features of a Cushite. Indeed, Albenda (1982: 8) writes, 'one foe still retained facial features which resemble those of an Upper Nile Nubian: a beardless face with a broad blunt nose, and small tight curls covering the head.' Reade (1976: 100) draws the same conclusion.

By the reign of the Assyrian king Sennacherib (704–681 BC), the Cushites were at open war with the Assyrians. In 702 BC a new Cushite king, Shebitku, became pharaoh. Sennacherib was trying to consolidate Assyrian control of Palestine, while the smaller rulers of these various Palestine states were plotting to overthrow Assyrian rule. One of the central players in this coalition was Hezekiah of Judah (2 Kings 18 – 20; Isaiah 36 – 39). Hezekiah and his coalition apparently persuaded Shebitku to support them in their attempt to throw off Assyrian control (Kitchen 1973b: 384–385).

In 701 BC Sennacherib sent an army to invade Phoenicia, Philistia,

---

[23] Cushites appear in the various lists four times; see J. Wilson (1972: 93). Albenda (1982: 8) also argues that Cushites were living in Nimrud during the eighth century. By the reign of Sennacherib (704–681 BC), however, Cush and Assyria were at war. Any Cushites residing in Assyria and advising on military matters would probably not have been there as representatives of the Cushite pharaohs in Egypt, who were in a fight for their lives with Assyria.

[24] Na'aman (1990: 217–218) argues that the Cushite king Piye is 'So, King of Egypt' mentioned in 2 Kings 17:4 as conspiring with Hoshea of Israel. Na'aman likewise concludes that the Cushite troops depicted in the Assyrian reliefs as fighting against the Assyrians in the 720 BC campaign of Sargon II suggests that the Cushite king, not the weak remains of the earlier Egyptian dynasty, had dispatched this army. Na'aman also provides an extensive bibliography on the portrayal of Cushites in the Assyrian reliefs.

and Judah. Shebitku sent an army under the titular command of his brother Tirhakah (Taharqa in Egyptian/Cushite sources), who would become pharaoh after Shebitku in 690 BC.[25] The Cushite–Egyptian force, along with the various allies of the coalition, first engaged the Assyrians at Eltekeh, where they were defeated but not destroyed. They retreated, while the Assyrians attacked the Judahite fortress of Lachish (Kitchen 1973b: 385; 2 Kgs. 18:13–16).

Assyrian reliefs portraying Sennacherib's siege of Lachish (701 BC) portray captured enemy soldiers that appear to be Cushites (Albenda 1982: 10). This suggests that, besides challenging Sennacherib in open battle, the Cushites had also lent their support to defending the Judahite fortresses. The strong implication of this observation is that Black Cushite troops and Jews from Judah were fighting side-by-side in an attempt to defend the town of Lachish.

After Lachish fell, Hezekiah paid tribute to the Assyrians,[26] but they advanced on Jerusalem anyway. The Assyrian commander delivered a speech to the defenders of Jerusalem (2 Kgs. 18:19–25; Isa. 36:4–10), mocking their reliance both on the Pharaoh of Egypt (the Cushite king Shebitku) and on their god. However, in the meantime, Tirhakah regrouped and advanced again against the Assyrians. They withdrew from the siege of Jerusalem to deal with Tirhakah. Sennacherib defeated Tirhakah, who then retreated back into Egypt (Kitchen 1973b: 385–386).

---

[25] A detailed discussion of the various views concerning Tirhakah's chronology (how can he be called king in 701 BC if he does not ascend to the throne until 690 BC?) is outside the scope of this book. See the discussions by Bright (1981: 286–287); Finegan (1959: 213); Hallo (1960: 34–68); and Honor (1926: 34). The best solution appears to be that of Kitchen (1973b: 161–172, 385–388), who argues convincingly that Tirhakah, the younger brother of the Pharaoh, was appointed commander of the expedition to Palestine and was the titular king of this expedition. Kitchen likewise rebuts earlier claims that Tirhakah would have been too young for such a task, demonstrating that he was probably 20–21 at the time (1973b: 385). See also the discussion by Cogan and Tadmor (1988: 246–251), who tend to agree with Kitchen.

[26] The biblical account (2 Kgs. 18:13–16) only mentions the silver and gold that Hezekiah took from the temple. Sennacherib's annals, however, provide a longer, more inclusive list. The Assyrian account cites the silver and gold, but it also lists numerous other precious or interesting items, many of which suggest an African origin: couches inlaid with ivory, chairs inlaid with ivory, elephant hides, and ebony-wood. See the full account of Sennacherib's siege, including the tribute list, in Pritchard (1969: 287–288). The fact that Hezekiah has treasures that are connected to Africa (ivory, elephant hides, ebony-wood) correlates well with our earlier observation that relations between the Cushites and the Judahites were close at this time. Perhaps these items had been given to Hezekiah as gifts by the Cushite Pharaoh. This is not certain – there were areas in the Ancient Near East other than Cush that had elephants and ivory – but Cush was definitely a major supplier of ivory at that time.

Sennacherib's annals do not mention Tirhakah by name, as later Assyrian annals do, but they do mention this event. According to Sennacherib's account, Hezekiah appealed to Egypt and Cush (both under Cushite rule) for help against the Assyrian siege, and the Cushite king responded with an army.[27] Sennacherib apparently turned from his siege of Jerusalem to defeat this Egyptian/Cushite relief expedition, and then returned to his siege, which proved unsuccessful.[28] The biblical account explains the reason: Yahweh killed a large portion of the Assyrian army overnight. The biblical record is clear in its stress that Yahweh – and he alone – was responsible for the deliverance of Hezekiah and Jerusalem (2 Kgs. 19:14–37).[29] For the purposes of this study, however, it is significant to note that Judah, while being ruled by the righteous king Hezekiah, was allied with a Black pharaoh and the Black Cushites against the Assyrians. Furthermore, the Cushite commander did march with his army against the Assyrians to relieve the siege of Jerusalem. This event was recorded twice (2 Kings 19 and Isaiah 37) and remembered in Jerusalem, thus providing another very positive point of contact between Judah and Cushite soldiers.

After Sennacherib's withdrawal, Tirhakah and the Cushites continue to be involved in Palestine, particularly along the coastal areas (Phoenicia) that controlled the trade roads (Redford 1992: 357–358). The next Assyrian king, Esarhaddon, attacks Tirhakah in 674 BC, but is defeated and retreats back to Assyria. However, Assyrian power was too great. Esarhaddon returned in 671 BC and drove Tirhakah out of Egypt. The Cushites withdrew up the Nile to Cush, behind the natural protection of the Nile's cataracts. For the next eight years

---

[27] For the Assyrian account see Pritchard (1969: 287–288). The term used for Cush is *Meluhha*. At this time in Assyrian history this term was used to refer to Cush. See Oppenheim (1977: 64, 408).

[28] At any rate, the accounts (Assyrian and Hebrew) agree that Sennacherib did not actually capture Jerusalem, but only 'shut up Hezekiah like a bird'. The annals of Sennacherib say nothing of the disaster described in 2 Kgs. 19:35–36 and Isa. 37:36–37, but the king of Assyria would hardly record such a disastrous event. The biblical account of Sennacherib's assassination in 2 Kgs. 19:37 does not appear in the Assyrian annals either, but a later reference in the annals of Ashurbanipal seems to corroborate the story, stating, 'The others, I smashed alive with the very same statues of protective deities with which they had smashed my own grandfather Sennacherib'.

[29] Redford (1992: 353), always sceptical of any divine activity in the texts, suggests that the strong response by the Cushites was the reason for Sennacherib's permanent withdrawal from Palestine. It is interesting to note that the Assyrians do not venture down to tangle with the Cushites for another twenty-six years. Esarhaddon invades in 674 BC (and is defeated by Tirhakah).

the Cushites played a dangerous game of cat and mouse with the Assyrians. When the Assyrian army moves into Egypt, the Cushites retreat to the safety of Cush. When the Assyrian army leaves, the Cushites sweep back down the Nile, destroy the small Assyrian contingents left behind along with any puppet government structures, and re-establish control over Egypt. When the Assyrian army returns to put down the rebellion, the Cushites fall back again up the river to Cush.[30] Finally, in 663 BC, the Assyrian king Ashurbanipal, after driving the Cushites out of Egypt once again, destroyed the temple city of Thebes, the base of Cushite power in Egypt.[31] The Cushites never again controlled Egypt or engaged in empire building, although they continued to carry out trade and commerce with both Egypt and other nations of the Ancient Near East.

Postscript: Cushite soldiers in the ANE after the monarchy

In 663 BC an Egyptian family from Lower Egypt regained control of Egypt with the aid of Greek and other mercenaries. Egypt then began to strengthen its southern frontier against the Cushites. Under Psamtek I, however, a large contingent of Egyptian troops defending the southern border defected to Cush, settling among the Cushites and intermarrying with them. They were perhaps unhappy with the preference given to mercenary troops of other nationalities (H. Hall 1970: 293–294). Egypt later (590 BC) settled Jewish mercenary soldiers on the isle of Elephantine on the Nile as a frontier garrison against the Cushites.[32] This settlement no doubt provided another point of contact between Jew and Cushite. Indeed, the name *Cushi*, 'the Cushite', appears in the Aramaic Elephantine texts (Porten and Yardeni 1993: 280).

During the Persian period, Cambyses conquered Egypt and prepared to invade Cush. Herodotus provides a fascinating account of an envoy sent by Cambyses with gifts to the Cushite king for the purpose of spying out the situation. The Cushite king rejects the gifts and defies Cambyses. He hands the Persian envoy a Cushite bow – for

[30] An interesting connection is that in 667/666 BC Ashurbanipal took Manasseh of Judah along with him as he drove the Cushites south and recovered Egypt (Pritchard 1969: 294).

[31] For a discussion of this period see Kitchen (1973b: 393–397).

[32] See Williams (1973, 95–96); the *Letter of Aristeas*, 13; and Herodotus, *History*, 2.161.

which the Cushites were famous – and states that when Cambyses comes back with an entire army strong enough to draw that bow then the Cushites might respect them. According to Herodotus, Cambyses then tries to invade Cush, but the expedition ends in total disaster.[33] The Persians, however, do gain control of Egypt all the way up the Nile to Elephantine, which bordered on Cush. This influence put the Cushites in constant contact with the Persians. Indeed, Herodotus states that Cushites served as mercenaries in the army of the Persian king Xerxes. Herodotus describes the troops as clad in leopard and lion skins, and armed with extremely long bows.[34]

The Greeks were also familiar with Cushite soldiers. Numerous articles of Greek art from the sixth and fifth centuries BC portray Black soldiers with Negroid features (Snowden 1970: plates 17–22). Most of the contact between the Greek world and Black Africa came through Cush via Egypt and the Nile. It is likely, therefore, that these Black soldiers in Greek art were Cushites, serving as mercenaries throughout the Greek world.

Snowden suggests that the Negroid stone figures on Cyprus from the time of the Egyptian occupation (568–525 BC) indicate that Cushite troops were also used in the Egyptian invasion and administration of Cyprus. Likewise the Blacks depicted on a Minoan fresco imply that Cushites may have come to Crete as auxiliaries. Cushites also served in Hannibal's army. The famous Carthaginian war elephants probably came from Cush as well. War elephants are depicted on several Cushite reliefs, especially at Meroe (1970: 122–123, 130).

Conclusions

Although historical records of the Ancient Near East are by nature sketchy and incomplete, it is significant to note the regularity and consistency with which Cushites appear as soldiers throughout the region. Not only did Cushites carry out campaigns as part of their own armies, but they also served in the armies of Egypt, Israel, Assyria, Persia, Greece, and Carthage. Apparently they were well known in the ancient world as soldiers, and they appear regularly in history in this role, both in the biblical record and in the historical

---

[33] See Herodotus, *History*, 3.152–153. In an inscription the Cushite king Nastesenen speaks of defeating *k-m-b-s-u-d-n*. Hall (1970: 312–313) argues that this is a reference to Cambyses. Gray (1969: 20–21), disagrees, citing Reisner, who maintains that Nastesenen was much later than Cambyses.

[34] See Herodotus, *History*, 3.379; and Gray (1969: 21–22).

records of others. Throughout the entire period of the Israelite/ Judahite monarchy (1020–587 BC) Cushite soldiers were frequent visitors in Israel and Judah.

Furthermore, once the Cushites gained control of Egypt, they established close, friendly relations with Hezekiah, king of Judah. Trade and commercial relations apparently also flourished during this time. When Judah was threatened by Assyria, the Cushites fought alongside the Judahites in defence. Indeed, they even sent out a large army to relieve the siege of Jerusalem. These events were important enough that they were recorded in both 2 Kings and the book of Isaiah.

This historical background is important, for it demonstrates that the Black Africans from Cush played a frequent and very important role in the biblical story. A clear and correct understanding of the biblical books of this period requires that one grasp the multi-ethnic world in which the biblical story took place. This historical background of the monarchy will also be critical to our understanding of the prophets, in the chapter that follows.

Chapter Six

Racial issues in the prophets

Introduction

The prophets speak often of Israel's relationship with the foreign nations of the world. They likewise address Yahweh's relationship, both present and future, with these same nations. The description and development of these two relationships has implications for our theological view of racial issues. Sharpening the focus from ethnic tensions and divisions in general onto our current Black–White tension and division in the Church today are those prophetic texts that address the ancient Black Cushites. There are several significant passages in the prophetic literature that incorporate these Black Africans into the prophetic message. Cush plays an important role in Isaiah, Amos, Zephaniah, and Jeremiah. Thus in this chapter we want to explore two basic themes: theology regarding the nations, and, within that parameter, theology regarding the Cushites.

Judgment and blessing in Isaiah

The prophet Isaiah lived and preached during a time of great political upheaval and turmoil for Israel and Judah (740 BC to 687 BC). In fact this period was characterized by frequent wars and invasions. Dominating the political landscape of Isaiah's life and the first 39 chapters of his book were the imperial aspirations of the superpower to the north, Assyria. In addition, as discussed in Chapter 5, Egypt, the power to the south, was challenging the Assyrian expansion into Palestine, with Judah and Israel caught in the middle. Likewise, as discussed in Chapter 5, it is critical to the historical context to remember that the Cushites began fighting the Assyrians in Palestine as early as 720 BC. By 710 BC the Cushites were in control of Egypt and by the close of the century they were at open war with Assyria. Thus during practically all of King Hezekiah's reign (715–687 BC), the focal period for the first half of Isaiah, the Cushites were major geopolitical players in Palestine, contesting with Assyria for control of the region. Isaiah mentions Cush or the Cushites eight times, which comes as no surprise because of the major role they played in Judah's affairs. However, references to *Egypt* during Hezekiah's reign must also be understood in the context of the ruling Cushite pharaohs. Armies from Egypt during the Twenty-fifth Dynasty would have been under Cushite command and would have had large contingents of Black Cushite soldiers, probably forming the most critical elements of the army.

This Cushite presence and involvement is an obvious point of background discussion for Egyptologists who deal with this period (Kitchen 1973b: 362–398, for example). Yet the historical background discussions by most biblical commentators on Isaiah are strangely silent about the Cushites and the Cushite control of Egypt during this time. In the introductory discussions regarding the historical background of Isaiah, the Cushite rulers of Egypt are not even mentioned by Oswalt (1986: 4–13), Motyer (1993: 20–21), Goldingay (2001: 28–29), or Watts (1985: 82–83). A few commentators mention that the monarchs of Egypt at this time are 'Ethiopian', but they give no historical discussion or context in which to understand such statements (Grogan 1986: 6; Wolf 1985: 21–23).[1] Yet a thorough understanding of the historical context for the book of Isaiah is critical to developing accurate theology from individual texts.

The book of Isaiah contains texts that relate to the issue of race in two basic areas. First, the book mentions the Cushites eight times, so these texts should be informative for us regarding attitudes and theology in Isaiah's day concerning these Black African foreigners. Second, the book of Isaiah advances the concept of equal salvation for all peoples and nations more than any other prophetic book (House 1998: 293–294). The prophet paints an eschatological picture of people from all nations blending together with the remnant of Israel as the true people of Yahweh.

As mentioned above, the period surrounding the end of the eighth century BC was characterized by war and turmoil. Much of the book of Isaiah deals with judgment on the various nations involved in this warfare.[2] Likewise, much of Isaiah also focuses on Yahweh's

---

[1] One of the few writers who provides a significant – but still incomplete – discussion of the political situation in Egypt is Gottwald (1964: 162–163).

[2] This is a strong reminder and clarification that the inclusion of all peoples into one 'people of God' does not imply a theological universalism. The Gentile nations are blended into the people of God because they become true worshippers of God. When

judgment on Judah, a judgment arising from her infidelity to Yahweh. However, regularly interspersed between the texts of judgment are texts of eschatological re-gathering and restoration. Part of this picture is the addition of all the nations into the true worship of Yahweh. Thus Isaiah's vision of the future involved a picture of God's people that was decidedly multinational.

Isaiah 2:2–4 (compare also Micah 4:1–3) presents this vision early in the book:

> In the last days
>
> the mountain of the LORD's temple will be established
>   as chief among the mountains;
> it will be raised above the hills,
>   and all nations will stream to it.
>
> Many peoples will come and say,
>
> 'Come, let us go up to the mountain of the LORD,
>   to the house of the God of Jacob.
> He will teach us his ways,
>   so that we may walk in his paths.'
> The law will go out from Zion,
>   the word of the LORD from Jerusalem.
> He will judge between the nations
>   and will settle disputes for many peoples.
> They will beat their swords into ploughshares
>   and their spears into pruning hooks.
> Nation will not take up sword against nation,
>   nor will they train for war any more.

'All the nations' and 'many peoples' stream to Yahweh to worship and learn from him. As the book of Isaiah unfolds, this picture will be repainted many times (Westermann 1991: 90–94; Köstenberger and O'Brien 2001: 45–50), and the mix of peoples worshipping together will be described: a Jewish remnant, the hated Assyrians, the Egyptians, and the Black Cushites.

---

in opposition to God, the nations, as well as Israel and Judah, face judgment, and the prophets state this quite clearly. However, the time is coming, declare the prophets, when the nations and the remnant will both turn to Yahweh through the work of the Messiah.

Isaiah 11:10–12 contains the first actual reference to Cush in the book.

> In that day the Root of Jesse will stand as a banner for the peoples; the nations will rally to him, and his place of rest will be glorious. In that day the Lord will reach out his hand a second time to reclaim the remnant that is left of his people from Assyria, from Lower Egypt, from Upper Egypt, from Cush, from Elam, from Babylonia, from Hamath and from the islands of the sea.
>
> > He will raise a banner for the nations
> > and gather the exiles of Israel;
> > he will assemble the scattered people of Judah
> > from the four quarters of the earth.

The reference to Cush in verse 11 comes within the context of describing the 'four quarters of the earth' (11:12) from which the remnant will be gathered during the reign of the coming Messiah (Stump/Root of Jesse, 11:1, 10). As Assyria represents not only the superpower, but also the far northern regions, so Cush represents not only a geopolitical power, but also the far southern regions. The range of countries mentioned indicates that the exiles will return from all over the world (Oswalt 1986: 287; Childs 2001: 104). However, the text also states that the coming Davidic kingly Messiah will be a banner raised for the *nations* (11:10, 12), who will also gather to seek him.[3] The connection between the nations in this passage and the remnant of Israel and Judah is not extremely clear. Motyer (1993: 125) understands the gathering of the nations around the banner of the Messiah as an indication of Gentile inclusion. The connection between 11:11 and 11:12 suggests that the Messiah will bring both exiles and Gentiles together. Watts suggests that the nations are playing a role in the re-gathering of scattered Israel (1985: 179). Thus as the Gentiles are brought into the true worship of Yahweh through the advent of the Davidic Messiah, they (the Assyrians, Cushites, i.e. the people of the four corners of the world) will also be instrumental in bringing about the eschatological re-gathering of Israel and Judah.

---

[3] The NIV's translation of *dāraš* as 'to rally' is unexpected. The word normally means 'to seek' or 'to inquire'. See Goldingay (2001: 85).

In Chapters 13 – 27 the book of Isaiah focuses on the theme of Israel and the nations (Seitz 1993: 115–27). Within this unit, Isaiah 18:1–3 presents another specific and significant reference to Cush.

> Woe[4] to the land of whirring wings
>   along the rivers of Cush,
> which sends envoys by sea
>   in papyrus boats over the water.

> Go, swift messengers,
> to a people tall and smooth-skinned,
>   to a people feared far and wide,
> an aggressive nation of strange speech,
>   whose land is divided by rivers.
> All you people of the world,
>   you who live on the earth,
> when a banner is raised on the mountains,
>   you will see it,
> and when a trumpet sounds,
>   you will hear it.

The historical setting for chapter 18 involves the international plots and political intrigue that took place during the reign of Hezekiah. Cush, the ruler of Egypt and the dominant power in the south, was scheming with Hezekiah and his neighbours to forge an alliance in order to rebel against the Assyrians. Envoys would have been busy travelling back and forth between Jerusalem and Egypt.

Isaiah, of course, not only in these chapters but elsewhere throughout the book, chastens Judah for putting faith in such alliances rather than in Yahweh. This is a major theme throughout Isaiah 1 – 39. Both Childs (2001: 135–136) and Sweeney (1996: 256–257) stress that Isaiah 18 is not a proclamation of judgment on Cush, but rather judgment on Judah – a judgment that Cush will see and respond to positively (18:7). Thus the translation of the opening particle *hôy* should be translated merely as an interjection ('ah') rather than as a judgment term ('woe') as the NIV translates. This is the translation favoured by Childs (2001: 134); Sweeney (1996: 257); and Jenni (1997:

---

[4] NIV's translation 'woe' is misleading; see the discussion below.

357), as well as the NRSV, NASB, and the Jewish Publication Society's Tanakh.[5] Watts (1985: 245) likewise dismisses the notion that this term implies a judgment on Cush. He argues that it is merely a 'cry of dismay' over the coming delegation.

Isaiah 18:1–2a clearly identifies Cush as the region which has sent envoys abroad by boat. What is not clear is who the messengers in 2b are and to whom they are sent.[6] Although a wide range of views has been proposed,[7] the most convincing position is that of Childs (2001: 138) and Sweeney (1996: 257). They argue that 18:2a ('which sends envoys by sea') is a reference to Cushite envoys coming into the Palestine region. The command in 2b ('Go, swift messengers'), however, is directed to Judah's envoys, who are to travel to Cush ('a people tall and smooth-skinned') and to proclaim the message described in 18:3–6. The message is addressed to all the nations of the world, telling them to look for Yahweh's signal banner (note the connection with the term 'banner' in 11:10 and 11:12, where the banner is the Messiah's). Childs writes:

Then they will recognize Yahweh according to his action. Far above the fever of busy diplomatic intrigue, God views the world in calm rest from his heavenly dwelling before he acts. At the right time, just before the harvest, he will trim the shoots with the pruning hooks and hack off the spreading branches.

---

[5] Thus the NIV's editorial heading, 'A Prophecy Against Cush', is likewise inaccurate and misleading. Worse is the NLB translation, 'Destruction is certain for the land of Ethiopia.' The exact same particle *hôy* appears but three verses earlier in 17:12. In that text NIV translates it as 'Oh' and NLB as 'Look!' It is unlikely that the same introductory particle means 'oh' or 'look' in one verse, but 'woe' or 'destruction is certain' three verses later. The recent NET Bible has also replicated this mistranslation in its attempt at dynamic equivalence, 'The land of buzzing wings *is as good as dead.*' For a detailed discussion on this particle see Jenni (1997: 357–358).

[6] In 18:2 the text reads, 'Go, swift messengers, to a nation tall and smooth, to a people feared far and wide'. Traditionally this has been understood as messengers being sent to Cush, a country of people 'tall and smooth', a possible reference to skin colour. However, the Hebrew word translated as 'tall' normally means 'to draw out', and nowhere else in the Bible is it translated as 'tall'. It is, on the other hand, often used of drawing bows. Therefore this reference may perhaps be more of a play on the Cushite fame with the bow – calling them the 'drawn ones' perhaps – than any reference to their height (although Herodotus does mention the height of the Cushites). Likewise, the term translated 'smooth' literally means 'the ones who have been polished'. It can also mean 'the bald ones'.

[7] Watts (1985: 245–246), for example, identifies the Assyrians as those receiving the envoys, while Oswalt (1986: 360), on the other hand, suggests that the destination of the envoys is to a future, figurative people.

In the context of the chapter the imagery can only mean that of judgment against Judah, not Ethiopia. God will not support the planned rebellion, which will surely fail.

(2001: 138)

Isaiah 18:7 then indicates that the Cushites will respond to Yahweh's action, acknowledging his sovereignty as Lord by bringing tribute to him on Mount Zion (Childs 2001: 138; Westermann 1991: 91–92). This text may refer to the events of 701 BC. After Yahweh miraculously delivered Jerusalem by smiting the Assyrian army (Isaiah 36 – 37) foreign envoys, no doubt, came to Jerusalem (the Babylonians, for example, in Isaiah 39). The Cushites may have been part of this response. However, this text may also refer to eschatological events as well, epitomizing that time of future Gentile inclusion when the Gentiles come streaming to Jerusalem (see the discussion on Zeph. 3:10, below) (Wolf 1985: 122). This would imply that, besides being historically involved, the Black Cushites also play a symbolic role. They are representative or paradigmatic of the Gentile inclusion into Israel.[8]

Isaiah 18, 19, and 20 focus specifically on Cush and Egypt. While the exact literary connections between the chapters are disputed, it appears that they are at least connected thematically. Isaiah 20:1–6 warns the Egyptians and the Cushites that Sargon the Assyrian king will defeat them.[9] Likewise, Isaiah 19:1–15 prophesies judgment on Egypt.[10] However, Isaiah 19:19–25 moves beyond the impending judgments and looks to the eschatological future. The Assyrians and the Egyptians will join Israel in worshipping Yahweh, and the prophet even refers to these foreign nations in traditional covenant terms ('my people'). Westermann writes that this text parallels 2:1–4 and contains some of the 'most daring' universalistic language in

---

[8] Sweeney (1996: 260, 262) writes, 'Cush is representative of the nations at large.' The point of the passage has to do with all nations and not just Cush. 'The prophet maintains that Cush and the nations at large will recognize YHWH's power even if Israel does not.'

[9] This defeat is connected to the rebellion and battle at Ashdod (712/711 BC). For the importance of this event in the geopolitical intrigues of the day, see Spalinger (1973: 95–101).

[10] Egypt was overrun by numerous kings and armies throughout the eighth and seventh centuries, so it is difficult to be specific in identifying which judgment was in view here. Watts (1985: 252–253) presents a plausible case for seeing this prophecy of judgment on Egypt as being fulfilled by the conquest of Egypt by the Cushites.

Scripture. God's power to save and to bless is extended well beyond Israel to all peoples (1991: 93).[11]

This theme of blessing for the nations and the inclusion of the nations into the worshipping people of God is expanded and developed in the second half of Isaiah (40 – 66). Although the historical context of these chapters moves from the Assyrian crisis to the Babylonian crisis and even beyond, the theme of saving and gathering the peoples and nations of the earth along with the remnant of Israel is repeated in even more striking terms. The task of being a 'light to the nations' and of bringing salvation to all the peoples of the earth is assigned to the Messianic Servant of Yahweh (42:6, 49:6) (Westermann 1969: 211–212; Oswalt 1998: 293).[12]

In the latter half of Isaiah, the Cushites – along with the Egyptians – are once again used to symbolize the extent of Yahweh's ingathering of the nations. Isaiah 45:14 states:

This is what the LORD says:

'The products of Egypt and the merchandise of Cush,
    and those tall Sabeans –
they will come over to you
    and will be yours;
they will trudge behind you,
    coming over to you in chains.

---

[11] Although this was a common view in OT scholarship during much of the twentieth century – and is still the consensus view of evangelical scholarship – toward the end of the last century this position was challenged, and currently outside of evangelicalism there is quite a range of viewpoints on this issue. See Blenkinsopp (1988: 83–103); Van Winkle (1985: 446–458); and Gelston (1992: 377–398). One of the stronger critics of the traditional view is Gowan (1998: 156–157) who writes, 'There is no hint of the near equality of Israel and the other nations found in Isa. 19:19–25.' Gowan argues against the idea of a true Gentile inclusion into the people of God. The only 'universalism' in Isaiah, he states, is that the nations will see what Yahweh does for Israel and that this will be proof that Yahweh is God alone. However, I do not find Gowan's argument convincing. Likewise, Clements (1996: 57–69) argues that the 'light to the nations' motif is one of the themes that connects the three major sections of the book of Isaiah. Clements writes 'the nations are expected to participate in Israel's salvation, not simply as onlookers and spectators, but directly as those who will enjoy its benefits' (1996: 68–69).

[12] Israel apparently also was assigned a role in bringing the nations to Yahweh, although this understanding is likewise challenged by several of the authors cited in the previous footnote. Oswalt (1991: 88–92) and Kaiser (2000), on the other hand, argue that Israel herself was included in the mandate to reach the nations and to bring them to Yahweh as true worshippers. However, Köstenberger and O'Brien (2001: 35) maintain that this overstates the case. They write, 'To contend that Israel had a missionary task and should have engaged in mission as we understand it today goes beyond the evidence.'

They will bow down before you
　and plead with you, saying,
"Surely God is with you, and there is no other;
　there is no other god.'"

First of all note that 'the products of Egypt' and 'the merchandise of Cush' are figures of speech for the people from these wealthy regions.[13] This is clear from the pronouns and actions that follow ('they will come . . . they will bow down,' etc.). Thus the text is referring to the actions of Egyptians, Cushites, and Sabeans.[14] Isaiah is saying that the time is coming when all peoples, regardless of how far away they are, or how wealthy they are, or how big they are,[15] will recognize the sovereignty of Yahweh (Oswalt 1998: 215; Childs 2001: 355). Likewise these nations appear to come voluntarily; the mention of chains is either a figure of speech indicating their 'voluntary submission and glad surrender' (Oswalt 1998: 215; Motyer 1993: 363–364) or simply a reference that they had been in chains (metaphorically) prior to this event (Childs 2001: 355).[16]

[13] North (1964: 155–156) suggests a different pointing from the MT, thus taking these words as collectives, 'the toilers and the merchants'. Either way, he argues, the reference is primarily to the people and not the products.

[14] The Sabeans are apparently the inhabitants of Seba (or perhaps Sheba – in early Hebrew there was no written distinction between *s* and *sh*). The use of this term in Scripture points to two different locations for these people, one in southern Arabia and one adjacent to or even part of Cush. In this text, with its association to Cush (see also Isa. 43:3) the reference is clearly to a group of people near Cush, who are, most likely, also Black Africans. This is the position that Childs appears to take when he refers to the people in this verse as 'African tribes' (Childs 2001: 355). For a discussion on the two geographical areas of the Sabeans see Müller (1992: 1064). Likewise, these two different locations have given rise to differing views on just where the Queen of Sheba (2 Chronicles 9, 1 Kings 10) actually ruled. Although there is a valid argument that she was from Black Africa, the evidence seems stronger that she lived in southwest Arabia, and the majority of OT scholars maintain this view. See the discussions on both sides by Ricks (1992: 1170–1171); Ullendorf (1974: 104–114); Van Beek (1974: 40–63); Cogan (2000: 315); and Felder (1989: 22–36).

[15] The Sabeans are referred to as 'men of stature' or, literally, 'men of measurement'. Many commentators thus make a connection back to the alleged fame of the Cushites for great height as alluded to in Isa. 18:2 ('a people tall and smooth') (Oswalt 1998: 215; North 1964: 157–158). However, the phrase used here differs from the one used in 18:2, and it is used in reference to the Sabeans rather than the Cushites. In other biblical usages this particular phrase 'men of stature' is used of warriors that are extraordinarily big and, by implication, dangerous opponents (an Egyptian in 1 Chron. 11:23; a Gittite in 1 Chron. 20:6 and 2 Sam. 21:20; the inhabitants of the Promised Land or the Nephilim in Num. 13:32).

[16] Melugin (1997: 260–264) disagrees and notes that the servitude of the nations to Israel is a consistent theme in Chapters 40 – 55. He acknowledges the universal

The Egyptians, Cushites, and Sabeans are also apparently the representative people referred to in Yahweh's profound statement eight verses later (45:22–23):

> Turn to me and be saved,
>   all you ends of the earth;
>   for I am God, and there is no other.
> By myself I have sworn,
>   my mouth has uttered in all integrity
>   a word that will not be revoked:
> Before me every knee will bow;
>   by me every tongue [lāšôn] will swear.
> They will say of me, 'In the LORD alone
>   are righteousness and strength.'

Childs claims that these verses take the theme of salvation beyond anything seen so far in the book: 'The old division between Israel and the nations has been forced to give way before the salvation that God has both promised and achieved.' Childs notes that this is not a universal statement of blanket salvation for everyone, for there are still those who defy and resist Yahweh. But there is 'no longer any division along ethnic, national, or geographical lines'; rather, the 'offspring of Israel' is now defined in terms of those who find in God their righteousness and strength. They shall triumph and exult, indeed from 'all the ends of the earth' (2001: 355–356).

This theme is repeated clearly in Isaiah 66:18–24, the closing unit of the book. Childs (2001: 542) writes that this final unit is a summary of eschatological themes that run throughout the book. Isaiah 66:18

---

salvation of the nations as well. However, he argues that these two concepts (salvation and servitude of the nations) are unresolved in Isaiah, remaining in tension. Melugin also suggests that, although the theme of salvation for the nations can definitely be found in Isaiah, it may be an overstatement to call Isaiah the 'high-water mark' of biblical testimony on this theme. The 'high-water mark' of salvation for the nations, continues Melugin, is to be found in the relationship between Genesis 1 – 11 and Genesis 12:1–3. He writes, 'Genesis expresses more explicitly and clearly than Isaiah 40 – 55 that Israel was chosen for the sake of the *world* and that justice for Gentiles is central to the purposes of Yahweh the creator and universal lord.' As can be seen from the discussion in Chapter 3, I agree with Melugin's understanding of Genesis 1 – 12, and I do see those chapters as foundational to the concept; indeed, the rest of Scripture appears to allude back to these chapters frequently on this issue. Yet I would see the book of Isaiah as *complementing* this theme by painting powerful images of peoples of all nations streaming to worship Yahweh. Genesis 1 – 12 provides an intellectual framework for this concept, but Isaiah really adds the emotional punch.

states, 'And I, because of their actions and their imaginations, am about to come and gather all nations [gôy] and tongues [lāšôn], and they will come and see my glory.' There is probably an intertextual allusion in this verse to Genesis 10 and 11. Recall that in Genesis 10 the division of the peoples of the world was structured by summary statements employing the categories 'families/clans, languages [lāšôn], territories, and nations [gôy]' (Gen. 10:5, 20, 31).[17] As discussed in Chapter 3, tightly connected to Genesis 10 is the Tower of Babel story (Genesis 11), where God scatters the people across the face of the earth. The use of nation, language, and gathering in Isaiah 66:18 suggests that the prophet is painting an eschatological picture in which the coming Messiah reverses the division described in Genesis 10 – 11 and brings about the promised blessing of Genesis 12:3 by gathering the peoples of the world to him in true worship.

A further radical element is added to solidify the extent of the Gentile (i.e. the nations') inclusion. In 66:21 Yahweh states that he will choose some of these Gentiles to be priests and Levites, allowing them the special privilege of leading in worship and teaching, a privilege to which even most natural-born Israelites could not aspire (Goldingay 2001: 373).[18]

However, as we saw in earlier passages of Isaiah, this is not a blanket proclamation of salvation for all peoples, regardless of their attitude toward Yahweh. The final verse (66:24) is one of judgment on those who have not accepted the Messiah and have rebelled against Yahweh (House 1998: 296). Oswalt (1998: 387) summarizes the implications for this unit by writing:

> The message of God is not for the descendants of Jacob but for the world, and those of the world who respond to it are the true children of Jacob. The message has been given the Israelites as a trust to be proclaimed. It is not national election or cultic righteousness that makes people the servants of the Lord, but obedience to his Word (cf. 40:8; 55:11). But this theme is not limited to this last division of the book; it is part

[17] J. Scott (1995: 13–14) notes that Isa. 66:19 refers to six groups of people from the Table of Nations in Genesis 10: Lud (following the LXX, i.e. Libya) from Shem; Put from Ham; and Tarshish, Tubal, Meshech, and Javan from Japheth.

[18] Recall our discussion in Chapter 4 regarding Phinehas ('the Negro'). Phinehas was one of the most significant priests in Israel's history and tradition. With a name that means 'the Negro', one might speculate whether he foreshadows this particular prophecy.

and parcel of the whole book, as is indicated by its appearance in the introduction (2:2–5). From the very outset Israel is expected to be the means whereby the nations are drawn to the mountain of the house of the Lord to learn the Torah of God.

Thus, throughout the book of Isaiah, one of the consistently recurring themes is the vision of a future time when all peoples of all nations and languages will be united together as the true worshipping people of God. In the first half of Isaiah, in the context of the Assyrian–Cushite-Egyptian geopolitical struggle to control Palestine, Isaiah paints his ingathering picture with these nationalities. Later the picture is broadened to add the Babylonians, and the final unit of the book connects back to Genesis 10 and includes all peoples and languages. The book of Isaiah stresses that the Messianic message and the salvation of God is designed for all peoples. Black Africans (the Cushites) are clearly portrayed as part of the worshipping people-of-God mix. For the Church today to continue to divide along racial lines and to continue to maintain a racial division is to be out of step with the prophetic picture of God's future plan, in which all his people worship him together as one family.

Amos: Are you the same to me as Cushites?

Throughout the first eight chapters, the book of Amos consistently proclaims judgment on Israel. It is not until Chapter 9, in the final verses of the book, that the theme of hope and restoration is mentioned. As the book makes the transition from judgment to hope and restoration, an unusual verse appears (9:7) which mentions the Cushites:

> 'Are not you Israelites
>   the same to me as the Cushites?'
>   declares the LORD.
> 'Did I not bring Israel up from Egypt,
>   the Philistines from Caphtor
>   and the Arameans from Kir?'

Earlier expositors of this verse tended to view the Cushites in a very negative sense; thus they interpreted the analogy between Israel and Cush as likewise something negative.[19] Note, for example, the blatantly racist statements of Harper (1905: 192) regarding this passage in an early volume of the prestigious *International Critical Commentary*:

> Israel, says the prophet, is no more to me than the far-distant, uncivilized, and despised black race of the Ethiopians [i.e. Cushites] . . . No reference is made to their Hamitic origin, or their black skin; and yet their color and the fact that slaves were so often drawn from them added to the grounds for despising them.

Likewise, even as recently as 1969, Mays (157), in the much-respected *Old Testament Library* commentary, writes: 'On the evidence one can say no more than that the Cushites were a distant, different folk whom the Israelites knew mostly as slaves . . . What the comparison does is to humiliate Israel completely with respect to Yahweh . . .' Mays' *evidence* is lacking and he does not discuss anything regarding the situation in the Ancient Near East during the time of Amos. As in the case of earlier White scholars, Mays apparently ignores the actual historical context and starts with the assumption that because these people were Black they must be associated with slavery. Without doing any solid historical research, he has proceeded to interpret the text on the basis of this assumption, therefore repeating the biased and prejudiced theological errors of his predecessors.[20]

---

[19] For a discussion regarding how this verse has been abused throughout recent history, see Rice (1978: 35–44) and Holter (2000: 115–118).

[20] Evangelical writers are not immune from this tendency. McComiskey, for example, does not make the slavery-association mistake, but he does write an incredibly uninformed explanation of Cush in this text. He states, 'Cush was a territory roughly corresponding to Ethiopia and Nubia. It is infrequently mentioned in the OT. This country seems to have been chosen because of its great distance from Israel. It lay at the outer extremities of the important nations of the ancient Near East. At the time of Amos, it was probably considered an insignificant region' (1985: 327). McComiskey's first statement makes little sense – Cush, Ethiopia, and Nubia are different terms used throughout history to refer to the same region. Cush is mentioned 54 times – perhaps that qualifies as infrequent, but I doubt it. As far as lying at the outer extremities of the *important* nations and being insignificant, it should be pointed out that at the time of Amos (760 BC) the Cushites had long since pushed the Egyptians out of Cush and were seriously challenging them for control of Upper Egypt. At this time Cush was a major producer of gold in the Ancient Near East; was probably exporting horses to Assyria; and apparently had significant envoy representation as far away as Assyria. By 750 BC the Cushites controlled Upper Egypt; in 728 BC they conquered the Delta (Lower Egypt), thereby controlling all of Egypt. Certainly the Egyptians did not consider them insignificant.

There is absolutely no evidence anywhere in the Ancient Near East that the Cushites' reputation was associated with slavery. As mentioned in Chapter 2, the only reputation of the Cushites that appears frequently in the Ancient Near East is as soldiers, particularly bowmen. For most of the last century White biblical scholarship has overlooked this fact and has frequently lapsed back into the 'slavery' assumption regarding the Black Cushites. This phenomenon has been noted several times in other parts of this book, in order to highlight the presuppositions of racial bias that still reside in the field of biblical and theological studies. It is hoped that, if nothing else, this repetitive exercise will challenge the readers of this book to question their inherited presuppositions regarding race, and to replace those inaccurate presuppositions with careful historical research and exegesis.

Recently numerous Old Testament scholars have reassessed this text and have come to dramatically different conclusions from those of their predecessors. Gowan (1996: 424), for example, concludes that this text points to the fact that Yahweh was not a national deity belonging only to Israel, but that all nations belonged to Yahweh, even to the ends of the earth. In addition, Gowan offers a strong rebuttal (and rebuke) of earlier racist interpretations such as Harper's, charging them with reading their own 'modern' bias into their understanding of the text.

Because this text lies between the judgment passages of Amos 1–8 and the restoration passages of Amos 9:11–15, commentators are still divided on the main point of this passage. However, a significant number of writers do note the connection between the Cushites, Egyptians, Philistines, and Arameans of 9:7 and the reference to 'all the nations' in 9:12 (Andersen and Freedman 1989: 905). Viewed in light of this connection, the focus of the passage would be on the universal aspect of Yahweh's sovereignty. The relationship that Yahweh has with Israel is also available to all the other nations, and Cush is a prototypical example of all these other nations (Brueggemann 1997: 520; Limburg 1988: 124; R. Smith 1972: 138). Andersen and Freedman (1989: 906) sum up the main thrust of this text, stating:

It means not that Yahweh has not special interest in Israelites, and that they are like Cushites to him, that is, remote and unimportant, but rather that just as there is a special relation between Yahweh and Israel there will be a comparable relation with the Cushites, who also belong to him and who represent

118

a whole group of nations who also belong to him and will become his publicly and formally.

Amos 9:7, therefore, is not a negative text criticizing Israel, but a positive text pointing to the inclusion of the nations addressed in 9:12. Amos, then, alludes to the Cushites in a similar fashion to that of Isaiah, citing them as a prime example of part of the eschatological blend that will compose the true people of God.[21]

The prophetic voice in Psalms

Several passages in Psalms address both the Cushites and the rest of the nations in much the same manner as the prophetic books do. Because of this similarity – and because the material is not extensive enough to warrant a separate chapter on Psalms – they are included in this chapter along with the prophetic material.

Several psalms reflect the anticipation that the nations will one day join in praising and worshipping Yahweh (Ps. 67; 86:9–10; 117:1–2). The psalm that develops this theme most extensively is Psalm 67.

> May God be gracious to us and bless us
>   and make his face shine upon us,
> that your ways may be known on earth,
>   your salvation among all nations.
>
> May the peoples praise you, O God;
>   may all the peoples praise you.
> May the nations be glad and sing for joy,
>   for you rule the peoples justly
>   and guide the nations of the earth.
> May the peoples praise you, O God;
>   may all the peoples praise you.

---

[21] It is significant to note that Brueggemann, in his *Theology of the Old Testament*, emphasizes the importance of Amos 9:7. Brueggemann (1997: 520–522) offers an extended discussion of this verse – along with Isaiah 19 – in his chapter entitled 'The Nations as Yahweh's Partner'. Thus Brueggemann's extended treatment of this text underlines the point that many of the texts that we are dealing with in this chapter are not 'obscure' passages buried in the depths of the OT, but rather 'central' passages, especially to those striving to formulate theology. Brueggemann spends even more time on this passage in his article, '"Exodus" in the Plural' (1998: 15–34), where he notes that Amos 9:7 argues against the tendency to wed Yahweh to any specific ethnic community, as Israel was prone to do (27).

Then the land will yield its harvest,
   and God, our God, will bless us.
God will bless us,
   and all the ends of the earth will fear him.
                                        (Ps. 67:1–7)

Indeed one or more of the terms 'nations', 'peoples', or 'ends of the earth' appears in nearly every verse (2, 3, 4, 5, 7). Brueggemann writes: 'the psalm envisions a whole earth and all its peoples now gladly affirming Yahweh's sovereignty and gratefully receiving from Yahweh all the blessings of a rightly governed creation' (1997: 500–501). Davidson suggests that this brief psalm is the antidote for Israel's occasional drift into narrow exclusiveness. 'The blessing which God's people have received and confidently expect to continue to receive is a blessing to be shared. Here is a faith crying out to be universalized' (1998: 209).

Two texts in Psalms mention Cush specifically. The first is Psalm 68:31–32:

Envoys will come from Egypt;
   Cush will submit herself to God.

Sing to God, O kingdoms of the earth,
   Sing praise to the Lord.

This text first of all reminds us of the close connection in many biblical texts between Egypt and Cush. The first two lines are apparently structured in synonymous parallelism. Davidson (1998: 216) posits that these verses invite the whole world to embrace the God of Israel. Thus this text presents a similar vision to that in Isaiah: a future time when the peoples of the earth will join in as true worshippers of Yahweh.

The other text that mentions Cush is Psalm 87:4, 6:

I will record Rahab and Babylon
   among those who acknowledge me –
Philistia too, and Tyre, along with Cush –
   and will say, 'This one was born in Zion.'

The LORD will write in the register of the peoples:
   'This one was born in Zion.'

Tate (1990: 385–393) entitles this psalm 'Zion: the Birthplace of All Nations'. He states that it is Yahweh's intention to bring people from far and wide, from a diversity of nations, to be 'citizens' of Zion, part of the big family of God.[22] The point is not that they will actually be born in Zion, but that God will consider them as such and register them as such. As with other texts that we have explored in this chapter, this one appears to describe a fulfilment of Genesis 12:3, in which the nations of the earth will be blessed through the 'seed' of Abraham (McCann 1996: 1024). The major focus of the 'blessing' in this text is on the inclusion into the metaphoric kinship or family of God.

In both of these texts from Psalms it is significant that the Black Cushites are used as a central focus of the 'salvation for the nations' theme, a role they also play in the prophetic literature. This frequent usage of Black Africans as prototypical people in the make-up of the family of God underscores the multi-ethnic, or even 'multicoloured', view that the Old Testament regularly paints of the true worshippers of God.

Zephaniah and the name *Cushi*

The book of Zephaniah is important to our discussion for two main reasons. First, Zephaniah's ministry and message are set during the early years of Josiah the king (around 640–630 BC). This identifies him as the next prophet to follow Isaiah. Remember, as discussed above and in Chapter 5, that the Cushites ruled Egypt from 715 BC until 663 BC, during which time relations between Cushite-ruled Egypt and Judah were close, both commercially and militarily. Indeed, throughout the first half of the seventh century BC the Cushites maintained a strong presence throughout Palestine. The end of Cushite rule in Egypt was marked by the tumultuous destruction of Thebes by the Assyrians in 663 BC, a scant thirty years or so before the prophetic ministry of Zephaniah began. This significant event marked the high point of Assyrian expansion and, ironically,

---

[22] Kraus argues that this text refers to Israelites of the exile, scattered among the nations, and not to the people of the nations themselves (1989: 188). Kraus's view, however, goes against the normal reading of the text; while his view is plausible, the majority of commentators disagree and maintain the understanding that the nations of the world are referenced and not the Israelites of the exile. See, for example, Booij (1987: 19–21); Tate (1990: 385–393); McCann (1996: 1024); Mays (1994: 280–281); and Davidson (1998: 288).

the beginning of the Assyrian decline. Zephaniah writes in this context.[23]

The other reason that Zephaniah is important to our study is the fact that, in three short chapters, the book mentions Cush or the Cushites three times. This is not entirely surprising, in light of the historical context; the Cushite–Assyrian struggle was the major geo-political reality that dominated the lives of the three or four genera-tions in Judah immediately prior to Zephaniah. Indeed, as in Isaiah and in Jeremiah, the Cushites play an important role in Zephaniah, and thus this book is also particularly significant to our study.

The first reference to Cush is in the superscription of the book (Zeph. 1:1), where the genealogy of Zephaniah is given. 'The word of the LORD that came to Zephaniah son of *Cushi*, the son of Gedaliah, the son of Amariah, the son of Hezekiah, during the reign of Josiah son of Amon king of Judah.' In addition to the fact that Zephaniah's father was named *Cushi* ('Cushite'), the genealogy of Zephaniah is unusual in the prophetic literature because it goes back *four* generations, a feature unique among the identifying lineages of the prophets. Scholars are divided on the reason. Those who identify the Hezekiah of Zephaniah's lineage with King Hezekiah see the royal connection as a reason for the extra-long genealogy. It is pos-sible that the reforms of Hezekiah may be implicitly connected to the forthcoming reforms of Josiah, thus giving a reason for connecting Zephaniah back to his royal ancestor. Also, note that Hezekiah was the king during the great Assyrian–Cushite collision (715–687 BC), the events of which provide much of the background for the oracle in Zephaniah 2:1–3:13.

On the other hand, several scholars question whether this Hezekiah is to be identified with the famous king. They suggest that the citing of four generations of ancestors was required in order to establish Zephaniah's legitimate Judahite heritage, a legitimation that was required precisely because his father was named 'Cushite'. The evidence, however, appears to weigh in favour of identifying Zephaniah's ancestor Hezekiah with the earlier king.[24]

However, we are still left with determining the implications of Zephaniah being the son of a man named *Cushi*. Although we are not

[23] For further discussion on the Cushite–Assyrian context of Zephaniah see Floyd (2000: 182, 203–213, 225–228); Bennett (1996: 661, 670–671); Christensen (1984: 669–692); and R. W. Anderson (1995: 45–70).

[24] See the discussion on this issue by Barker and Bailey (1998: 383–385); Floyd (2000: 182); and Berlin (1994: 63–68).

certain of the reason behind this name, we can be fairly certain that the Hebrew term *kûšî* (lit. 'Cushite') makes reference to the country of Cush, south of Egypt, and that the owner of such a name would be connected *in some way* to this region.[25] This is particularly true during the seventh century BC, when Cush was a major world power. This historical connection becomes even more probable if we attempt to assign a date for the birth of Zephaniah's father. If we estimate the beginning of Zephaniah's ministry in 630 BC, assume that he is at least 30 at the beginning of his ministry, and assign a 25-year span between father and son, then his father would have been born around 685 BC.[26] Remember that although Sennacherib chased the Cushites down into Egypt in 701 BC, the Cushites re-emerged as a central power in the region shortly afterwards. Indeed, Tirhakah defeated the Assyrians in 674 BC and sent the army of Esarhaddon retreating back into Assyria. In 667/666 Ashurbanipal marched an Assyrian army back into Egypt to subdue Tirhakah, and the Assyrian king took along a large number of vassal kings from Palestine, including Manasseh (Pritchard 1969: 294). So, within this context of Cushite diplomatic, commercial, and military activity in Judah, a boy was born and named 'Cushite'. Thus the historical evidence weighs heavily in favour of the view that the name *Cushi* is connected in some sense to the historical Cushites of the seventh century BC.[27]

[25] Roberts (1991: 166) makes a strange, somewhat contradictory statement about this name. First of all he writes that it is impossible to know whether or not this reference has anything to do with the bearer's nationality. Then to substantiate this point, he suggests that *Cushi* may have simply functioned like the nickname 'Tex'. It seems to me that his illustration serves to *disprove* his point rather than support it. If we encounter someone named Tex in Los Angeles, is it likely he is from Boston? Is it not more likely that he is from Houston or Dallas? The reason we call people 'Tex' is precisely because they are from Texas. Note how this identical connection played out in the movie *Forrest Gump*. Forrest, while writing home to Jenny about the men in his squad in Vietnam, gives their names and their homes. 'There is Dallas from Phoenix and Cleveland from Detroit . . . and Tex . . . I don't remember where Tex is from.' At this point the audiences break out in laughter, because it is obvious to everyone (except Forrest) that Tex is from Texas.

[26] The helpful idea of attempting to place the birth of the individuals named *Cushi* into a specific historical time frame in order to shed light on the possible meaning of their name is taken from R. Anderson (1995: 53–54).

[27] Several recent commentators, however, have argued either that the name carries no significance or else that any attempt to determine that significance is merely speculation (Robertson 1990: 252; Roberts 1991: 166). Berlin (1994: 67) maintains that there is no connection between *Cushi*, the father of Zephaniah, and the historical country of Cush. Likewise she sees no connection between this name and the other references to Cush in the book of Zephaniah (2:12, 3:10). Does such a disconnection as Berlin suggests not reflect a disregard of both the historical context and the literary context? Also disregarding historical context (and common sense) is Bentzen (1952: 153), who

Zephaniah's father, however, is not the only one during this time frame with the name *Cushi*. In Jeremiah 36:14 the court official who functions as the intermediary in the struggle between King Jehoiakim and Jeremiah is identified as Jehudi ('Judahite') son of Nethaniah, the son of Shelemiah, the son of *Cushi*. Jehoiakim reigned from 609 BC to 598 BC. If we start with the year 600 BC, and if Jehudi, an important court official,[28] is middle-aged – say 40 – and we again assume 25 years between father and son, then his great-grandfather *Cushi* would have been born around 715 BC, just as the Cushites were coming to power. The length of years used in these calculations, of course, is merely an approximation. Other logical assumptions likewise still place this Cushi within the time frame of the Twenty-fifth Dynasty, when the Cushites ruled Egypt and meddled in the political affairs of Palestine. For example, if Jehudi is only 25 and the generational gap is 20 years, then Cushi was born in 685 BC, about the same time as Zephaniah's father. R. W. Anderson (1995: 54–55) and Blenkinsopp (1996: 113) both suggest that these two genealogies may refer to the same individual; however, this connection is tentative at best. The mention of two people in the text with the same name born around the same time period (within 40 years or so?) does not necessarily mean that they are the same person. On the other hand, even in spite of the very rough dating approximation of each, it is fairly certain that both of them were born and lived during the time of Cushite influence in Palestine. Thus it is probable that the reason for naming these two individuals *Cushi* was probably the same reason, and very likely tied to the historical context of Cushite presence and influence in Judah.

Other evidence to be taken into account in our discussion is the meaning and purpose of genealogies. R. Wilson (1994: 213) states that genealogies can express kinship connections. These connections

---

goes to the other extreme, assuming without any evidence that the term 'Cushite' must imply 'slave'. He writes, 'His father is called *Cushi*, i.e. the Ethiopian, the Negro. This perhaps implies that he was of a slave family.' Once again we see that throughout the first half of the twentieth century, numerous European – Bentzen is Danish – and American scholars often made the quick and unwarranted assumption that all Black Africans (Cushites) in the Scriptures must be connected to slavery. I would once again suggest that this type of associational thinking falls into the category of racism. Furthermore, I would suggest that this type of racist undercurrent continues to lurk in subtle forms, often unconsciously, throughout the pages of Euro-American biblical scholarship.

[28] R. P. Carroll (1986: 659) states that the citation of a three-generation genealogy suggests a very important person, puzzling as that may be in this context.

can be biological, but they can also reflect 'status, economic, or geographical relations'. Thus the genealogy of Jeremiah 36:14, which starts with *Cushi* ('Cushite') and ends with *Jehudi* ('Judahite') may perhaps suggest the possibility of something more than mere biological lineage. And it is also possible that the author is using the genealogy for his literary purpose as well (to be discussed below). However, in another work R. Wilson notes that *linear* genealogies, such as these two, usually have a fairly narrow purpose: to ground 'a claim to power, status, rank, office, or inheritance in an earlier ancestor.' These claims, R. Wilson states, can be made by both rulers and office-holders of all types (1992: 931).

Thus, according to R. Wilson, the earliest ancestor would be the most important one in the genealogy. This makes sense for Zephaniah, who appears to trace his ancestry back to the righteous King Hezekiah. But what of Jehudi? His lineage is traced to *Cushi*. Several scholars argue that the purpose of the four-generational genealogy of Jehudi was to show that although one of his ancestors was a Cushite, he, after three generations of Yahweh-believing forefathers, was now a bona fide, 'naturalized' Judahite (Holladay 1989: 258; Berridge 1992: 674; Ward 1962: 819). However, this understanding does not coincide with the normal usage of linear genealogies as explained above by Wilson. The normal manner of understanding the genealogy would be to place the emphasis on the earliest forefather, *Cushi*. It is Jehudi's connection – not his generational distance – with *Cushi* that his genealogy stresses, if we assume that this genealogy is used in a manner consistent with the rest of the Old Testament and the normal usage in the Ancient Near East.[29]

The answer may be a literary one, for Jeremiah 36 has numerous parallels and literary connections with the chapters that follow. In Jeremiah 36 there is major conflict between Jeremiah and Jehoiakim the king. This is paralleled by the conflict between Jeremiah and Zedekiah in Chapters 37 – 38. In both stories, not only the king, but also the ruling nobles of Judah are involved (see the discussion below on Ebed-Melech). Both stories have a mediator between the king and

---

[29] Rice (1975: 106–107) offers one of the more plausible alternative explanations for a four-generation genealogy ending with *Cushi*. Rice notes that the names of Jehudi's father Nethaniah and his grandfather Shelemiah both show up in other places in Jeremiah (Nethaniah, 40:8; Shelemiah, 36:26). Thus Jehudi cannot be clearly identified merely by his father or his grandfather. The narrator must go back one more generation for clarification, to an ancestor named *Cushi*, who, Rice argues, is an African from Cush.

Jeremiah. In chapter 36 the mediator is Jehudi the son of . . . *Cushi*. In chapter 38 the mediator is Ebed-Melech the Cushite (*Cushi*). In the centre is Chapter 37. Note the numerous parallels between this chapter and the events surrounding the Assyrian siege during Hezekiah's reign, over one hundred years earlier.[30] In both stories the king calls on the prophet to pray; the enemy (Assyria, Babylonia) besieges Jerusalem, withdraws, and then returns; an Egyptian/ Cushite army marches out in relief, but to no avail; a speech is given to tell the Judahites that Egypt/Cush will not help. The differences, of course, are the point. Isaiah's word to Hezekiah is one of deliverance and hope, while Jeremiah's word to Zedekiah is one of judgment. But note how Hezekiah's siege is brought into the context of Zedekiah's. Is it mere coincidence that Cushites, who played such a major role in Jerusalem's struggle against the Assyrians, should be mentioned twice in the context of Jerusalem's fall to the Babylonians? As discussed below, Ebed-Melech the Cushite does not relieve the city Jerusalem, but he does save the prophet Jeremiah. Furthermore, Yahweh proceeds to deliver Ebed-Melech because of the Cushite's trust in him (Jer. 39:15–17). Indeed, Ebed-Melech is one of the few in Jerusalem who are delivered. So, I would suggest that Jehudi's lineage becomes significant to the story in Jeremiah 36 precisely because he was descended from one named *Cushi*. Perhaps the narrator includes this extra-long lineage to connect Jehudi the intermediary to the theme of Cushite involvement in the defence of Jerusalem, and to remind the readers of Hezekiah's wise faith in contrast to Zedekiah's foolish obstinacy.

Now let us return to the question raised earlier. Having addressed to some extent the purpose for the genealogies, we still need to explore the reasons why someone in Judah might have the name *Cushi*.[31] First of all, keep in mind the historical context, as discussed above. At the time these two were born, there was a strong military

---

[30] Both Holladay (1989: 287) and Clements (1988: 218) comment on the parallel between Zedekiah in Jeremiah 37 and Hezekiah in 2 Kings 19/Isaiah 37, but neither develops the observation.

[31] *Cushi* also occurs in the Elephantine texts as a personal name among the Jewish settlers/mercenaries who lived on the Isle of Elephantine (Porten and Yardeni 1993: 280). The Isle of Elephantine was on the Nile River at the southern border of Egypt, very close to Cush. The same name occurs in Assyrian literature as *Kusaya*; see Tallquist (1914: s. v. *Kusaia*) and Dalley (1985: 46). The Greek equivalent term *Aethiops* (Ethiopian) also appears as a proper name. *Aethiops* of Corinth is credited with the founding of Syracuse (734 BC). See Athenaeus 4.167; cited by Snowden (1970: 103).

and commercial Cushite presence in Judah. In this context there are at least four plausible reasons for naming someone *Cushi*: the individual was *actually* a Cushite from Cush; the individual had a Cushite mother, father, or grandparent, and therefore *looked* like a Cushite; the individual had Judahite parents, but was *born* in Cush; or the individual was named *in honour* of the Cushites, since they were a powerful military ally in the struggle against the Assyrians. Since numerous Cushite soldiers, diplomats, and traders were in Judah, and likewise, Judahite diplomats and traders must have been in Egypt and Cush, any of the four scenarios described above would have been possible.

The main point to be drawn from these two people named *Cushi* is that the record they left further underscores the close and positive relationship that Cush had with Judah during the first half of the seventh century BC. Likewise these texts add dimension to the ethnic picture of ancient Israel. Black Africans were in and around Jerusalem regularly, and their presence and influence left strong imprints on the story of God's people.

Cush, however, plays a role in the book of Zephaniah much wider than the prophet's genealogy, for Cush is also included in the prophetic message. Cush is mentioned both in a judgment passage (2:12) and in a restoration/ingathering passage (3:10). Floyd (2000: 182) writes that there is probably a connection between the implied Cushite aspect of Zephaniah's ancestry and the message regarding Cushites in the book. Thus, as we attempted to do in combining the literary and historical elements in Jeremiah 36–38, Floyd suggests that historical background and literary purpose are working together. Zephaniah's Cushite ancestry, Floyd states, 'would be consonant with the pivotal historical role that is subsequently assigned to Yahweh's overthrow of the Cushites in the main body of the book and also consonant with the subsequent designation of "the rivers of Cush" as the southernmost extent of the cosmic context in which Yahweh acts' (2000: 182).

An analysis of the actual texts referring to Cush supports this synthesis. Zephaniah 2:12 reads, 'You, too, O Cushites, will be slain by my sword.' Yet the following verses (2:13–15) then proceed to pronounce judgment on *Assyria*. The English translations are somewhat misleading in their rendering of 2:12. In the Hebrew text of Zephaniah 2:12 there is no future tense verb (Hebrew imperfect), but rather a verbless clause and a pronoun (in contrast to the numerous imperfect – i.e. future – verbs in the following verses that deal with

Assyria). Literally, the text reads, 'You also, O Cushites; Slain of my sword are they.'[32] This is not a future prophecy but rather a statement of current fact. Floyd correctly identifies this as a reference back to the final defeat of Cush at the hands of the Assyrians, when Ashurbanipal completely devastated Thebes in 663 BC during the generation prior to Zephaniah (2000: 212–213).[33]

The oracle in Zephaniah 2 moves around the four points of the compass: Philistia to the west (2:4–7); Moab and Ammon to the east (2:8–11); and then the two great imperial powers of the seventh century, Cush to the south (2:12), and Assyria to the north (2:13–15). Floyd (2000: 212–213) writes,

> Assyria and Ethiopia [Cush] represent the distant imperial powers on the north–south axis partly for historical reasons. From a late-seventh-century Judahite perspective the point at which Assyrian hegemony reached its greatest extent, i.e. the Assyrian defeat of Egypt's Ethiopian dynasty, was ironically also the point at which Assyrian power finally became over-taxed. It is thus implied in 2:12 that the fall of Thebes in 663 BC marked the beginning of the end for Assyria.[34]

Thus, as in Isaiah, the Cushites, as an imperial Gentile power that did not acknowledge Yahweh, fell under the same judgment of Yahweh that the other powers experienced. Yahweh judged Cush through the Assyrians, whom he had raised up, but then Yahweh likewise used that action by the Assyrians as the basis for pronouncing and predicting judgment on the Assyrian empire as well.

---

[32] When the predicate is followed by the pronoun in a verbless clause, the structure is called a 'clause of classification'. Waltke and O'Connor (1990: 8.4.2) write that such a clause answers the question, 'What is the subject like?' Thus the grammar implies the question, 'What are they (i.e. the Cushites) like? They are slain of my sword.' Thus Floyd (2000: 226) translates, 'Also you Ethiopians! (They are [already] slain by my sword!).' Besides Floyd, this type of present-tense translation is followed by practically every major commentator – Berlin (1994: 104); R. Smith (1984: 134); Patterson (1991: 348); Robertson (1990: 309); J. Smith (1911: 231–232) – as well as the LXX, which translates the verse with present tense *este*. In light of this virtual unanimity among the commentators, it is unusual that English translations continue to use the future tense.

[33] Haak (1995: 238–251) and Berlin (1995: 175–184; 1994: 112–113) present alternative views. Haak argues that Cush refers to a tribe in northern Arabia, while Berlin, arguing from Genesis 10, identifies Cush with Mesopotamia. Floyd (2000: 206–213) presents a very convincing rebuttal of both views.

[34] The connection between the destruction of Thebes and the prophetic end of Assyria is also made in the book of Nahum.

Cush, however, reappears in Zephaniah 3:9–10, this time in a passage describing the future ingathering of Yahweh's people:

Then will I purify the lips of the peoples,
    that all of them may call on the name of the LORD
    and serve him shoulder to shoulder.
From beyond the rivers of Cush
    my worshippers, my scattered people,
    will bring me offerings.

After prophesying destruction to various nations and destruction to Jerusalem, the prophet turns to Yahweh's great plan of restoration for both groups. Zephaniah 3:9–13 is a promise of salvation both for the people of Israel (3:11–13) and for all the peoples of the earth (3:9–10) (R. Smith 1984: 140–141). Indeed, the terms used in 3:9–10 appear to echo terms found in the Tower of Babel story in Genesis 11 (Achtemeier 1986: 82; R. Smith 1984: 140–142; Floyd 2000: 235). The languages (lit. 'lips') of the peoples were confused in Genesis 11 but purified in Zephaniah 3:9; thus in the prophetic future the effects of the Tower of Babel will be reversed (Floyd 2000: 235). The phrase 'my scattered people' (lit. 'daughter of my scattering') may also connect to the scattering of people in Genesis 11 (R. Smith 1984: 142). Just as Yahweh's judgment entailed the break-up and destruction of international order, including Judah, so too the future picture of salvation 'entails the future possibility of a new more just existence for all peoples' (Floyd 2000: 236). As in Isaiah, Zephaniah paints a picture of a new world order in which there is unity of the nations based on a universal recognition of Yahweh. This picture focuses on a region 'beyond the rivers of Cush' from which Yahweh's scattered people (those from Genesis 10–11 as well as people of Israel) will stream to Yahweh to worship him. The rivers of Cush probably refer to the natural significant rivers in the region of Cush (the White Nile, the Blue Nile, and the Atbara).[35] 'From beyond the rivers of Cush' then refers to Cush itself and Black Africa beyond. Thus, for Zephaniah, Cush becomes a paradigm for the inclusion of foreign people into the people of God. The mixing of Black Africans shoulder to shoulder

---

[35] Floyd (2000: 213), however, maintains that the rivers of Cush could also refer to the description of the rivers in the Garden (Gen. 2:13). Floyd suggests that as Zephaniah paints the colourful future picture of salvation in which all people come together to serve Yahweh, he uses the imagery of the Garden.

with the remnant of Israel in worship of Yahweh is at the core of the prophetic imagery regarding the fulfilment of God's great salvific plan for the ages.

As demonstrated earlier, throughout the Old Testament foreign peoples are blended into the stream of the 'people of God' through two avenues. One is historical, for foreigners (and especially Cushites) are frequently incorporated into Israel/Judah by means such as faith, intermarriage, or naming. However, the other avenue is eschatological: a future, glorious inclusion of the nations into the people of God, an inclusion based on faith. Zephaniah proclaims both aspects: the first through his physical father named *Cushi*, and the second through his prophetic picture of Yahweh's great future ingathering of all the peoples, even those from beyond the rivers of Cush.

Ebed-Melech the Cushite

Of all the episodes in the Old Testament in which Black Cushites appear, the story of Ebed-Melech is perhaps the most detailed and the most dramatic. Thus it is also one of the most significant texts for our study.

Ebed-Melech plays a key role in the story of Jeremiah and in the tragic account of the fall of Jerusalem, as recorded in Jeremiah 38 and 39. As Jeremiah had predicted, because of Judah's covenant violation and her refusal to repent, the Babylonians invaded, and in 588–587 BC Nebuchadnezzar laid siege to Jerusalem. Jeremiah preached to the inhabitants of Jerusalem that it was futile to resist Nebuchadnezzar because Yahweh had raised him up to judge Judah. This message was extremely unpopular with the Hebrew officials who were engaged in the defence of Jerusalem. They accused Jeremiah before King Zedekiah, who promptly decreed that these officials could do with Jeremiah as they pleased. With royal permission, they seized Jeremiah and lowered the prophet into a mud-bottomed cistern, ostensibly to let him die there (Jer. 38:1–6). In essence, the entire nation had rejected Yahweh's prophet and his message. No one from Judah interceded for Jeremiah.

Indeed, help for Jeremiah came from an unlikely source. A foreigner – a Black foreigner – called 'Ebed-Melech the Cushite' interceded for Yahweh's prophet, securing permission from the king to rescue Jeremiah from the cistern. This action probably saved Jeremiah's life (Jer. 38:7–13).

Who was Ebed-Melech and what was he doing in Jerusalem in

587 BC? The text stresses his Cushite nationality, referring to him as 'the Cushite' *four* times (38:7, 10, 12; 39:16). No doubt, to the inhabitants of Jerusalem the term 'Cushite' would have elicited images of Black Africans. In Jeremiah 13:23 the prophet asked rhetorically, 'Can the Cushite change his skin or the leopard his spots?' The point of this question was that some things in life are unchangeable. The sinful behaviour of Judah, Jeremiah continued, was so habitual and so entrenched that it had become as unchangeable as skin colour. Of interest to this study is the observation that the reference to the Cushites' skin was apparently proverbial (Clements 1988: 87).[36] This implies that Cushites were known in Jeremiah's Jerusalem; that they were known for their dark skin colour; and that they were known well enough that popular proverbs arose about their skin colour.[37] As a Cushite living in Jerusalem, Ebed-Melech may have been a specific part of the avenue through which the city became familiar with Cushites (along with the general history of contact between Cush and Judah, as discussed in Chapter 5). Or perhaps Ebed-Melech was part of a larger Cushite contingent stationed in Jerusalem. If so, their unique dress and skin colour would probably have generated great interest on the part of the inhabitants.

The mention of Cush also suggests an Egyptian connection. In the early years of the sixth century, Cush was still closely interrelated to Egypt both culturally and militarily, although neither controlled the other at this time. As demonstrated in Chapter 5, Cushites were frequently employed in the armies of the ANE, and especially in the armies of Egypt. Furthermore, Egypt was the major military ally of Judah in Zedekiah's rebellion against Babylonia. The identification of Ebed-Melech as a Cushite in Jerusalem during the Babylonian siege suggests a connection with the Egyptian army.[38]

In Hebrew Ebed-Melech's name means literally 'servant of a king'.

---

[36] As discussed in Chapter 2, the Greeks also had proverbial statements about the Cushites' black skin colour and the difficulty of changing it. See Snowden (1983: 7).

[37] As discussed earlier in this chapter, note that Zephaniah, a contemporary of Jeremiah, mentions Cush or Cushite three times in his three short chapters, adding further evidence that the people in Jerusalem at this time were quite familiar with Cushites.

[38] If we were reading a story that took place in London in 1944 and we encountered an American in the story, we could probably safely assume that he was connected to the military in some way, and that he was probably a soldier. Furthermore, if he had direct access to Winston Churchill, we could suppose with some certainty that he was either a high-ranking soldier or else a high-ranking official related to the military in some manner.

131

Holladay suggests – without citing any evidence – that this name may have been given to him because no one in Jerusalem could pronounce his Cushite name. Holladay – among others – also suggests that Ebed-Melech's name indicates that he was Zedekiah's servant or slave (1989: 289). As we have encountered in numerous other texts discussed in this book, scholars often appear overly quick to assign Cushites to a 'slave' status without first doing proper historical and exegetical study. As demonstrated below, the evidence *against* Ebed-Melech being a slave is overwhelmingly strong.

First of all, identifying Ebed-Melech as a slave simply does not accord well with the events of the story. Could a slave approach the king and criticize his actions? And would the king then acquiesce? Indeed, Holladay notes the astonishing boldness of Ebed-Melech's action: a 'slave' approaching the king in public as he sits 'at the gate'.[39] Furthermore, although in the Masoretic Text (MT) Ebed-Melech says, '*these men* have done wrong,' in the Septuagint (LXX) he says, '*you* have done wrong.' In Jeremiah the LXX is arguably the superior text. Holladay states that Ebed-Melech was stronger in his accusation of Zedekiah than Nathan was of David in 2 Samuel 12 (1989: 289).

Yet do *slaves* speak with such boldness? Holladay tries to account for this boldness by suggesting that Ebed-Melech was a 'personal servant' of Zedekiah. But the question remains: why accuse Zedekiah in public? And why such a passive response by the king? Holladay (1989: 289) attempts to explain that the king's lack of anger at Ebed-Melech's indictment indicated his recognition of the truth in the accusation. Yet is it in Zedekiah's character to reverse policy and to thwart the intentions of the powerful officials in the city simply because of truth?

Furthermore, there is a serious exegetical or semantic problem in associating the name Ebed-Melech with the idea of a slave or a personal slave-like servant. Semantically, it is questionable whether the phrase 'servant of a king' implies anything to do with slavery. The tendency of interpreters in this text is to isolate the single word 'servant' from the phrase – and thus from the critical context – of the entire phrase, 'the servant of the king'. True, the term 'servant' (*'ebed*) by itself can refer to an individual with slave-like status. However, the phrase 'servant of a king' or 'servant of the king' carried no such implication. Everyone in the kingdom was a 'servant'

---

[39] The phrase 'sitting at the gate' refers to a king or other official holding a public court at the gate of the city.

of the king. This term, when used in the context of a ruler, implied submission to the ruler, not slave social status. Thus Moses, Joshua, and David, the greatest leaders of Israel, are frequently called 'servants' of Yahweh without any implication of 'slave' status. Indeed, the term 'servant' in the context of these great men implied a leadership role (under Yahweh).[40]

Likewise, in the Egyptian literature – and the Cushites are integrally related culturally to the Egyptians – high government officials frequently referred to themselves as 'servants' of the king or pharaoh. An inscription on the statue of Nebwawi, a high priest under Thutmose III, refers to him as 'the king's servant'. In another text, Nebwawi states, 'I was a servant, useful to the king.' Another high Egyptian official, Senmut, is called 'his true servant', alluding back to the king (Breasted 1906: II:181, 179).

Most conclusive, however, is the occurrence of the term 'servant of the king' or 'servant of such-and-such king' on Israelite and Judahite seals. In a 1995 article in *Biblical Archaeology Review*, Lemaire cites several such seals (49–52).[41] In addition to this, in their book *Forty New Ancient West Semitic Inscriptions*, Deutsch and Heltzer (1994: 41) add to this list, noting that there are a total of eleven bullae and seals from Judah alone that have the phrase 'servant of the king'. They also cite one Ammonite seal and two Edomite seals with the same phrase. Lemaire (1995: 50) stresses that the term 'servant' in these contexts is not a reference to a lower echelon of society, but, in fact, an indication of 'a high ranking official, a "minister," either of a god or a king'. Deutsch and Heltzer draw the same conclusion: that in ancient Israel and Judah, the title 'servant of the king' referred to a relatively high official (1994: 39).[42]

---

[40] Zevit (1969: 74–77), citing Greenfield (1967: 117–119) in support, argues that *'ebed* in Jeremiah should be translated as 'vassal'. Zevit notes an Ugaritic letter (UT 2062) from the king to an official named Yadan who is referred to as *'bd.mlk* (ebedmelech).

[41] Shema, servant of Jeroboam; Abyaw, servant of Uzziah; Ushna, servant of Ahab; Yehozarah, servant of Hizqiyahu (Hezekiah).

[42] Lemaire (1995: 51) also draws an interesting distinction between when the king's proper name is mentioned (i.e. 'servant of Jeroboam'), and when the ruler is simply referred to generically ('servant of the king'). The seals and bullae that mention Judahite kings specifically by name are all from the *eighth century*. However, Lemaire writes that in Judah during the *seventh century*, 'the custom was to identify a person by his title alone – for example, *'bdhmlk*, "servant of the king."' The Ebed-Melech in the book of Jeremiah appears in the early part of the sixth century, yet probably received his name (or is it his title?) back in the seventh century. Thus the use of the generic *mlk* in his name matches the particular form of this title that appears in seals of this particular century.

These Judahite inscriptions discussed by Lemaire, Deutsch, and Heltzer are *strong* evidence that the phrase 'servant of the king' referred to an official, rather than to a slave. This is also the conclusion of N. Fox (2000: 53–63), who provides an extensive study of this term. Fox concludes that this title could be used of a wide range of offices in the court, but generally given only to someone of 'high status and in close proximity to the king: a prince, an army officer, or another minister of state' (2000: 62). Applying N. Fox's definition of the term to Ebed-Melech certainly fits the actions of both Ebed-Melech and Zedekiah in the Jeremiah narrative much better than the 'slave' interpretation, and the epigraphic evidence appears to be quite conclusive.

Ebed-Melech is also called an 'official' or 'officer' (*sārîs*) in the royal palace.[43] This term can carry the meaning of 'eunuch', although the more likely nuance here is 'official' or 'officer'. Numerous texts in the Hebrew Bible use *sārîs* in contexts that imply a nuance of 'official' rather than 'eunuch' (although the two meanings do overlap in some instances, where 'eunuchs' are used as officials).[44] However, in several instances *sārîs* refers specifically to military officers. In 2 Kings 25:19 the term carries this meaning.[45] The text in Jeremiah 52:25 also requires that *sārîs* refer to a military officer ('the *officer* in charge of the fighting men').

In the immediate context of the Ebed-Melech story, *sārîs* is also used of two Babylonian 'military' officers. In Jeremiah 39:3, Sarsekim is called *raḇ-sārîs*, or 'chief officer', as is Nebushazban in 39:13. Holladay notes that this title was a military or diplomatic title (1989: 291). Within the book of Jeremiah the term *sārîs* is never used in a context that requires a meaning of 'eunuch', but it occurs in numerous places where the context suggests a high-ranking individual with military responsibilities.

It is also probable that a word play is taking place in Jeremiah 38 and 39 between the words *sārîs* and *śar* or *śārîm* (the plural form).

---

[43] The term *sārîs*, however, is absent altogether in the LXX rendering of Jer. 38:7, which, as mentioned above, in Jeremiah is a tradition not easily dismissed. Numerous scholars suggest that in Jeremiah the LXX is the superior text. Holladay (1989: 266) for example, follows the LXX.

[44] Thompson (1980: 639) cites instances where *sārîs* refers to royal officials in Egypt (Gen. 37:36; 39:1; 40:2,7), in Assyria (2 Kgs. 18:17; 20:18), in Babylon (Jer. 39:3, 13; Isa. 39:7; Dan. 1:3, 7–11), in Persia (Esther 1:10, 12), and in Jerusalem (Jer. 29:2; 34:19; 41:16; 52:25; 2 Kgs. 23:11; 25:19).

[45] See Schneider (1964: 766). See also Johnston (1997: 290) and Patterson (1980: 635), who argue that *sārîs* should not be translated as 'eunuch' unless the context demands it.

Both words can refer to officials or to military officers. Certainly Ebed-Melech (*sārîs*) is contrasted with the officials or officers (*śārîm*) of Jerusalem.[46] Twice in 38:4 the Jerusalem *śārîm* refer to Jeremiah in a belittling manner, calling him 'this man'. Ebed-Melech, by contrast, refers to them, the *śārîm*, as 'these men', but Jeremiah he calls 'the prophet' (38:9). The *śārîm* accuse Jeremiah of seeking *rā'â* (evil, harm, ruin) for the people (38:4). Ebed-Melech accuses them of having already committed *rā'â* (38:9) by what they did to Jeremiah.

Both of the terms *sārîs* and *śārîm* are also used frequently in these two chapters to contrast the Jerusalem officers and the Babylonian officers. Thus in 38:4 the Judahite *śārîm* (officers) are the ones who put Jeremiah in the cistern. Ebed-Melech the *sārîs* is the one who pulls him out. Jeremiah 38:17, 18, and 22 all refer to Babylonian *śārîm*. Jeremiah warns Zedekiah that he must surrender to these *śārîm* if he and Jerusalem are to survive. Ironically, however, Zedekiah seems to be more concerned about his own *śārîm* (38:25, 27), and he begs Jeremiah not to reveal to them the prophecy of judgment he delivered to Zedekiah in 38:17–23. Yet, as the reader knows, it is the Babylonian *śārîm* and *sārîs* that Zedekiah should be worried about. In 39:3, after the walls are breached, a group of Babylonian officers, referred to as *śar* and *sārîs*, enter triumphantly and take their seats in the gate, in contrast to Zedekiah, who had been sitting at the gate in 38:7. In 39:13 another group of Babylonian officers is mentioned, again referred to either as *sārîs* or *śar*. Ironically, these *śārîm* and the one *sārîs*, like Ebed-Melech, are involved in rescuing Jeremiah (39:13–14).

So, to summarize the word play, the Judahite *śārîm* are against Jeremiah, and they throw him into the cistern. Zedekiah fears these *śārîm*. The Cushite *sārîs* rescues Jeremiah from the cistern, but the prophet must still stay in the courtyard of the guard. The final rescue comes from the Babylonian *śārîm* and *sārîs*, who replace Zedekiah in the gate and free Jeremiah from the courtyard of the guard.[47]

---

[46] Brueggemann (1991: 146) suggests that this term refers to the influential group of individuals in Jerusalem who seemed to control policy. Some translators have opted for 'princes' (NIV). In Jeremiah 39 the term is clearly used to refer to Babylonian military officers. However, in the Ancient Near East, as in other cultures as well, the wealthy, influential nobles were precisely the ones who received military commands. Few nations could afford a standing, professional officer corps.

[47] Very little study has been done exploring the literary role of the *sārîs* in the Hebrew Bible. However, Morris notes that individuals who are called *sārîs* appear in favourable roles in the narratives about Joseph, Daniel, and Esther. He underscores several other similarities in these three stories (foreign courts, jealous officials,

How do the factors discussed above assist in understanding Ebed-Melech? In summary, note the following points. First, Cushites appear frequently throughout the Ancient Near East, usually as soldiers. Second, Judah had a military alliance with Egypt, which regularly used Cushite soldiers and Cushite commanders. Third, the name Ebed-Melech does not suggest that he was a slave or personal servant, but rather that he had a high official position. Fourth, the term *sārîs* in the context of Jeremiah 38 and 39 also implies that Ebed-Melech was an official, and probably a military officer. Fifth, the action of Ebed-Melech – his bold public accusation of Zedekiah, followed by Zedekiah's compliance – implies that he had considerable political clout.

The most plausible explanation that accounts for these data is to understand Ebed-Melech as a military officer. Perhaps he led a contingent of Cushite soldiers. He may even have been in charge of the royal bodyguards. He is probably the ranking representative of the Egyptian army in Jerusalem, the equivalent of a modern military attaché. This would explain why he could obtain an audience with Zedekiah and why Zedekiah acquiesced so quickly. With the powerful army of Nebuchadnezzar at the gates of Jerusalem, Zedekiah could not risk offending the Egyptians and the Cushites, the only allies he had who could possibly offer any tangible military help.[48]

Jeremiah 39:15–18 adds an important postscript. Yahweh spoke to Jeremiah, promising that Ebed-Melech would survive, even though Jerusalem would fall to the Babylonians. The reason for this, Yahweh stated, was that Ebed-Melech 'trusted' in Yahweh. At a time when the entire Hebrew nation was being judged because of disobedience and covenant violation, a Black Cushite was delivered because of his faith. Brueggemann (1991: 159–161) notes that Ebed-Melech was singled out as an exception because of his trust in Yahweh. Indeed, he is specifically contrasted with Zedekiah. Yahweh did for Ebed-Melech exactly what he would not do for Zedekiah: save him from the Babylonians. 'Trust,' Brueggemann continues, 'as evidenced by Ebedmelech is a limit and

---

appearance before foreign kings with whom they find favour, deliverance from destruction), and suggests that they belong to a similar literary genre, which he calls 'The Hebrew Courtier Tale'. See Morris (1994: 69–85). The Jeremiah–Ebed-Melech story contains several remarkably similar elements.

[48] The story drips with irony as well. Judah relied on Egyptian military strength rather than on Yahweh, and thus they perished. Jeremiah, on the other hand, relied on Yahweh, and preached that Egyptian military might would be of no help whatsoever. Jeremiah is delivered, ironically, by Ebed-Melech, who is probably the ranking representative of the Egyptian military in Jerusalem.

alternative to Babylonian power and devastation.' Ebed-Melech thus becomes the representative of an important remnant – the remnant of faith. The destruction of Jerusalem by Yahweh is not 'morally indifferent or undifferentiated'. Acts of faith and trust are salvific. Ebed-Melech represents such action (1991: 159–161).

Several scholars have noted the similarity between the 'salvation oracle'[49] given to Ebed-Melech in Jeremiah 39:16–18 and the 'salvation oracle' given to Baruch in Jeremiah 45:1–5 (Schulte 1988: 257–265; Seitz 1983: 3–27). Both texts contain the phrase 'but you shall have your life as a prize of war' (39:18; 45:5). Schulte notes that when the prophets gave personal oracles to individuals, these oracles were usually oracles of judgment. The oracles given to Ebed-Melech and Baruch were unusual in that they were oracles of deliverance. Schulte also observes that when judgment oracles were delivered to kings, the king was usually representative of a larger group. Judgment on the king implied judgment on the king's nation (1988: 257–258). This suggests, perhaps, that oracles of salvation given to individuals such as Ebed-Melech also referred to the broader group that the individual represented. The implications of this observation suggest that Ebed-Melech, as the recipient of a salvation oracle, represents a larger group in a prophetic sense. Specifically he represents the Black nation of Cush (the text stresses his nationality). Generally, however, he represents the broader group of all Black Africa, and, even broader, he represents all Gentiles who trust in God.[50]

---

[49] In Jeremiah 39:17 Yahweh promises to 'rescue' and 'save' Ebed-Melech because of his trust in Yahweh. The final phrase of the verse literally reads, 'oracle of Yahweh'. Most English translations render this as 'declares the LORD', which perhaps misses some of the formal structure of the pronouncement.

[50] Seitz (1983: 17–18) argues that Baruch and Ebed-Melech are 'types' modelled on Caleb and Joshua: individuals exempted from national judgment because of faith, who provide continuity and transition to a new generation of faith. This is similar to Brueggemann's view that Ebed-Melech represents the remnant of faith. Both Seitz and Brueggemann, however, skip over the stress in the text on Ebed-Melech's nationality. He is a Black Cushite and this aspect is stressed in the text. If he is indeed a soldier, as this chapter argues, then he is also contrasted with the other salvation oracle recipient, Baruch, who is a peaceful Hebrew scribe. The one who represents the remnant of faith is not only a Gentile, but also a Black soldier. Stulman (1995: 65–85) also makes some interesting and relevant observations concerning the book of Jeremiah. Stulman notes that the book of Jeremiah presents a 'topsy-turvy' world where the insiders (priests, prophets) become outsiders (like the Barbarians) while the outsiders (the Babylonians) seem to enjoy the favour of Yahweh. Indeed, they become the 'servants' of Yahweh (1995: 73–74, 84). Stulman does not address Ebed-Melech, but the story of this Cushite certainly supports Stulman's view. As a Cushite, Ebed-Melech would been the consummate 'outsider', yet he becomes the prototypical man of faith whom Yahweh delivers – one of the 'insiders'.

A future, fellow Cushite, the so-called 'Ethiopian eunuch' of Acts 8, will fulfil a similar role in the New Testament (see Chapter 8). The 'Ethiopian eunuch' of Acts 8 and the Roman military officer Cornelius in Acts 10 will combine to represent the spread of the gospel to the nations in the Book of Acts. Ebed-Melech, 'Ethiopian' (i.e. Cushite) in nationality and military officer in occupation, appears to foreshadow them both. Another interesting parallel between Ebed-Melech and the 'Ethiopian eunuch' is that in each story the Black African believes God's messengers precisely at the time when Israel rejects them and persecutes them. Ebed-Melech is introduced into the story as the leaders of Jerusalem arrest Jeremiah and throw him into a pit. The Ethiopian eunuch is introduced as the leaders of Jerusalem execute Stephen and begin a persecution of the new Church (Acts 7:54 – 8:3).

Thus, as in the much later story of the Ethiopian eunuch in Acts 8, it is highly significant theologically that it was the foreigner Ebed-Melech the Cushite who acted positively in obedience to Yahweh while the rest of the nation continued in hostile disobedience. While the entire nation of Judah was disobedient to Yahweh, it was a Black Cushite who confronted the king and delivered Jeremiah.

In summary, Ebed-Melech was a Black man from Cush. He was not a slave but rather a high-ranking official. He was also probably a soldier, most probably the commander of a Cushite/Egyptian unit assisting in the defence of Jerusalem. He is contrasted with Zedekiah and the Hebrew 'princes' in Jerusalem. They opposed Jeremiah and his message from Yahweh, and thus they perished. Ebed-Melech, on the other hand, trusted in Yahweh and defended Jeremiah, and thus he was delivered. Ebed-Melech, a Black soldier, also represents the people of faith. He foreshadows the future inclusion of the nations that is prophesied by Isaiah and others, an inclusion of both Blacks and Whites, an inclusion based not on nationality or ethnicity, but on faith.

Conclusions

Several important conclusions relating to race emerge from our study of the prophets. First of all, the prophets emphasize that God cannot be tied to any ethnic community. Thus it is critical for the Church today to grasp the significance of the fact that God is not a Caucasian or a God only for Caucasians. Neither is he an American or a God primarily for Americans. Quite to the contrary, Yahweh is the God of all the peoples of the world. Likewise, the people of God are clearly portrayed as a wide-ranging ethnic mix. The biblical picture of this blended mix includes Black Cushites as one of the critical components. In fact, the Black Cushites generally function in the prophetic picture as representatives of the rest of the nations of the world.

Also, as mentioned earlier, Israel related to the nations of the world in two ways. First, throughout the narrative story of Israel, foreigners are regularly incorporated (literally) into Yahweh's people. Second, the Old Testament paints an eschatological picture that fulfills Genesis 12:3 and brings all the scattered people of Genesis 10 back together into one people of God (Köstenberger and O'Brien 2001: 35).

A synthesis of the prophets' theology toward the foreign nations follows much the same twofold pattern. First of all, references to the Black Cushites appear in several genealogies, which incorporated them, at least literarily, and probably also biologically, into Israel and Judah. Also, when Yahweh delivered an oracle of salvation to Ebed-Melech and then saved him from the destruction of Jerusalem, this special relationship strongly implies that Ebed-Melech became one of the few true people of God in Jerusalem at that time.

Second, of course, is the eschatological picture. The prophets frequently proclaim that in the future Yahweh will bring all peoples together in true worship in climactic fulfilment of Genesis 12:3. This gathering includes the faithful remnant of Israel along with Black Cushites, Egyptians, and even hated enemies like the Assyrians: that is, all the nations of the world. Thus we see that the eschatological family of God as portrayed by the prophets is clearly multi-ethnic.

Chapter Seven

The ethnic make-up of the New Testament world

Introduction

The ethnic and political boundaries within the biblical world never remained static, but during the four hundred years that preceded the New Testament era numerous tumultuous events occurred that had a significant impact on the ethnic composition of the world into which the gospel exploded. The Persian Empire, which dominated the eastern end of the biblical world at the close of the Old Testament period, was checked by the rising power of the Greek city-states, and then overrun completely by Alexander the Great. In a few brief years Alexander swept across all of the Ancient Near Eastern regions except Cush. Alexander, and the empires established by his generals upon his death, unified (to a certain degree) the entire region from Macedonia to India with a common Greek culture. In the first century BC, however, the political remnants of Alexander's conquests were in turn subdued by Roman expansion. During the entire New Testament era, the Romans were in firm control of the Mediterranean world and of much of the rest of the Ancient Near East.

However, numerous other events took place during this time frame that affected the ethnic make-up of the region. Migrations and invasions occurred, such as that by the Celts into Macedonia and Asia Minor. Merchant-driven colonization occurred; Jews were scattered throughout the region; Roman soldiers and foreign auxiliary soldiers retired and settled in areas away from their homes; and slaves were captured from a variety of areas of the Roman frontier and transferred throughout the Empire to be incorporated into the diverse mix of peoples that inhabited the cities of the first century AD.

Traditionally, biblical scholarship has tended to overlook much of the ethnic diversity in the New Testament world. Discussions generally cover the Greco-Roman culture and the Jewish Diaspora, assuming subconsciously that the New Testament world consisted of only two ethnic groups: Jews and Greco-Roman Gentiles. Occasionally the 'Barbarians' are included as another group. But there still seems to be an underlying assumption in much of the literature that everyone who was not Jewish or 'Barbarian' was 'Greco-Roman', as if this were a monolithic ethnic group. However, while there was definitely a Greco-Roman culture, there was not really any Greco-Roman ethnic group.

So although the writers of the New Testament do use the standard generalization of 'Greeks, Jews, and Barbarians,' the New Testament itself also reflects the reality of numerous different peoples and ethnic groups. Acts 2, for example refers to the languages of the Parthians, Medes, Elamites, Cretans, and Arabs, as well as the languages spoken by the residents of Mesopotamia, Cappadocia, Pontus, Asia, Phrygia, Pamphylia, Egypt, and Cyrene. Other texts refer to Samaritans, Ethiopians, and Cypriots. An elder in the early church was 'Simeon called *Niger* [black].' Peter addresses his first epistle to the believers in Pontus, Galatia, Cappadocia, Asia and Bithynia. Furthermore, although in New Testament studies much is often made of Paul's ability to communicate in Greek with almost everyone in the cities he visits, in Lystra the people switch to the Lycaonian language in their accusations against him. The majority of people in these provinces were neither Greek nor Roman, although many of them spoke Greek as their second language. Who were these people? This chapter attempts to present a brief overview of the extremely complex ethnic world in which the gospel was planted and took root during the first century AD.

The Greco-Roman world (Greeks and Barbarians)

As the Romans built their empire in the years just prior to the birth of Christ, they inherited a certain unifying Greek culture that they in turn assimilated into their way of life. Thus, throughout the diverse Roman Empire, many people adopted this common culture and language and became known as 'Greek' (*hellēn*). The basis for inclusion into this Hellenistic culture, however, was not birth but rather education (E. Ferguson 1993: 9).[1] As the New Testament era dawns the educated people of the Roman Empire viewed the people of the

[1] E. Ferguson (1993: 9), among others, cites the famous lines by Isocrates: '. . . the name "Hellenes" suggests no longer a race but an intelligence, and the title "Hellenes" is applied rather to those who share our culture than to those who share a common blood.' Cited from *Panegyricus* 50.

world in two categories: Greeks and Barbarians.[2] Hengel (1980: 55) points out that these were 'blanket' terms that were used loosely. A 'Barbarian' was a person, whether 'cultured' or not, who spoke a 'foreign' language. The term 'Greek' did not refer to a people, but rather to a community of various peoples who spoke the same language and embraced certain aspects of the same culture. Although entrance into this group was via education and not birth, the 'Greeks' were nonetheless contemptuous of the 'Barbarians'. Prejudiced thinking among the educated elite – and most of the literary records we have were produced by them – tended to follow this cultural classification rather than racial or ethnic classifications.

Yet the Greco-Roman cultural assimilation was largely an urban phenomenon that was strongest among the upper classes; it did not necessarily transfer out into the countryside of the Roman provinces. Local rural people kept their languages, religions, customs, and values, even as their upper classes were integrated into the Greco-Roman system (Jeffers 1999: 48–49).

Within the framework of this 'common culture', the Greco-Roman cities of the New Testament era also experienced quite a significant amount of ethnic mixing. Several factors contributed to this. First of all, the *Pax Romana* created a climate in which trade flourished: thousands of ships were sailing the Mediterranean, and merchants brought products (and people) from Africa, Britain, India, and even China (Casson 1959: 223–239).

Second, the Roman army contributed to this mix through its stationing and retirement policies. The Roman army used large numbers of foreign 'auxiliaries' to supplement the Roman legions. These foreign units, however, were always stationed away from their native land. After serving twenty-five years they were given Roman citizenship; they often settled (and married) in the foreign land where they had been serving. Likewise, even ethnic Roman soldiers often retired and settled away from Italy. These soldiers frequently intermarried with women from the regions where the troops served or settled (E. Ferguson 1993: 51).

---

[2] Initially, the Romans were included in the category of 'Barbarian'. As their political power grew and as they embraced more and more of Greek culture they moved into a middle category between the Barbarians and the Greeks. The Romans themselves viewed the world in this way. Cicero, for example, divided the world into three parts: Romans, Greeks, and Barbarians. Eventually, however, the upper class of Romans began to refer to themselves as Greek (*Hellēn*), and the term 'Greek' became connected to the cultural status of the upper class (Hengel 1980: 65–66).

Third, large numbers of slaves were displaced throughout the Empire. In the Roman world of the New Testament era slavery was very common,[3] and slaves came from all areas of the Roman frontier. Although the majority of slaves were from the eastern frontiers of the Empire, Germans, Gauls, and Britons from the west were also common. These slaves, however, were not isolated in ethnic communities but were integrated into the ethnic mix of the Greco-Roman world (E. Ferguson 1993: 56–59).

Finally, ethnic Greeks and ethnic Romans who immigrated to other lands frequently intermarried with local people. For example, during the first century of Ptolemaic rule large numbers of ethnic Greeks immigrated to Egypt, especially to Alexandria. These Greeks created a powerful new elite overlaid on top of Egyptian society. However, the upper class of Egyptians merged into this class as well, and numerous mixed Greek–Egyptian marriages took place (Bowman 1986: 122–125).

The Jewish Diaspora

Large numbers of Jews had been relocated outside of Palestine by the Assyrians in 722 BC and by the Babylonians in 587 BC. During the Persian period their dispersion continued, and they spread throughout the Persian Empire, sometimes moving voluntarily and sometimes forced to relocate. By the time of Alexander, Jews were residing in most regions across the Persian Empire (Bickerman 1988: 37).

A new series of forced relocations occurred as the Persian Empire broke up and the Ptolemies and Seleucids carved up Alexander's conquests. Many Jews residing in Babylonia were moved to Asia Minor. In one recorded instance, for example, Antiochus III resettled 2,000 Jewish families in Lydia and Phrygia (Bruce 1992a: 230).[4] To the south Ptolemy I shipped thousands of Jews to Egypt, particularly to Alexandria. By the time of Christ, Alexandria had over 150,000 Jews, the largest Jewish population outside of Palestine (E. Ferguson 1993: 381; Jeffers 1999: 275; Borgen 1992: 122–123). There were also large

---

[3] Jeffers (1999: 221–222) notes that there were two or three million slaves in Italy at the time of Christ, and that throughout the Roman Empire slaves probably constituted at least 10% of the population.

[4] For a thorough discussion on Jews in Asia Minor see Levinskaya (1996: 137–152) and Bickerman (1988: 91–100).

numbers of Jews in Rome (Levinskaya 1996: 167–193; Leon 1960: 1–45) and in Cyrene (Yamauchi 1992: 9–10). In fact, E. Ferguson concludes that as many as two thirds of the Jews in the New Testament world lived outside of Palestine and that they may have constituted as much as 7% of the population in the Roman Empire (1993: 403–404).

Unlike many of the other groups scattered across the Roman Empire, the Jews resisted total assimilation into the Greco-Roman culture, even in the urban areas. They did embrace Greek rather than Aramaic as their primary language, and there was a certain degree of intermarriage, particularly in Alexandria (Bowman 1986: 123–124; Bickerman 1988: 249–251). However, religiously and ethically they maintained their boundaries and retained a strong ethnic identity.[5] Because the Jews had allied with Rome during the first century BC, especially during the time of Julius Caesar, they had received a privileged position in the Roman Empire, exempting them from worshipping Roman deities and participating in pagan religious festivals (E. Ferguson 1993: 404–405; Jeffers 1999: 215–216). Thus, with official Roman sanction, the Jews were able to retain their own religion and, to a certain degree, their own distinctive culture.[6] So, while the Greeks of the New Testament world viewed the world as divided into two groups – Greeks and Barbarians – based on education and culture, the Jews divided the world into three groups: Jews (an ethnic distinction), Greeks, and Barbarians (an educational or cultural distinction) (Hengel 1980: 65).

Judaism in the first century AD, however, was not entirely monolithic, and there were several 'schisms' or 'branches'. Of interest to our study are the Samaritans, because the tension between the Jews

---

[5] Of course Jews reacted to the pressure of 'Hellenization' in different ways. In this reaction there were some Jews at each extreme end of the spectrum (total assimilation, total rejection). However, most Jews remained in the middle, trying to belong to the Greek culture while still retaining an ethnic and religious identity. They tended to follow Hellenistic ways so long as those ways did not appear to threaten Judaism (Cohen 1987: 27–46). However, LaGrand argues that the Jews of the first century probably had notions of racial purity that were similar in some respects to modern concepts (1999: 35). Jeremias notes that in Jerusalem this concept was the strongest, and that only families that were 'racially pure' could belong to the 'true Israel'. Jeremias states, 'Up to the present, it has not been sufficiently recognized that from a social point of view the whole community of Judaism at the time of Jesus was dominated by the fundamental idea of the maintenance of racial purity' (1969: 270).

[6] The degree to which the Diaspora Jews did or did not assimilate into the Greco-Roman culture is discussed in some detail by Hengel (1980) and Bickerman (1988), among others.

and the Samaritans had an ethnic component as well as a religious one. Traditionally, the origin of the Samaritans has been connected to the fall of the Northern Kingdom Israel in 722 BC. The Assyrians deported many of the Israelite inhabitants but also resettled other non-Israelite people into the region. According to this view, the Samaritans were the descendants of this Jew and non-Jew mixture. Toward the end of the twentieth century, however, it became apparent that this view was an oversimplification of a complex – and somewhat obscure – process, and most scholars today have qualified the traditional view by the addition of other historical aspects.[7]

Yet, whatever their exact origins were, it is clear that during the first century AD there was a mutual animosity between the Samaritans and the Jews of Judea. Mainstream Judaism apparently viewed the Samaritans as a 'mixed' people who worshipped incorrectly. Thus the mainstream Jews of the New Testament era felt both a religious and a racial superiority to the Samaritans, and this attitude surfaces as a background for several New Testament texts (E. Ferguson 1993: 378, 499–501).

Black Africa (Cush, Meroe, Ethiopia)

As discussed in Chapter 2 and referenced throughout Chapters 3–6, a Black African nation was located along the Nile, just south of Egypt. This civilization was an identifiable entity from as early as 2000 BC and continued to flourish until around AD 400. The Hebrew text of the Old Testament, as well as the Assyrian literature and much of the Egyptian literature, referred to this kingdom as Cush. The capital of Cush was originally located at the city of Kerma. Later in history the Cushites moved their capital south along the Nile to Napata. Finally, during the sixth century BC the capital was moved further south to Meroe, although the city of Napata continued to be

---

[7] See the discussions by Williamson (1992: 724–728); R. T. Anderson (1992: 940–947); and especially the major work on the Samaritans by Crown (1989). Anderson's introductory statement is instructive: 'The Samaritans are not easily brought into sharp focus. Sources are often contradictory, sketchy, or nonexistent. It is problematic how distinct the Samaritans are from the Jews of different periods, what constitutes the basic distinguishing focus, or how much interaction existed between the Samaritans and other sects based on the Mosaic Pentateuch. The geographical origin of the people called Samaritans has been seen in Mesopotamia and both N and S Palestine, raising the question whether their basic characterization is geographical, ethnic, or doctrinal' (1992: 941).

important (O'Connor 1993: 70–71). Many historians and writers will thus refer to this phase of Cushite history as the 'Meroitic Kingdom'.[8]

However, the Greeks referred to the entire region south of Egypt by the term *Aithiops*, from which comes the modern word 'Ethiopia'. The Romans generally employed the same designation, although later Roman writers will often use the term 'Nubia', derived from the Noba tribe that also lived in the region earlier known as Cush. The modern country of Ethiopia, located east of ancient Cush, is not the point of reference when the classical Greek and Roman writers use the term *Ethiopia*.[9] In general the Greek term *Ethiopia* refers to Black Africa: that is, everything south of Egypt. However, the vast majority of Greek and Roman contact with Black Africa was via the kingdom of Meroe (i.e. the descendant of Cush), and, in general, the term Ethiopia as used by the classical Greek and Roman writers can be taken as a synonym for the region defined by the names Cush, Meroe, or Nubia.[10]

Therefore, when the Old Testament was translated into Greek during the second century BC the translators used the Greek term *Ethiopia* to translate the Hebrew word *Cush.* Likewise, the writers of the New Testament will use the Greek term *Ethiopian* to refer to the people who live along the Nile south of Egypt: that is, the ancient Cushites. In keeping with the normal Greek usage I will also use the term Ethiopia interchangeably with the term Meroe in Chapters 7 and 8 to refer to the Black African nation that lay just south of Egypt, referred to earlier in this book as *Cush.*

The Kingdom of Meroe (Ethiopia) managed to maintain independence throughout the Greco-Roman period. Alexander the Great easily conquered Egypt in 332 BC but he did not advance south beyond the cataracts on the Nile into the territory of the Ethiopians.

---

[8] The many excellent recent works that cover the history of Cush also address the Meroitic period. See Török (1997); Welsby (1998); Yamauchi (2001); Burstein (1997; 2001); and O'Connor (1993).

[9] The region in East Africa defined as modern Ethiopia does play an important role in the region a few hundred years later as the kingdom of Axum. In fact, it was the invasions and incursions by Axum that hastened the end of the Meroitic kingdom in the fourth century AD. Later in history the general region that was controlled by Axum became known as Abyssinia, a term that some modern Ethiopians still use in reference to themselves. Early in the twentieth century this country in East Africa took on the name Ethiopia. See the discussion on the history of Axum by Burstein (1997: 77–100).

[10] See the detailed discussion of the Roman usage of the term *Aethiops* by L. Thompson (1989: 57–62).

Likewise, upon Alexander's death in 323 BC and the assumption of Egyptian rule by the Ptolemy family, the Ethiopians maintained independent status and continued to trade with Egypt and the rest of the Mediterranean world (Burstein 2001:149–150).

Upon the defeat of Anthony and Cleopatra (the last Ptolemaic monarch) in 30 BC Rome assumed direct rule of Egypt. Although there was some minor fighting along the border between Rome and Meroe off and on from 30 BC until 20 BC (Jameson 1968: 71–84), eventually peace was established through diplomacy (J. Anderson 1971: 242–243). The Ethiopians at Meroe obtained very favourable terms from the Romans in a treaty signed in 20 BC, under which the Ethiopians were not required to pay any tribute at all to the Romans. Peaceful relations between Rome and Meroe continued for the next three centuries (Yamauchi 2001a: 43–44), allowing Ethiopian emissaries and merchants to travel and trade throughout the Mediterranean world. Indeed, this was a time of prosperity for Meroe, as trade between sub-Saharan Africa and the Roman world flourished, with the Ethiopians at Meroe playing the 'middle man' (Burstein 2001: 138). Although the Ethiopians adopted much of Greek culture, they also retained and developed much that was unique to their own civilization, including their own unique writing script.[11]

Thus Black Ethiopians from the kingdom of Meroe were actively interacting with the Mediterranean Roman world as the Christian era dawned. Snowden (1970: 15–99; 2001: 251–252) and L. Thompson (1989: 57–156) cite a multitude of Roman texts that refer to Ethiopians. Snowden (1970: 22–99) also offers artistic evidence, presenting clear portrayals of 'Negroid' Black Africans in Greco-Roman art of the classical period.[12] The Roman world encountered Black Ethiopians as merchants and traders, soldiers, slaves, and former slaves who had become freedmen. Indeed, Black Ethiopians appeared in Roman society at all levels: soldiers, slaves, freedmen, officials, nobles (Snowden 2001: 267).[13] In addition,

---

[11] Most educated Ethiopians of this era probably knew Greek as well as Meroitic, and they may also have known Latin. The Ethiopian 'eunuch' of Acts 8 (see Chapter 8) was probably reading Isaiah from the Greek Septuagint.

[12] Snowden (1970: 15–99) cites the specific names of 49 individuals in Greco-Roman literature that are Ethiopian. He also presents 77 pictures of 'Negroid' people in Greco-Roman art.

[13] See also the discussion of relations between Meroe and the Greco-Roman world by L. Thompson (1969: 34–35).

intermarriage between these Black Africans and the rest of the Greco-Roman Mediterranean world was not only common but rather the norm. Thus these Blacks were continually being assimilated into the genetic melting-pot of the Roman world (L. Thompson 1989: 84). L. Thompson presents clear evidence that children of mixed marriages were not classified as *Ethiopian* unless they physically looked like an *Ethiopian*, and, unlike in contemporary America, these children almost always moved into the mainstream of the Roman world (L. Thompson 1989: 73–77). As mentioned earlier, the degree to which any given society accepts intermarriage between ethnic groups and likewise embraces the offspring of such marriages as full, normal members of the society is probably a good indicator of how much or how little racial prejudice exists within that society.

Snowden (2001 and 1970) and L. Thompson (1989) have both surveyed the classical Greco-Roman literature extensively to try to determine the attitude of the Greco-Roman world toward Blacks. Although these two authors occasionally disagree and argue with each other, they both arrive at the same basic conclusion.[14] Thus L. Thompson argues that Roman attitudes toward all 'others' reflected common ethnocentrism and not racial prejudice *per se*. That is, they perceived themselves as superior to *all* those who were different, and thus the Romans occasionally would criticize or mock those groups that differed from them (1989: 19). Thompson writes:

Roman attitudes towards Aethiops, even at their most negative, have nothing to do with the familiar modern phenomenon of *race* and are of a kind very different from those commonly described by social scientists by the terms 'racist', 'racial prejudice', 'color prejudice', and 'racism'.

(1989: 157)

---

[14] For a discussion of the history regarding the view of the Greco-Roman world toward Blacks, see L. Thompson (1989: 21–24). Basically, earlier writers put forward the view that the Greeks and Romans had a totally negative and derogatory view toward Blacks; indeed, one that was similar to the racial prejudice of many Whites today. Snowden, through two influential books (1970, 1983), piles up a substantial amount of evidence that dismantles that view, and he argues that there was no racial prejudice in the Greco-Roman world at all. Thompson (1989) likewise rejects the first view, but he feels that Snowden has oversimplified the issue. The Greco-Roman world had its prejudices, Thompson argues, but those prejudices were aimed at anyone who was different, and thus were not racially focused or racially defined.

Snowden's conclusions are similar. He states:

> Both the Greeks and the Romans, in spite of ideas and con-
> cepts which a few scholars have described as negative and det-
> rimental to blacks, had the ability to see and to comment on
> the obviously different physical characteristics of blacks
> without developing an elaborate and rigid system of discrimi-
> nation against blacks based only on the color of the skin.
> Color, in spite of the existence of black-white symbolism, the
> somatic norm image, and the like, did not acquire in the
> Graeco-Roman world the great importance it has assumed in
> some post-classical societies either in the self-image of many
> peoples, or in the denial of equality to blacks in theory and
> practice. The Greeks, Romans, and early Christians were free
> of what Keith Irvine has described as the 'curse of acute color-
> consciousness, attended by all the raw passion and social prob-
> lems that cluster around it'.

$$(2001: 268)^{15}$$

In conclusion, we see that Black Africans from the kingdom of
Meroe (previously Cush) could be found throughout the Mediterranean world during the first century AD. Indeed, as discussed in the
chapters that follow, the New Testament bears witness to this rela-
tively common presence of Blacks (the Ethiopian 'eunuch' of Acts 8;
Simeon who was called *Niger* in Acts 13:1). Although probably not
common in the rural hinterlands of the Roman Empire outside of
Egypt or North Africa, Blacks from Meroe nonetheless were prob-
ably in most major cities of the Mediterranean. In addition, these
Black Africans could be found in many units of the legions of the
Roman army stationed on the frontiers from eastern Anatolia to
Britain.

North Africa (Berbers, Phoenicians, Greeks, and Romans)

The make-up of the North African population during the first
century AD was considerably different from what it is today. The Arab
conquest of North Africa did not take place until the end of the

---

[15] Snowden is quoting Irvine (1970: 19).

seventh century AD,[16] so during the New Testament era there were practically no Arabs residing in this region. The original inhabitants of North Africa (the modern countries of Libya, Tunisia, Algeria, and Morocco) were called 'Libyans' by the ancient Egyptians. As discussed in Chapter 2, the Egyptians of the ancient world categorized their foes into three groups: the Asiatics to the north, the Cushites to the south, and the Libyans to the west.[17] The Libyan civilization west of Egypt was apparently indigenous to the area; at least, they inhabited this region for as long as we have any historical or archaeological records. Their exact origins are unknown, but probably they developed as a mix of Black African, Semitic, and Egyptian elements. Bullard (2001: 184–185), for example, suggests that during the period 5500–3000 BC 'Negroid tribes' migrated northward toward the Mediterranean coast and intermarried with people of Asian (Semitic) and Egyptian origins.[18] Brett and Fentress (1996: 12–15) note that there is archaeological evidence of people living in North Africa as early as 7000 BC. From what little evidence exists from this era, the population appears to have been a mixed group with several different racial features, perhaps related to the same peoples that migrated and settled in the Nile Valley. In the highland areas lying inland and south of the Mediterranean coast there is evidence of an early neolithic civilization. Both skeletal remains and art frescoes in caves point to a 'Negroid' composition of this group (Brett and Fentress 1996: 18; J. Ferguson 1969a: 3–4).

Yet by the end of the second millennium BC the frescoes in this area began to show different people as well – tall light-skinned men with long hair and pointed beards (Brett and Fentress 1996: 19). These individuals are similar in appearance to the Libyans portrayed in Egyptian art of this period mentioned above. Brett and Fentress suggest that this mountainous area was originally inhabited by Negroid peoples, but that during the second millennium a new warrior aristocracy – the people shown in Egyptian art – gained control of the region and began to mix with the local population (1996: 19–21).

[16] For a discussion of the Arab conquest of North Africa and of the resultant Arab–Berber alliance that invaded Spain, see Carmichael (1967: 93–103).

[17] See Leahy (2001: 290–293) and Baines (1996: 378–384) for details on Libya's connections with ancient Egypt.

[18] Ghaki (1987: 85) suggests that, in addition to these elements, there may have also been a mixing with groups migrating south from Iberia as well as from Sicily and Sardinia. But he notes that by the second millennium BC there was an ethnic identity – at least, a collection of related tribes – that can be called Libyan or Berber.

The modern descendants of these ancient Libyans are known as Berbers; they live today in many of the North African countries, and are found as far south as northern Nigeria (the nomadic Tuaregs). The name 'Berber' was a derogatory term applied to these people by the Romans (i.e. from the Latin for 'barbarian'). The Berber language (still spoken today) has been classified as Afro-Asiatic and it is similar to ancient Egyptian (Brett 1981: 100; Bullard 2001: 184). Although this region has been occupied and colonized by numerous groups throughout history (Phoenicians, Greeks, Romans, Byzantine Greeks, and Arabs), the Berbers maintained their ethnic identity and were not subsumed into these outside cultures, although some degree of intermarriage with these 'visitors' definitely occurred at different times throughout history. Modern Berbers in the northern areas of the Mediterranean coast are fairly light-skinned, but the Tuaregs, a Berber group who live further south, are darker in complexion.

The probable ancestors of the Tuaregs were a Berber tribe that the literature of the Greco-Roman period refers to as the Garamantes (Picard and Picard 1968: 92). Snowden (1970: 112) notes that some classical writers called the Garamantes people 'Ethiopians', probably indicating that these writers associated these people with Black Africa.[19] However, Snowden also notes that some writers did not make this association. Thus Snowden concludes that this group was probably a 'mix' (1970: 112).[20] Indeed, excavations of tombs from the city of Garama/Germa during the early Roman period reveal both people with 'Negroid' features and people with 'Mediterranean' features (Brett and Fentress 1996: 23–25).

Likewise the Roman literature also refers to the Berber Nasamones as a tribe of *Ethiopians*, suggesting at least a similarity of skin colour. Other Berber tribes were also described in these terms. The Berber Asphodelodes were said to resemble Ethiopians, and the Berber Gaetulians were called 'the black Gaetulians' (*Melanogaetuli*), probably indicating a dark complexion (L. Thompson 1989: 62).

During the eighth century BC Phoenician (ancient Canaanite) ships

---

[19] See the discussion of this text by L. Thompson (1989: 36–37), who is cautious about identifying the 'black' character in the text with the marauding Garamantians of the text.

[20] Modern Tuaregs, at least the ones I encountered during my travels in Niger Republic, tend to have sharper noses and thinner lips than the Black Africans of the sub-Sahara, but they also have darker skin than the Mediterranean Arabs. On the streets of New York City people would probably assume they were light-skinned African-Americans.

from cities along the Palestinian coast (Tyre, Sidon) were sailing regularly into the western end of the Mediterranean Sea. By the seventh century they had established several colonies in North Africa. The most significant colony was Carthage, located in the modern country of Tunisia. These Phoenician colonists were Semitic, descendants of the ancient Canaanites, and they followed Canaanite religion and culture. Although during the first several hundred years the Phoenicians paid the Berbers 'rent' for using the site, eventually the power of Carthage grew and subdued most of the Berber tribes. From a shipping-related colony Carthage developed into a major economic and military power, incorporating much of the western North African coast as well as part of Iberia, challenging first the Greeks and then the Romans for domination of the western Mediterranean area. The Carthaginians also participated in significant trading operations with sub-Saharan Africa, both by sea along the Atlantic coast and by land across the desert (J. Ferguson 1969a: 5–9).

At the end of the third century BC Hannibal led an army of Carthaginians and allies – including many Berber tribes, such as the Numidians – in an invasion of Italy itself.[21] L. Thompson (1989: 59) states that the Romans allude to *Ethiopians* in the Carthaginian army. Whether these are Berbers or Cushites is not clear. In addition, a new and terrifying element of Hannibal's army was the use of war elephants. Snowden (1970: 130–131) presents a convincing argument that the elephants and the handlers (mahouts) came from Ethiopia (Cush). Thus it appears that Black Africans from Ethiopia (Cush), along with the 'mixed' Berbers, were part of Hannibal's army and played a significant role in his invasion of Italy. Eventually, of course, Rome prevailed, capturing Carthage in 146 BC and later adding the entire North African Mediterranean coast to the Roman Empire.

Meanwhile, by the end of the seventh century BC Greek settlers had also established colonies to the east of Carthage, particularly at Cyrene, now in the modern country of Libya (White 2001: 216). By the time that the Greek historian Herodotus visited in 440 BC, Cyrene had developed into a strong centre of Greek culture. Many of the Greek colonists, however, took Libyan (Berber) wives, and admitted the children of these marriages into full citizenship. As mentioned above, after the death of Alexander, one of his generals, Ptolemy I, took control of Egypt. Ptolemy I seized Cyrene in 322 BC and

---

[21] Hannibal's cavalry consisted almost entirely of Numidian Berbers. For a detailed discussion of the rise and fall of Carthage see Picard and Picard (1968).

resettled a number of captured Palestinian Jews there (Yamauchi 1992: 9).[22] By the time Rome gained control of Cyrene in the early first century BC serious tensions had surfaced between the growing Jewish population and the Greeks. In 74 BC the Romans officially annexed the area, calling it Cyrenaica (Yamauchi 1992: 10).

At the dawn of the New Testament era, the fertile strip of land along the North African coast was part of the Roman Empire and was providing a large portion of the imported grain that Rome required. Numerous colonies of Roman military veterans were established in this region during the Roman occupation. However, although there had been Phoenician, Greek, Jewish, and Roman colonists settling in this area for centuries, the vast majority of the population remained Berber (Brett 1981: 102). In general, the colonists resided in the coastal cities, which by the New Testament era were typical Greco-Roman cities. But just beyond the fertile strip of land along the coast lay the frontier of the Empire and the limits of Roman control. The Berber tribes controlled this area, and the Romans dealt with them more as allies than as vassals.

As time passed, the Berbers were integrated to a moderate degree into the Greco-Roman urban society. Numerous aristocratic Berbers, especially those in the urban areas, assimilated into the Roman culture, often taking Roman names and speaking Latin. Thus these Berbers often remain invisible to the historian (Brett and Fentress 1996: 53). The 'lower' social levels of the cities also became populated with Berbers, who also generally dominated all farm work. Later in history, Christianity swept through this region and was embraced by many of these urban Berbers. By the fourth century AD North Africa had 600 bishops, more than Gaul and Egypt combined (Bullard 2001: 198). Out of this Christian community several significant Church Fathers emerged: Tertullian, Cyprian, and Augustine, whose mother was Berber (Power 1999: 353; J. Ferguson 1969b: 184).

In AD 429 the Vandals conquered North Africa and settled in the area, to be followed by the Byzantines in AD 533. Finally, the Arabs swept across the region at the end of the seventh century AD. Although Greco-Roman culture disappeared with the Arab occupation, the Berbers retained their identity and their language, even down to today.

---

[22] See also the discussions regarding citizenship (Kwapong 1969: 99–109) and Jews in Cyrene (Smallwood 1969: 110–113).

Anatolia (Celts and others)

The term 'Anatolia' refers roughly to the region covered by modern Turkey, from the Mediterranean and the Black Sea to the Euphrates and the Syrian Desert (Mitchell 1993:1). The term 'Asia Minor' is often used in reference to the same general area.

The history of the region is rich and complex. The Hittites inhabited and controlled the area from the fifteenth century BC until around the twelfth century BC, when the Phrygians began migrating to Anatolia from the Balkan area. The Phrygian kings, many with the dynastic name 'Midas', ruled until the collapse of the Phrygian empire at the end of the seventh century BC, when they were overrun by the Cimmerians and Scythians from the northeast (Mitchell 1993: 1; Bruce 1992b: 365–366; Cunliffe 1997: 172). Anatolia then fell under the control of Persia, but the Persians did not settle there in any great numbers.

In addition, throughout the first millennium BC, Greek colonists established Greek cities along the western coast of Anatolia. The western coastal area of Anatolia became more and more 'Hellenized' as the years passed. Alexander swept through Anatolia in the fourth century BC and, upon his death, his successors (the Ptolemies of Egypt and the Seleucids of Antioch) fought over control of it (Bruce 1992b: 366). Alexander's conquest continued the spread of Greek culture to the region, especially in the cities along the coast. The Greek language became firmly established as the *lingua franca* of the region, especially for traders and merchants. Toward the end of the third century BC, the Seleucid king Antiochus III settled 2,000 Jewish families from Babylon in Lydia and Phrygia to help pacify the area and keep it loyal to him (Bickerman 1988: 92–93; Bruce 1992a: 230).

In the first millennium BC the Celts inhabited much of northern Europe, from France to Romania. In 400 BC they began migrating southward and eastward, moving through Macedonia, northern Italy, and Greece. In 280–270 BC they crossed over into Anatolia and settled in the region. They became known in the Greco-Roman world as Galatians (Mitchell 1993: 13–19; Cunliffe 1997: 68–90). They fought and traded with the people of the surrounding areas, especially the small kingdoms of Pergamum, Bithynia, Pontus, and Cappadocia, and they intermarried with the Phrygians, who still inhabited the area where they had settled (Mitchell 1993: 29; Cunliffe 1997: 176–177).

The Roman Empire then expanded into Anatolia: from 163 BC to

63 BC the Romans slowly gained control of the region, often aided by the Galatians. In 25 BC the Romans created the province of Galatia (Mitchell 1993: 30, 61) along with the other provinces of Asia Minor (Asia, Phrygia, Bithynia, Lycaonia, Cappadocia, Pontus). Mitchell (1993: 5) notes that these Roman divisions were political, and that they cut across cultural and ethnic lines. In addition, more than anywhere else in the Roman Empire, the boundaries and borders of these provinces were frequently changing. The province of Galatia, for example, contained primarily ethnic Celts (with some intermarriage) in the northern regions of the province and primarily ethnic Phrygians in the south.[23]

Most studies of Anatolia during the first century focus on the coastal cities, which were largely Greco-Roman. However, the vast majority of the population resided in villages all across the interior. Many, many tribal languages (including Celtic) continued to be spoken. No doubt many peasants, especially those with dealings in the city, knew Greek as their second language, but there were also probably some in the villages who knew no Greek at all. When Paul arrived, the ethnic, or even the linguistic, situation was extremely complicated (Mitchell 1993: 170–175).

Conclusions

The story of the New Testament took place in a world with a wide range of ethnic diversity. Although the educated population of the Roman Empire tended to refer to themselves as 'Greeks', in reality they were made up of dozens of different Indo-European, Asian, and African ethnic groups. And while many people in the urban areas were assimilated into the Greco-Roman culture, the countryside tended to remain more diverse, reflecting the ethnic composition that pre-dated the Romans. Jews were present in large numbers in most cities and, by and large, retained their ethnic identity. Likewise, Black Africans from Meroe (in Greek, *Ethiopians*) and Berbers from North Africa also interacted frequently with the first century AD Mediterranean world. This was the diverse world to which Paul and the Apostles proclaimed the gospel.

---

[23] This ethnic distinction enters into the discussion of Paul's use of the term 'Galatians'. Hansen probably represents the emerging consensus that Paul is addressing the cities in the southern region of the Galatian province. Since they inhabited the province of Galatia, they could properly be called Galatians, even though ethnically they were probably not Galatians (Celts) but rather Phrygians (1994a: 378–389).

Chapter Eight

Race and the theology
of Luke-Acts

Introduction

More than any of the other gospel writers, Luke includes aspects of race in the most central elements of his theology in Luke-Acts.[1] Indeed, one of the main issues that Luke addresses is the question, 'How did the hope of God open up to include all races . . . ?' (Bock 1994: 1). Likewise, regarding this theme, Bock later comments, 'This racial concern, observed throughout Luke's Gospel, indicates how God's plan includes all races.' Bock also identifies the racial theme as central to Acts (1994: 28, 35). In similar fashion Witherington stresses that Luke was concerned to show the gospel spreading both ethnically and socially to all people. He writes: 'The universalization of the gospel will embrace not only all ethnic diversity in the [Roman] Empire but also people up and down the social scale' (Witherington 1998a: 72).

Yet Luke is also concerned with discipleship and Christian community. God's plan is not just that the gospel will go to all peoples, but that all peoples will be brought together through the gospel to form one people in Christ. Tannehill states that it is Luke's 'conviction that God is calling the peoples of the world to share in a community that includes their enemies and reconciles them with those who worship and live in other ways' (1990: 2). Thus the universalistic elements of Luke's theology have implications not only for missiology, but also for ecclesiology ('how we do church') and social interaction within the Church.

The other gospels

This chapter focuses on Luke-Acts because the theology of Luke-Acts speaks most directly to the issue of race within the Church. This

---

[1] Most scholars concur that Luke and Acts should be read and interpreted together as a single story, even though they are separated in the canon (Johnson 1991: 4; Tannehill 1990: xiii; Green 1997: 6).

narrow focus is not to imply that the other gospels do not speak at all to this topic. Quite to the contrary, Matthew, Mark, and John all address related issues, particularly the universalistic aspect of salvation being offered to 'all the nations'. These three books will often connect to either the Abrahamic promise (Gen. 12:3, 22:18, 26:4) or the Isaianic expansions of this promise that envisaged the eschatological gathering of the nations along with Israel.[2] We will discuss them only briefly.

Matthew begins with a reference to Abraham, implying an allusion to the Genesis promise of blessing for the nations,[3] and closes with the Great Commission ('make disciples of all nations'). Brown suggests that Matthew – who addresses a church of both Jews and Gentiles – wants to demonstrate that the mix of Jew and Gentile in the Church had always been Jesus' concern. This point is stressed, Brown argues, especially in the 'infancy narratives' (1993: 47). Keener (1999: 45) notes that the Gentile mission is a recurrent theme throughout the book of Matthew. One of the more significant texts is Matthew 8:11, where Jesus tells a centurion that 'many will come from the east and the west, and will take their places at the feast with Abraham, Isaac, and Jacob in the kingdom of heaven. But the subjects of the kingdom will be thrown outside . . .' Blomberg (1992: 26) suggests that the tension within the book of Matthew between particularistic passages (to the Jews only) and the universalistic passages (to all the nations/Gentiles) forms one of the most foundational or overarching themes of the book.[4]

Because interracial marriage is such a sensitive, yet critical issue for the Church today, it is appropriate for us also to examine the genealogy of Jesus in Matthew 1. Included in Jesus' genealogy are four unusual women: Tamar (1:3), Rahab (1:5), Ruth (1:5), and Bathsheba (1:6). Ancient Jewish genealogies normally did not include women, so Matthew's reference to them is most unusual (Keener 1999: 78–79; Brown 1993: 71). Furthermore, if Matthew simply wanted to include women for the sake of having women in the list, he could have cited

[2] LaGrand (1999: 107–108) provides a summary of how Jesus' ministry to the nations is presented in each of the gospels.

[3] Davies and Allison (1988: 158) and Brown (1993: 68) argue that this mention of Abraham implies a connection to the Abrahamic promise of 'all the nations will be blessed in you' and thus 'serves to announce the evangelist's interest in the salvation of the Gentiles.'

[4] For discussions on Matthew and the promise to the nations see LaGrand (1999); Köstenberger and O'Brien (2001: 87–109); and Jeremias (1958).

Sarah, Rebekah, or one of the other respected matriarchs. Obviously Matthew was attempting to say something theologically by his inclusion of these four most unusual women in the lineage of the Messiah. Two common aspects connect the four women: first, all of them have some type of scandal attached to their entry into their Israelite marriages; and second, all of them have Gentile origins or connections. As mentioned in Chapter 2, Tamar and Rahab were Canaanites, and Ruth a Moabitess. The ethnicity of Bathsheba is not known, but she was married to Uriah the Hittite, and thus had been united to a Gentile. Note that Matthew underlines this fact by mentioning her former husband Uriah in 1:6. Both Brown (1993: 73) and Hagner (1993: 10) posit that Matthew's purpose in listing these women included both of these aspects.[5] Keener (1999: 79–80) and LaGrand (1999: 171) both note that the point of Jewish genealogies at this time was to establish 'racial purity' along the lines of the model given in Ezra-Nehemiah. The inclusion of these Gentile women in the lineage would have been shocking to most Jewish readers. Keener writes, 'Matthew seems to highlight the mixed nature of Jesus' lineage purposely.' These references, Keener continues, imply an 'allusion to the Gentile mission (2:1–2; 24:14; 28:19), which speaks to disciples of their responsibility to cross cultural boundaries to spread Christ's gospel' (1999: 80).

Yet Matthew may be implying even more than Keener suggests. Interracial marriage does more than merely cross over cultural boundaries; it goes a long way toward removing the boundary. Thus it is suggestive that Matthew used the interracial marriage phenomenon in Jesus' lineage to introduce the 'inclusion of the Gentiles' theme. Within the Church that Matthew addressed, there were both Jews and Gentiles. Paul had already proclaimed that Jew and Gentile were one in the Lord, but it is extremely likely that Jewish families were still reluctant to allow their Christian children to marry Gentiles; generations and generations of family and cultural tradition had ingrained into these Jewish families that interracial marriage was wrong. It is possible, then, that Matthew is saying more with these women in Jesus' genealogy than just that the gospel is for the Gentiles, too. He may be arguing with residual Jewish attitudes in the Church and reinforcing Paul's theology that Jew and Gentile are one in the Lord (and

---

[5] The Catholic scholar Brown also insists on a parallel between these women and Mary, the mother of Jesus. He finds in it the commonality that all of them take an active role in God's plan and are thus to be seen as instruments of God's providence (1993: 73).

thus can, and should, intermarry). The implications for the Church today are obvious. Many White Christians today, like the Jewish Christians of the first century, carry generations of cultural baggage regarding racial intermarriage. Matthew, on the other hand, tells them that Jesus Christ was a descendant from several racially mixed marriages, as scandalous in that day and time as some interracial marriages can be in the world today. Perhaps the subtle theological sub-point of Matthew 1 is that racially mixed marriages among God's people are a normal part of the new community that Christ creates in the world.

In Mark the stress on the nations is not as pronounced as in Matthew, and Mark does not directly connect Jesus' mission to Abraham. Nonetheless, in the book of Mark, Jesus does occasionally refer to the 'blessing on all the nations', usually in an eschatological context. Also, in Mark 11:17 Jesus quotes from Isaiah 56:7, 'My house will be called a house of prayer for all nations.' Likewise Jesus' statement in Mark 13:10 ('and the gospel must first be preached to all the nations') does reflect Jesus' concern for the nations.[6]

Finally, the book of John likewise echoes the universal aspect of the gospel message. In John 4, Jesus shares with the Samaritan woman at the well. This encounter results in numerous Samaritans placing faith in Jesus and proclaiming him to be 'the Saviour of the world' (4:39–42). The Samaritans will be discussed in more detail below, but it is significant, as Carson (1991: 232) notes, that this first 'cross-cultural' evangelistic encounter was undertaken by the Lord himself, thus establishing the pattern he lays down in Acts 1:8.

In John 10:16 Jesus mentions that he has 'other sheep'. Within the context of John 10 this appears to be a clear reference to the Gentiles (Carson 1991: 388; L. Morris 1971: 512). Witherington (1995: 190) writes: 'Thus the ultimate vision held out here is for one flock to be produced of both Jewish and Gentile believers in Christ'. Likewise, the inclusion of all peoples into Jesus' new kingdom of God is implied in John 12:20–26 (Carson 1991: 435–436). When told that Greeks had come seeking him, Jesus responded that the 'hour has come for the Son of Man to be glorified,' thus indicating that Jesus saw their coming as the heralds of the climax of his ministry (Carson 1991: 435–436; Beasley-Murray 1987: 211).[7]

---

[6] See Köstenberger and O'Brien (2001: 73–86); LaGrand (1999: 105–111); and Jeremias (1958: 64–73).

[7] For further discussion on these Johannine texts in regard to Jesus' Gentile mission see Köstenberger (1998).

Luke: Abraham and the blessing for all nations

One of the ways that Luke advances the theology of salvation for all peoples is by showing continuity with the Old Testament regarding Abraham and the blessing for all nations. In Chapter 3 we discussed the important role that Genesis 10 – 12 plays in biblical theology. Genesis 11 recounts the Tower of Babel story, which ended with God scattering the world's people. They divide into the families, languages, lands, and nations that are described in Genesis 10. The Tower of Babel story marks the culmination of the consistent sin and rebellion of mankind demonstrated in Genesis 3 – 11. The promise to Abraham in Genesis 12:1–3 is God's gracious response to the human catastrophe of Genesis 3 – 11. In 12:3 God promises that all the 'families of the earth' will be blessed in Abraham. This promise is repeated in Genesis 18:18, 22:18 and 26:4 in a slightly varied form. In those verses God promises that 'through your offspring all nations [Gk. LXX *ethnē*] on earth will be blessed.' This theme was intensified by Isaiah and the prophets as they wedded the inclusion of the nations with messianic expectations.

Luke connects his theology firmly to this theme. Abraham's name occurs twenty-two times in Luke-Acts, underscoring the huge role that he plays in Luke's work (Bock 1994: 160). From the beginning of the story, Luke connects the coming of Christ to the promise made to Abraham. In Luke 1:54–55 Mary states:

> He has helped his servant Israel,
>   remembering to be merciful
> to Abraham and his descendants for ever,
>   even as he said to our fathers.'

Zechariah likewise relates the coming Messiah to the Abrahamic promises, proclaiming:

> to show mercy to our fathers
>   and to remember his holy covenant,
>   the oath he swore to our father Abraham.
>   (Luke 1:72–73)

Thus Luke introduces his narrative as a continuation of the story 'rooted in the Abrahamic covenant' (Green 1997: 57).

Johnson underlines how important God's promise to Abraham is in Luke-Acts. God's fulfilment of his promises to Abraham is 'the essential message of Luke's narrative for Gentile Christian readers' (1991: 42–43). In Acts 3:25 Peter quotes directly God's promise relating to the peoples of the earth, stating, 'Through your offspring all peoples on earth will be blessed.' Johnson argues that the references to Abraham in Luke 1 must be viewed in light of this later identification in Acts, one that makes the first Christians the seed of Abraham to whom the promised blessings are delivered (1991: 46).

The universalistic scope of Christ surfaces again in Luke 2:30–32 (Witherington 1998a: 69). Simeon, the righteous man at Jesus' dedication, declares:

> For my eyes have seen your salvation,
>   which you have prepared in the sight of all peoples,
> a light for revelation to the Gentiles
> and for glory to your people Israel.

Bock (1994: 243) argues that the phrase 'all peoples' in verse 31 refers to both Jews and Gentiles, and that the two verses together indicate that 'participation in that salvation also extends to every racial group.'

The Abrahamic promise of blessing to all nations is alluded to once again in Luke 24:47 (Köstenberger and O'Brien 2001: 125). In this text Jesus tells his disciples that 'repentance and forgiveness of sins will be preached in his name *to all nations*, beginning at Jerusalem.' Köstenberger and O'Brien argue that the phrase 'all the nations' connects both to the Abrahamic promises and to the Isaianic prophecies that envisage 'all the nations' streaming to Jerusalem in the last days (2001: 125). Bock points out that not only does this text proclaim that the message of hope is to go out to all nations, but also this universal scope is part of God's plan. 'God always intended to offer salvation to all races through Jesus' (1996: 1940–1941). This text, coming at the end of Luke, also anticipates the narrative in Acts, where the gospel does indeed go out to all nations[8] (Johnson 1991: 402–403; Tannehill 1986: 294–297).

---

[8] The tight continuity between Genesis and Luke-Acts regarding the nations is diffused somewhat by the different terms in English used to translate the one Greek term *ethnē*, an important term that occurs fifty-six times in Luke-Acts. Genesis 10 describes the people of the world as grouped by family, language, territory, and nation (Gk. LXX, *ethnē*). Likewise, Genesis 18:18, 22:18 and 26:4 speak of all the nations (Gk. LXX, *ethnē*) of the world being blessed in the seed of Abraham. To most of the

The theme of blessing – through the gospel of Christ – on all the nations continues with even more intensity in the book of Acts. In Acts 1:8 Jesus gives the disciples the programmatic command: 'You will be my witnesses in Jerusalem, and in all Judea and Samaria, and to the ends of the earth.' As discussed below, the movement from Judea to Samaria demanded that these early Christians cross over a longstanding ethnic, religious, and cultural boundary. Samaritans were loathed by the Jewish community. Also, as Witherington notes, the phrase 'ends of the earth' should not be taken as a reference to Rome simply because the book of Acts ends in Rome.[9] Rather, the phrase connects back to Luke 24:47 and the command to witness to 'all the nations' (1998a: 110; Moore 1997: 389–399). It thus denotes both geographical and ethnical universalism for the destination of the gospel.

In Acts 1:8 Jesus also ties the mission of his disciples to the empowering of the Spirit, a major theme that continues throughout the book of Acts. It is important that we as Christians today do not mythologize this connection. As discussed below, the ethnic and cultural boundary between the Jews and the Samaritans was every bit as rigid and hostile as the current boundary between Blacks and Whites in the most racist areas of the United States. Yet by the power of the Spirit, the layman Philip, followed by the apostles Peter and John, carried the gospel successfully across this cultural and ethnic barrier. Readers today tend to

---

first-century Greek-speaking world, *ethnē* was a loosely defined term that generally meant 'nation', but could be used of various groups of people. Greek-speaking Jews, however, added a new nuance to the semantic range of the word. To them the word could be used to refer to nations in general, but it could also be used in a very narrow theological and ethnic sense to refer to anyone who was not a Jew: that is, a Gentile. Used in this sense it was a negative term. In some contexts, it is difficult for English translators to know which English word, 'nation' or 'Gentile', best translates the term. Yet the intertextual and thematic connection between Luke-Acts and Genesis (and Isaiah) is broader than just that seen in texts that use the English word 'nation'. There are also allusions or direct connections to the Genesis promise of blessing to the nations (*ethnē*) to be seen in numerous passages that render the term as 'Gentiles'. Indeed, theologically there appears even to be some subtle semantic wordplay on the ironic difference between 'Gentiles' and 'nations', both of whom receive the gospel and become God's people in Luke-Acts.

[9] Barrett (1994: 80), among others, argues that the phrase 'to the ends of the earth' does indeed refer to Rome, but not to Rome as an end in itself; rather to Rome as a representative of the whole world. Ellis (1991: 123–132), arguing primarily from Greco-Roman usage, contends that the phrase refers to Spain, specifically to the city of Gades. However, Ellis' argument does not address the OT (Genesis and Isaiah) background of 'salvation for the nations', nor does he discuss the probable connection of Acts 1:8 to Luke 24:47. See the rebuttal by Moore (1997: 389–399).

gloss over the magnitude of Philip's work in Samaria, for we usually forget how much mutual animosity existed between the Jews and the Samaritans. Sociologically and missiologically, Philip's action was extremely profound, for he was able to put aside the generations of prejudice and hate that were an integral part of his own culture. The power of the Spirit in Philip's Samaritan mission was probably not limited to the working of miraculous signs (Acts 8:6–7), but was also actively involved in changing Philip's worldview and his inherited attitude toward the Samaritans. Likewise, if we Christians today are to have any hope of obeying the biblical command to form a unified people of God out of diverse ethnicities, we too must acknowledge and follow the critical leading and empowering of the Spirit.

The power of the Spirit is dramatically demonstrated in Acts 2 in the story of Pentecost. In Luke 24:47 Jesus had stated that repentance and forgiveness of sins would be preached in his name to all nations, beginning at Jerusalem. This thought is restated by Christ in Acts 1:8. The events in Acts 2 connect directly to Jesus' prophetic words as part of the unfolding fulfilment. Barrett (1994: 108) writes that demonstrating this fulfilment was one of Luke's major purposes in this text. The other major purpose, Barrett continues, was to teach that the Church, although located in Jerusalem at the beginning, was nonetheless in principle a universal society.

Acts 2:5 states that in Jerusalem there were Jews 'from every nation under heaven.' Luke emphasizes this point by listing the numerous nations that were represented (2:9–11). The stress that Luke places on the detailed listing of these nations suggests perhaps more than just a regathering of Diaspora Jews. Tannehill (1990: 27) concludes that although these people were Jews, they also functioned as representatives of their homelands, including the Gentiles there. Thus they provided a 'hint of the mission's power to cross ethnic and religious lines.' Similarly, Stott writes that the Pentecost event 'symbolized a new unity in the Spirit transcending racial, national and linguistic barriers' (1990: 68).

Furthermore, Luke's use of the phrase 'from every nation' in Acts 2:5 probably alludes back to the Abrahamic promise. As discussed above, the promise to Abraham forms a critical component in Luke's overarching theology, 'the essential message of Luke's narrative for Gentile Christian readers' (Johnson 1991: 42–43), and, as discussed above, it is implied in the imperative of Acts 1:8. In addition, the promise to Abraham regarding the nations/peoples of the earth is explicitly quoted in Acts 3:25.

With Abraham (Genesis 12) already in the context, the connection between the Pentecost event and the Tower of Babel episode (Genesis 11) appears to be quite plausible. Numerous scholars note that Luke may be presenting the Pentecost event as a reversal of the Tower of Babel (Witherington 1998a: 136; Barrett 1994: 119; Stott 1990: 68; Larkin 1995: 48; Kistemaker 1990: 79), although Barrett cautions against pushing the connection too far. However, note that others also see a relationship between the list of nations in Acts 2 and the list of nations in Genesis 10 (Stott 1990: 68; Köstenberger and O'Brien 2001: 134). At this point it is important for us to recall the relationship between Genesis 10, 11, and 12. Genesis 11 told the story of mankind's rebellion against God and the subsequent scattering, linguistically and regionally. Genesis 10 then described the result, with each region organized according to its families, languages (Gk. *glōssa*), territories, and nations (Gk. *ethnē*) – compare the same terms for language and nation in Acts 2:4, 5, 11. The answer to the scattering and alienation from God was revealed in the Abrahamic covenant in Genesis 12, with the promise, 'in you all the nations of the earth will be blessed.' The fact that central elements of these three critical chapters of Genesis all surface in the monumental event of Acts 2 cannot be accidental.

Noting the various connections between Acts 1 – 3 and Genesis 10 – 12 answers some of the objections of those who are reluctant to accept a connection between Pentecost and the Tower of Babel. Larkin (1995: 48), for example, sees the Tower of Babel element as a possible sub-theme but wonders why Luke does not make more explicit connections to Genesis 11 if that is the case. However, if we view Genesis 11 as part of the larger theological unit of Genesis 10 – 12, then we see that Luke does make numerous connections to that unit. It is the overall theme of Genesis 10 – 12, not just a reversal of the Tower of Babel, that is important to Luke.

Stott summarizes the theological truth of Pentecost by writing: 'Nothing could have demonstrated more clearly than this the multi-racial, multinational, multilingual nature of the kingdom of Christ.' Furthermore, Stott continues, this event not only connects back to Genesis 10 – 12 but points forward to the scene depicted in Revelation 7:9, where the redeemed will come from every nation, tribe, people, and language (1990: 68).

The Good Samaritan

As mentioned in Chapter 7, while the exact origin of the Samaritans is not completely clear, it is clear that the majority of Jews in Judea and Galilee hated them. For several hundred years animosity between the two groups had been growing, and this animosity exploded into serious violence in the first century AD.[10] Two events recorded by Josephus provide some context for the Jewish side of the hostility. First, while Coponius was procurator (AD 6–9) some Samaritans secretly joined some Jewish Passover pilgrims and entered the Temple with them. Once inside the Temple, they desecrated it by spreading human bones in the porticoes and in the sanctuary. This action was 'about the worst desecration possible' (Ford 1984: 83; Josephus, *Antiquities* 18:29–30). Second, in AD 51 people from the Samaritan village of Ginae murdered one or more – the sources contradict – Jewish pilgrims on their way to Jerusalem for the Passover. The Jews appealed to their Roman rulers for justice, but the Romans ignored them. An unruly 'mob' from Jerusalem then went down to Ginae, massacred all of the inhabitants, and burned the village to the ground. At this point the Romans intervened; they arrested and executed several of the Jews involved (Josephus, *Jewish Wars* 2:232–235; *Antiquities* 20:118–136; Tacitus, *Annals* 12:54). Keep in mind that prior to this time the Jews had been very supportive of Rome; indeed, this support was the reason for the special treatment that the Jews received throughout the Empire. Ford (1984: 86) and Rhoads (1976: 72) see the Samaritan Ginae incident as the turning point in Jewish–Roman relations and one of the critical events that led to the Jewish rebellion against Rome in AD 66.[11]

So, although the Ginae event occurred *after* Jesus told the Good Samaritan story, it does nonetheless illustrate the extreme hostility

---

[10] For a history of the hostility between the Jews and the Samaritans see Ford (1984: 79–86). See also Jeremias (1969: 352–358), who discusses the social attitude of the Jerusalem Jews toward the Samaritans. Jeremias notes that, in regard to social contact, the Samaritans were at the very bottom of the Jewish social scale.

[11] Mendels (1992: 300) and Hengel (1989: 346–348) also mention this event as one of the important conflicts leading up to the war. Hengel notes that the Jewish 'Zealots' tried to use this event as a pretext for drawing the entire Jewish population into a war with Rome (1989: 346). Obviously this event was not the only factor; the causes for the Jewish war against Rome were complex and many. Jewish–Roman relations had been deteriorating for some time. But it did obviously play an important role in the rising conflict between the Jews and Rome. See also the discussion by L. Levine (1992: 839–840).

that existed between the Jews and the Samaritans. The Ginae incident, however, occurred *before* Luke wrote Luke-Acts, and thus this
event – among other serious encounters between the Jews and
Samaritans – may have formed part of the context from which Luke
wrote. It is significant that outside of Luke-Acts the Samaritans are
mentioned only twice (Matt. 10:5; John 4). Luke, however, includes
six Samaritan episodes. Jesus rebukes James and John for wanting to
call down fire from heaven upon a Samaritan village that did not
welcome them (Luke 9:51–56). Jesus tells the story of the Good
Samaritan (Luke 10:25–37). Of ten healed lepers, only the Samaritan
leper returns to thank Jesus (Luke 17:11–19). Jesus tells the disciples
to be his witnesses in Jerusalem, and in all Judea and Samaria (Acts
1:8). In fulfilment of Jesus' words, Philip, Peter, and John preach in
Samaria and many believe and are filled with the Holy Spirit (Acts
8:4–25). As Paul travels through Samaria on his way to the Jerusalem
council, he tells the brothers there how the Gentiles had been converted, and these Samaritan brothers rejoice (Acts 15:3), probably a
subtle contrast to those in Jerusalem who were not as excited about
Paul's Gentile ministry. Clearly for Luke the Samaritans play an
important role in his theology, especially regarding the expansion of
the gospel.

Indeed, Jesus' model for the gospel expansion as he proclaims it in
Acts 1:8 required the early Jewish Christians first to take the gospel
to the hated Samaritans. Although the hostilities and animosities
between the Jews and the Samaritans are discussed at length as background for the Good Samaritan passage, few commentaries on Acts
mention it. Yet the expansion of the gospel into Samaria as described
in Acts takes place within a few years of Jesus' homily on the Good
Samaritan, and the prejudices between the groups had hardly abated
during that time. Therefore the phrase 'in all Judea and Samaria' can
hardly be relegated to a mere geographical description. If Jesus had
said, 'in all Judea and *Galilee*', then the emphasis would be geographical.[12] But when Jesus mentioned Samaria, he was, no doubt, making
a statement with strong ethnic connotations. Furthermore, if Acts 1:8
is read within the context of the gospel of Luke and the references to
the Samaritans within this gospel, then the ethnic animosities

[12] Barrett (1994: 80–81) notes that the inclusion of Samaria rather than Galilee is
surprising and unexpected. He attempts to address the problem by discussing whether
or not the Church was already established in Galilee or whether Galilee plays any role
in Luke's theology. So Barrett seeks the answer by discussing what is not said rather
than focusing on what *is* said: the mention of Samaria, a place that the Jews despised.

permeating the Jew–Samaritan relationship cannot be ignored, and Jesus' words must be understood within that context. Stott (1990: 42–43) comes close to making this point. He notes that the disciples' question about the restoration of the kingdom to Israel (Acts 1:6) betrays their narrow nationalistic focus. Jesus' answer, in contrast, stresses that his kingdom 'tolerates no narrow nationalism'. Stott (1990: 43) writes that Christ 'rules over an international community in which race, nation, rank, and sex are no barriers to fellowship.' Likewise, Stott notes the implied connection between Acts 1:8 and the fulfilment described at the consummation of his kingdom in Revelation 7:9, where 'the countless redeemed company will be seen to be drawn "from every nation, tribe, people, and language."'

Thus the proclamation of the gospel by Philip, Peter, and John to the Samaritans was, no doubt, an extremely difficult cross-cultural step for them to take. Throughout all of their lives they had been taught by their own culture to hate and despise the Samaritans. Yet in Acts 8, by the power of the Spirit, these early Christian preachers crossed over one of the central and most fixed ethnic boundaries of Judaism.

So the story of the Good Samaritan in Luke 10 plays an important role in the larger picture of Luke-Acts, as well as forming a backdrop for Acts 1:8 and the expansion of the gospel into Samaria in Acts 8. This argument grows stronger if we note the way in which this story is tied into the fabric of the surrounding context in Luke as well. First of all, in the preceding pericope, Jesus appoints seventy-two workers and sends them out ahead of him (Luke 10:1, 17). Most commentators view the number seventy-two (or seventy, as some NT manuscripts read) as significant, connecting back to the seventy-two (or seventy, as some OT versions read) nations of Genesis 10. Thus they argue that this text foreshadows the mission of the Church to the nations that later unfolds in the book of Acts (Nolland 1993: 549; Marshall 1978: 415; Green 1997: 412; Culpepper 1995: 219).[13]

In addition, the Good Samaritan story lies within a larger unit of Luke that is dealing with discipleship. The larger unit of Luke

---

[13] Luke 10:1 contains a difficult textual problem. One group of manuscripts reads '70' were appointed and another group reads '72' were appointed. The evidence is evenly divided. Johnson (1991: 167) opts for '70' and connects the number to the elders that Moses appointed in Exodus. Bock (1996: 994) opts for '72' but sees no symbolism in the number and no connection to the OT. However, Nolland (1993: 549) and Marshall (1978: 415) point out that in Genesis 10 the MT has 70 nations but the Septuagint has 72. Thus, they argue, the variation of manuscripts in Luke 10:1 reflects the variation of textual readings in the OT passage that Luke 10:1 was based upon.

9:51 – 19:10 is united by the theme of Jesus' trip to Jerusalem, but this large unit starts off by dealing with several key issues relating to discipleship. Marshall (1978: 402, 439), for example, entitles the first two sections as: 'The Duties and Privileges of Discipleship' (9:51 – 10:24); and 'The Characteristics of Disciples' (10:25 – 11:13), thus implying that discipleship is a central theme uniting this section. Culpepper (1995: 226) likewise sees literary connections between the Good Samaritan story and the episodes that surround it. In 10:21, for example, Jesus states that God has hidden things from the wise but revealed them to children. In the opening verses of the Good Samaritan story Jesus is questioned by one of the wise, an expert in the law. Furthermore, Culpepper notes the similarity between the Good Samaritan story and the following episode regarding Mary's failure to help Martha. Both stories, Culpepper suggests, 'illustrate the scandal that radical obedience to Jesus' commands requires' (1995: 226).[14]

The Good Samaritan story itself is undoubtedly familiar to the reader. An 'expert in the law' comes to test Jesus and asks him what he must do to inherit eternal life (Luke 10:25). Jesus responds by asking the expert what is written in the law. The Torah lawyer cites Deuteronomy 6:5, 'Love the Lord your God with all your heart and with all your soul and with all your strength and with all your mind,' and then tags on Leviticus 19:18, 'love your neighbour as yourself.' Jesus tells him that if he does this he will live. Yet the lawyer pushes

---

[14] A close narrative reading of this section suggests numerous other connections. In 9:37–45 the disciples are unable to cast out an evil spirit. In 9:51–56 Jesus is rejected by a village in *Samaria*. The disciples want to call down fire on this Samaritan village but Jesus rebukes them. The next pericope (9:57–62) deals with the cost of following Jesus. In 10:1–20 Jesus then sends out seventy-two on a mission to proclaim the kingdom of God. The Good Samaritan story occurs next, and deals with a primary social and cultural barrier that characterized Judaism (and Jesus' budding disciples): that is, they hated the Samaritans. This animosity, if left uncorrected, would no doubt hinder the spread of the gospel, for in the book of Acts the spreading of the gospel to the region of Samaria is a critical step. This cannot be coincidental.

In the wider context of Luke-Acts it is significant that the resurrected Jesus states, 'You will be my witnesses in Jerusalem, and in all Judea and *Samaria*, and to the ends of the earth.' Then in Acts 8, when the Jews in Jerusalem begin persecuting the Christians, Philip preaches the gospel in a city of Samaria. However, this time the Samaritans receive the message and the messenger. Note also that, this time, the disciple (Philip) is able to cast out demons (8:7). Note also the theme of joy (cf. Luke 10:21). Finally, this phenomenon is no longer limited to one city or village, for in Acts 8:25 Peter and John preach in many Samaritan villages. Is this thematic similarity regarding Samaria in Luke and Acts coincidence? Are the readers of Luke-Acts assumed to forget the earlier rejection of the gospel by the Samaritans and to forget the story of the Good Samaritan by the time they read of Philip's evangelization of Samaria?

further. Luke 10:29 states that the lawyer 'wanted to justify himself', so he asked, 'And who is my neighbour?' The term 'justify' in this context implies that the lawyer wanted to establish that his actions in this matter were righteous: that is, that he was indeed righteous regarding the commandment 'love your neighbour as yourself.' Marshall points out that the Jews interpreted the 'neighbour' of Leviticus 19:18 to mean fellow Jews. The Torah itself tended to expand this term to include the 'resident alien' (gēr), but Jewish usage explicitly excluded Samaritans and foreigners (1978: 444).

In response to the lawyer's question, Jesus tells the story of the Good Samaritan. This story might be better labelled an 'example story' rather than a parable, because there is not really any symbolic or metaphoric meaning in the story (Witherington 1994: 192). Hultgren classifies it as a 'Parable of Exemplary Behavior' (2000: 94).

As the story unfolds, at first it appears to be headed toward an anti-priest homily. A priest passes by the victim without helping him, as does a Levite. Yet Jesus' portrayal of these characters as priest and Levite is not directly related to their role as priest. Green suggests that Jesus uses these two individuals because 'they epitomize a worldview of tribal consciousness concerned with relative status and us-them categorizing' (1997: 430–431). That is, they represent the worldview that Jesus is dismantling.

The story takes a shocking turn when Jesus then introduces the hero of the story as being a 'Samaritan'. The contrast is emphasized in Luke's account by the emphatic position of 'Samaritan' at the beginning of the sentence (Marshall 1978: 449; Stein 1992: 317). To cast the hero of the story as a hated, despised Samaritan would have been an incredible shock to Jesus' audience.

Stott (1990: 200–202) cites several Jewish stories that are similar in some respects to the Good Samaritan story. In one, a rabbi helps a leper; in another, a rabbi helps a Roman who has been shipwrecked. Both stories show how a pious rabbi selflessly crossed over cultural barriers to help one who was less fortunate than he. Jesus' story, however, differs radically from this theme by placing the hated, despised one as the hero who does the helping. Thus Jesus kills two proverbial birds of prejudice with one stone. First, he is making the point that loving one's neighbour is to transcend all racial and cultural boundaries. Second, Jesus is challenging the Jews' stereotyped negative generalization of Samaritans by casting a Samaritan as the compassionate hero (Culpepper 1995: 230).

Because of the deep ethnic tension that existed between the Jews and the Samaritans, it is obvious that this story is directly addressing some ethnic issues. Culpepper (1995: 229) writes: 'Jesus demolished all boundary expectations. Social position – race, religion, or region – count for nothing.' Hultgren (2000: 100) likewise states that authentic love pays no attention to 'religious, ethnic, or cultural distinctions'. Stott (1990: 192) concludes that the story has to do primarily with the breakdown of barriers between insiders and outsiders. Marshall (1978: 450) writes: 'Implicitly, racial considerations are shown to be irrelevant . . . both the giving and receiving of mercy transcends national and racial barriers. All that remains is that men should put this into effect.' In defining the main point of the story Stein (1992: 319) states: 'Jesus and Luke sought to illustrate that the love of one's neighbor must transcend all natural or human boundaries such as race, nationality, religion, and economic or education status.'

This teaching of Jesus was both radical and upsetting. Green comments that if the lawyer took this encounter with Jesus seriously it would completely destabilize his worldview and 'challenge him to embrace the new world order propagated through Jesus' ministry' (1997: 426). Keesmaat (2000: 265) draws a similar conclusion, noting that Jesus' parables 'fundamentally reorder and reshape reality', challenging the worldview of his hearers.

If we readers today are to hear and follow Jesus it is imperative that we connect this parable to our situation and our worldview. Witherington (1994: 195) writes: 'When the dominion of God breaks into human lives and situations, old prejudices pass away and a new and shocking pattern of behavior comes to pass. Jesus is commending such a pattern of behavior here.' The relationship between Whites and Blacks in America, even within the Church, is remarkably similar to that between Jews and Samaritans of the first century: one that has historically been characterized by prejudicial animosity and distrust, with clear boundaries delineating 'them' from 'us'. The Good Samaritan story, especially when placed within the overall theology of Luke-Acts, likewise destabilizes our inherited 'Black–White' worldview, and challenges us to move beyond the 'us–them' mentality of our culture to an 'us–us, in Christ' unity that demolishes the ethnic boundaries of our society.

Yet Jesus does more here than just restructure our worldview, for this story also stresses the importance of action. The Samaritan hero actually helped the victim; he did not merely have compassion in his heart. Jesus likewise confronted the lawyer with the words, 'Go and do likewise.' Green (1997: 425–426) writes that it is the 'doing' that is the summation of the law. Indeed, throughout the book of Luke, 'hearing' is always authenticated by 'doing'. Therefore, if we Christians today are to hear Christ in this text, our theology *must* be reflected in our actions. We must *do* racial equality and not just *think* racial equality. The exemplary Samaritan in the story did not simply 'mind his own business'; he took risks and he sacrificed some of his own well-being in order to show love to his ethnically different neighbour. If we shirk the risks and dangers of breaking the ethnic barrier, and if we place our own well-being at the top of our priority list, hiding behind the self-righteous justification of 'minding my own business', then we become like the priest and the Levite, and not like the Good Samaritan. Thus we fail miserably in our attempt to hear and to follow Jesus. Yet if we allow ourselves to be filled with the compassion that Jesus gives; if we follow the leading and the power of the Spirit that led Philip to Samaria in Acts 8; if we dare to reject our inherited worldview and embrace instead the worldview of Jesus; and if we take serious social risks by actively shattering the ethnic barriers of our culture, then we have encountered Christ and have entered into the ranks of those who humbly follow him in both deed and belief.

The Ethiopian eunuch

In Acts 8, immediately after Philip's evangelistic success among the Samaritans, he encounters a man referred to as 'an Ethiopian eunuch, an important official in charge of all the treasury of Candace, queen of the Ethiopians.' As discussed in Chapters 2 and 7, the Greeks used the term 'Ethiopia' as a general term to refer to everything south of Egypt, i.e. all of Black Africa. However, most of their contact with Black Africans (Ethiopians) was with people from the ancient kingdom of Cush, the nation south of Egypt and along the Nile, just upstream of the cataracts on the Nile. As discussed in Chapter 7, by the first century AD the people of this kingdom had moved their capital to the city of Meroe, and this first-century nation is often referred to as the Meroitic Kingdom. Most 'Ethiopians' appearing in Greco-Roman literature are Black Africans from this region. However, there is no doubt whatsoever that the Ethiopian of Acts 8 is from the Black African kingdom of Meroe because of the reference to Candace (Gk. *Kandakēs*), the queen of the Ethiopians. Reisner (1923: 67) suggests that this is a Greek transliteration of *ktke*,

Meroitic for 'queen', and not a proper name, but rather a title. This same title occurs in Strabo's account of the Roman excursion up the Nile to Meroe by Gaius Petronius in 23 BC.[15] The Meroitic (Cushite) queen, called Candace, conducted all negotiations on behalf of Meroe. Haenchen (1971: 310) makes the identification of Candace with Cush, stating that this kingdom was always ruled by a queen mother. Reisner, however, points out that in a period of over 500 years, there were only five queens who actually ruled (1923: 67). Shinnie (1967: 61) cites Dunham as identifying the queen who would have been ruling during the time of the book of Acts as Queen Amanitare (AD 25–41). Others disagree, placing this queen earlier.[16] Although the precise identification of the queen is uncertain, there is little doubt as to her ethnicity and her country. She was a Black queen ruling over the Black African nation known earlier in history as Cush. Likewise the home and ethnicity of the Ethiopian eunuch in the story is clear; he is a Black African from the country along the Nile, south of Egypt.[17]

The Ethiopian in the story is designated as a 'eunuch'. In fact Luke stresses this title, referring to him by this term five times (8:27, 34, 36, 38, 39). This term was used both of people who were physically eunuchs and also of officials in general, with no connotations of physical definition. In this text, although the Ethiopian is an official, the fact that Luke uses another specific word for official (Gk. *dynastēs*) in 8:27 implies perhaps that this man was physically a eunuch. The theological point that Luke is probably trying to underline is that eunuchs were excluded from full membership in Israel. Even as a proselyte to Judaism – although keep in mind that the text never states that he was a proselyte – this man would have been restricted from full membership in several aspects (Witherington 1998a: 296; Polhill 1992: 223–224).

That an Ethiopian or Cushite was worshipping the Hebrew god and reading Isaiah is not as startling as it may at first appear. As mentioned in Chapter 5, at around 590 BC the Egyptians placed a Jewish settlement of mercenaries at the isle of Elephantine on the Nile as a frontier garrison to protect Egypt from the Cushites. The Cushites, therefore, would have had first-hand encounters with the Jewish

---

[15] Strabo, *Geog.* 17; cited by Reisner (1923: 73). This account is confirmed by Pliny, *Natural Hist.*, 6.35.4. See also Shinnie (1967: 19–21).

[16] Shinnie (1967: 61) presents the contrasting king and queen lists of Dunham and Hintze. See also Reisner (1922: 173–196).

[17] See the discussions in Witherington (1998a: 295–296) and Barrett (1994: 424).

religion at Elephantine, however corrupt it may have been. Also to be kept in mind is the fact that during the Meroitic period Cush was not an isolated, ignorant kingdom. No doubt the Cushites, famous for their religious piety, had access to the religious writings of all the nations of that day.

The actual story of the Ethiopian's conversion to Christianity is familiar. Philip, led by an angel of the Lord, left Samaria and went to the Gaza road, where he encountered this Ethiopian official in his chariot. After Philip explained 'the good news about Jesus' to him, they drove by some water and the Ethiopian asked, 'What is to prevent me from being baptized?' (8:36, NRSV). Polhill notes the theological significance of the verb in this question (*kōluō*, to hinder, forbid, prohibit), and suggests that Luke records this question for his Gentile Church audience, thus clarifying that no one is to be denied full membership into the Church through baptism. Remember that this official was a eunuch and was prohibited from full membership in Judaism. He was also from a region that lay outside the limits of the Roman Empire. Polhill summarizes by writing, 'The verb indicates that barriers have been removed, hindrances to the spread of the gospel to all people. In this case a double barrier of both physical and racial prejudice had fallen' (1992: 226).

Several commentators note the similarity between this story and one or more Old Testament stories, especially the Elijah narratives (Witherington 1998a: 219; Bruce 1988: 174). However, this story appears to connect intertextually much more with the story of Ebed-Melech in Jeremiah 38. In the Septuagint (the Greek translation of the OT) Ebed-Melech is identified as an Ethiopian, as is the official in Acts 8. Thus both men are Ethiopians from the same African nation on the Nile south of Egypt. Both are identified as 'eunuchs' (Jer. 38: 7; Acts 8: 27, 34, 36, 38, 39). Both of them believe in the prophetic message of God at a time when Jerusalem as a whole rejects it. This similarity in context is an important element. Ebed-Melech appears when all of Jerusalem has turned against God's messenger, the prophet Jeremiah. No one in Jerusalem listens to Jeremiah. In fact open persecution of the prophet breaks out. Jeremiah is arrested and thrown into an abandoned well. Of all the inhabitants in the city, only the 'Ethiopian' Ebed-Melech trusts in Yahweh (39:15–18) and is thus delivered from the destruction of Jerusalem. Note, then, the similarity in Acts 8. Stephen has been executed and a serious persecution has broken out against the church in Jerusalem. Keep in mind also that the rejection of the gospel by the Jews and the ensuing hostilities are a major theme for Luke in the book of Acts. Barrett writes that Luke uses the Ethiopian eunuch to introduce a major theme of his: the contrast between the Jews who reject the gospel and the Gentiles who accept it (1994: 424). During the persecution of the church in Jerusalem (8:1) the Ethiopian eunuch visits Jerusalem and on his way home he hears God's prophetic message from his messenger Philip. Like Ebed-Melech, this eunuch also believes. As mentioned in Chapter 6, the two individuals play similar roles: that of foreigners believing in God's message at a time when Israel not only disbelieves, but is also openly hostile to God's messengers.[18]

Whether or not the Ethiopian eunuch of Acts 8 relates to Ebed-Melech, the conversion of a Black African early in the book of Acts is significant. In Acts 1:8 Jesus tells the disciples that they will be his witnesses in Jerusalem, Judea, Samaria, and to the ends of the earth. The introductory verse in Acts 8:1 mentions the first three: Jerusalem, Judea, and Samaria. Witherington, citing several ancient Greek sources, posits that Ethiopia (Cush) represents 'the ends of the earth', and thus the conversion of the eunuch foreshadows the fulfilment of Jesus' mandate in Acts 1:8 (1998a: 290). Tannehill agrees, writing that this event is symbolic of the gospel's anticipated spread to the ends of the earth (1990: 107).

Pertinent to this study is the observation that this Black African believed, was baptized, and returned home before the conversion of Cornelius in Acts 10, who symbolized the Roman world. The Ethiopian eunuch was also converted several years before Paul received his Macedonian call to take the gospel onto European soil. Barrett (1994: 420) underscores the startling and theologically significant nature of the Ethiopian event by stating, 'His conversion marked an even more radical stage in the rise of the gentile mission than Peter's visit to Caesarea.' Polhill echoes this view, writing 'It is in any event of interest to note the first converted "foreigner" in Acts

---

[18] If Luke is indeed implying a connection to Ebed-Melech, then it is possible that this connection suggests a subtle foreshadowing of the fall of Jerusalem: that is, the inhabitants of Jerusalem in Ebed-Melech's day, in contrast to Ebed-Melech, rejected God's message and messenger and thus were destroyed. In like manner, the inhabitants of Jerusalem in the Ethiopian eunuch's day, in contrast to his faith, reject the gospel and thus will be destroyed. This connection is certainly tentative, but if Luke writes after the fall of Jerusalem and in the context of that fall (Witherington 1998a: 61; Bruce 1988: 12; Polhill 1992: 30–31; and C. Evans 1990: 6), then this connection is quite plausible. Note however, that the date of Luke-Acts is disputed and although most date Acts after the fall of Jerusalem, some argue for an earlier date (Bock 1994: 16–18; Ellis 1974: 55–60; and Marshall 1978: 35).

was an African, and one could say that the mission began there, long before Paul ever took it to European soil' (1992: 228).[19]

Although we do not know what happened to the Ethiopian official and whether or not he evangelized anyone in his home,[20] it is clear that by the fourth century AD Christianity was firmly established in his homeland (Cush/Meroe), an area inhabited by Black Africans. At the same time the gospel had also spread to Abyssinia (modern Ethiopia) and all along the North African coast (see Chapter 7). Thus it is clear that the African experience with the gospel can hardly be relegated to seventeenth, eighteenth, and nineteenth-century encounters with European slave traders and missionaries, as is sometimes alleged. From the very beginning of Christianity there were Black believers.

Furthermore, the conversion of this African was no mere coincidence. An 'angel of the Lord' directs Philip to the meeting place (8:26) and the Holy Spirit prompts him to approach the African man (8:29). Likewise, at the end of the encounter the Spirit takes Philip away. As in this entire unit of Acts, the Spirit plays a major role. So we can conclude that it was clearly part of God's plan for the gospel to reach this Black African in the most initial stages of the Christian evangelistic expansion. A Greek-speaking Semitic Jew led a Black African eunuch to Christ in one of the first evangelistic encounters recorded in Christian history, thus setting the stage for the explosion of the gospel into the world that took place over the next thirty years, and giving a foretaste of the mixed composition of the new people of God that will fill the kingdom of Christ.

---

[19] Some of the commentaries discuss whether this event or Cornelius' conversion in Acts 10 signifies the beginning of the Gentile mission. Haenchen, for instance, insists that Peter's experience with Cornelius is central to the Gentile mission in Acts and that the Ethiopian event must be peripheral (1971: 314). Tannehill (1990: 110), however, relates the two events coherently, writing: 'Its importance does not derive from the fact that Cornelius is the first Gentile converted. Rather, the two scenes of the Ethiopian Eunuch and Cornelius are related to each other according to a pattern established in the Samaritan mission and later repeated in Antioch (cf. 11:19–24): the new step is taken by someone other than the apostles, and the apostles must then catch up with the events that are happening independently of them. In the process the rightness of the new move is verified.'

[20] Although there is no evidence of a first-century church in Ethiopia/Cush, several Church Fathers credit the Ethiopian eunuch as being the first missionary there. Barrett (1994: 422) cites Irenaeus, *Against Heresies* 4.23.2, and Eusebius, *Ecclesiastical History* 2.1.13. Witherington (1998a: 301) cites Irenaeus, *Against Heresies*, 3.12.8–10.

Simeon called *Niger*

In Acts 13:1 Luke states that there were prophets and teachers in the Church at Antioch. He then lists five of them: Barnabas; Simeon who was called *Niger*; Lucius of Cyrene; Manaen, a member of the court of Herod the ruler; and Saul. Luke does not differentiate which of the men were teachers and which were prophets. Barrett (1994: 602) notes that each person on the list could be a prophet, a teacher, or both. Certainly the main point of the list is to reintroduce Barnabas and Saul, who frame the list, and who will become the central characters in the narrative to follow. However, Luke has been concerned throughout his two-volume work to present the people of God as multi-ethnic and diverse. So it is significant that Luke provides additional distinguishing information for the middle three names beyond the mere citation of their names. Larkin observes that the point appears to be that these leaders were culturally and socio-economically diverse (1995: 190). Thus, from the beginning, the leadership in the sending church of Paul reflected a wide diversity of ethnicity and social standing.

The prophet/teacher Simeon has the Latin surname of *Niger*, which means 'black'. While it is difficult to draw conclusions about the name *Niger* with absolute certainty, it is probable that this man was called *Niger* because he was Black and came from Africa. This is the view of most recent commentaries (Bruce 1988: 244–245; Witherington 1998a: 392; Johnson 1992: 220; Stott 1990: 216).[21] Stott (1990: 216) suggests that this is the same man as 'Simon of Cyrene', who carries the cross of Jesus in Luke 23:26; few other scholars, however, are convinced of this. Most note that there is simply no evidence for this connection. Furthermore, Witherington points out that the names are spelled differently (Simeon versus Simon), and that it would be unusual for Luke to use two different spellings within his own work for the same man (1998a: 392).

Although the text does not give us any other information on Simeon called *Niger*, there are several plausible explanations of how a Black African came to be in Antioch. As discussed in Chapter 2

---

[21] Barrett, on the other hand, states that although the name means 'black', nothing can be drawn about the man's origin (1994: 602). Neither Haenchen (1971) nor Conzelmann (1987) even discuss this leader of the Church. They also do not even mention that *Niger* means 'black', perhaps reflecting a lack of interest on their part in this subject.

and in Chapter 7, Black Africans from Cush/Ethiopia/Meroe were present throughout the ancient world during the entire biblical period. In the first century AD, many merchants, diplomats, and soldiers from Meroe travelled throughout the Roman Empire. Many Black Africans served as auxiliaries in the Roman army and, in accordance with the common practice of the day, retired at various locations across the Empire. So it would not be unusual to find a Black African in a cosmopolitan city such as Antioch during the first century.

The mention of a Black African as a leader in the Church in Antioch certainly has theological significance for Luke. Recall that in Acts 8 Luke provides a substantial discussion and description of the conversion of the Ethiopian eunuch, who was also Black. In Acts 8 this Black Ethiopian from Meroe becomes a Christian and returns to his country. In Acts 13, however, a Black African is now cited as one of the central leaders in the new, burgeoning Church in Antioch. So Luke shows clearly that not only is the gospel to go to all peoples, including Black Africans, but also that all people, including Black Africans, are to be integrally included into the Church, the new people of God. Moreover, as Acts 13:1 demonstrates, the multi-ethnic aspect of the early Church extended to leadership and not just membership.

Although Simeon called Niger is not a central character in Acts, his noted presence is important. The footprint in the sand that Robinson Crusoe found was but a small trace of another human, but it was, nonetheless, highly significant, for it established without doubt that someone else was there. The brief mention of Simeon called Niger is similar, for it establishes with high probability that Black Africans were part of the Christian Church and part of the Church leadership by the mid-first century AD. Thus the argument that Christianity only came to Black Africa through slavery and European exploitation is not accurate. Blacks were involved in the Christian Church and in the expansion of this Church from the very beginning.

Conclusions

Numerous important conclusions emerge from this chapter, providing us with significant theology on this issue for the Church today. Matthew underscores the mixed-marriage genealogy of Christ, pointing, of course, to the inclusion of the Gentiles, but also suggesting the acceptability of mixed marriages among the new people of God. In addition, along with Mark and John, Matthew includes the universality of the gospel message in his theology.

Of all the gospel writers, however, it is Luke, in his two-volume work, who focuses on the issue of ethnicity for the new people of God. First of all, Luke connects the theology of salvation for all peoples back to Genesis 10 – 12, showing that the expansion of Christianity to all peoples is a continuity and a fulfilment of these early chapters of Genesis. Thus the inclusion of ethnically diverse people into the people of God was always God's intention. Luke is also careful to note the important role that the Spirit plays in overcoming racial and cultural barriers and boundaries.

For Luke the Samaritans provide the first test case for crossing ethnic lines. He includes numerous passages dealing with the people that the first-century Jews hated. Luke stresses not only that the gospel demands to be proclaimed to all people of all ethnicities, but that the gospel also demands that all old culturally driven worldviews regarding racial prejudice be completely abandoned by the new people of God. Furthermore, the issue is not just *thinking* racial equality, but *doing* racial equality.

In the Ethiopian Eunuch story and through the mention of Simeon called Niger, Luke demonstrates that Black Africans were involved in the gospel expansion from the very beginning. Not only were they recipients of the gospel, as the Ethiopian eunuch illustrates; they were also leaders in the Church that spawned the major Christian expansion across the Mediterranean world, as Simeon called Niger illustrates.

As a pattern of true discipleship, Luke reminds the Church today that the gospel demands that we forsake our inherited culturally driven racial prejudices, and accept all people – especially those different from us – as integral parts of the Church. The demolishing of racial barriers within the Church is a task in which the Spirit leads us. I would also suggest that the inverse is true: flourishing racial prejudice within a church is probably indicative of the Spirit's absence.

The gospel therefore challenges each of us to do some serious Spirit-led soul-searching on this issue. Do our attitudes and actions toward those who are ethnically different reflect the prejudiced culture that we inherited, or do they reflect the new worldview of racial acceptance that the gospel proclaims and the Spirit empowers?

Chapter Nine

Race, Pauline theology, and the Apocalypse

Introduction

In Chapter 8 we explored issues relating to race in the gospels and in Acts, focusing in particular on Luke-Acts. In this chapter we will discuss racial issues as presented in the Letters of Paul and in the Apocalypse. Although texts that have implications for racial equality can be found throughout the New Testament, the strongest and clearest texts are found in Galatians, Colossians, Ephesians, and Revelation. We will therefore focus our study in this chapter on these four books.

An important goal to keep in mind is that we want to develop *theology* on this issue that is practical to the Church today. Thus when studying Paul it is imperative to move beyond a descriptive analysis of what Paul meant in the first century. Certainly it is critical to start with the descriptive analysis, but then we must move to find analogous situations to which the principles in the text speak today. The literature on Paul and Pauline theology is quite extensive, and the production of this literature shows no signs of slowing. Yet the vast majority of scholarly work in this area explores only the first-century situation: that is, the relationship between Paul, the law, Jews, and Gentiles. Thus they are largely descriptive, explaining the theology of Paul for the first century. They ask such questions as: what was Paul's view of the law? To what extent did Paul make a critique on Judaism?[1]

---

[1] Barclay (1996: 203–204) suggests that the new theological sensitivity to Judaism within New Testament scholarship has been a major driving force in recent Pauline studies. He notes that 'all are sensitized to the horrendous potential of anti-Semiticism in Pauline interpretation . . . Sanders' massive rebuttal of caricatures of Jewish "legalism" is evidently a product of the new spirit of understanding between Jews and Christians which characterizes our post-Holocaust, pluralistic world.' Even a casual survey of the recent literature reveals that concern over contemporary Jewish–Christian relations and attitudes form much of the context in which the discussion of Pauline theology takes place. While I acknowledge the importance of a proper understanding of Judaism by the Church today, I nonetheless wonder if this overwhelming

Very few move into analogous situations that apply to the Church today. Likewise, even the majority of New Testament theologies – as well as books on New Testament ethics[2] – tend to dodge the applicational implications of Paul's proclamation of unity in the body of Christ. It is obvious to most of New Testament scholarship that Paul passionately proclaims the unity of Jews and Gentiles in Christ. But so what? What does that first-century unity mean to the Church in the twenty-first century?

On the other hand, a few current commentaries on Galatians, Colossians, and Ephesians – especially the NIV Application Commentary Series, the Bible Speaks Today Series, and the New Interpreter's Bible – have attempted to carry the theology of Paul across the interpretative bridge of time and apply it to current situations in the modern Church. They have bucked the common trend and have moved their discussions beyond the Jews and Gentiles of the first century into application for the Church today. These are the sources that we will find to be the most helpful as we seek to apply the theology of Paul to the Church in our time, especially concerning the issue of race.

Galatians: Neither Jew nor Greek

Paul wrote Galatians as a response to the negative influence of 'Christian-Jewish missionaries' who had arrived in Galatia and were attempting to correct Paul's gospel by adding required elements of Judaism to the Gentile believers (Dunn 1993: 11). At the heart of

---

stress in academia is slightly skewed from the central problems the Church today actually struggles with. Jewish–Christian relationships today are an important theological issue that does need to be dealt with, but I suspect that it plays a larger role in the life of the academy than it does in the life of the Church as a whole. Thus I suspect that New Testament scholarship has tended to follow the major contemporary concerns of its academic guild instead of centring its study within the context of issues (like racial reconciliation) that may be more critical to lay people in the Church. Indeed, Barclay writes: 'Interpreting Paul as a cultural critic and exploring his vision of community in which there is "neither Jew nor Gentile" is an agenda still largely unaddressed by Pauline scholars' (1996: 206).

[2] R. B. Hays (1996: 441) is a significant exception. He writes: 'Thus the New Testament makes a compelling case for the church to live as a community that transcends racial and ethnic differences ... Where the identity of the community is understood in these terms, participation in any form of ethnic division or hatred becomes unthinkable, and ethnic division within the church becomes nothing other than a denial of the truth of the gospel. That is why racism is a heresy. One of the church's most urgent pragmatic tasks in the 1990s is to form communities that seek reconciliation across ethnic and racial lines.'

Paul's defence is a clarification of what 'justification by faith' truly means. For Paul, once this doctrine was clearly understood, then the equal standing of all believers (by faith alone) before God would become clear as well.

Hansen (1994b: 25) points out that by addressing 'justification by faith' Paul addresses both a theological and a social problem. The Church's misunderstanding of justification led to a social stratification within the Church, a stratification that was contrary to the unity in Christ that lay at the heart of the Christian faith. Translating this theology for the Church today, Hansen writes, 'If a church does not defend in practice the equality and unity of all in Christ, it implicitly communicates that justification is not by faith but by race, social status or some other standard' (1994b: 25).[3]

The theme of the unity of all believers in Christ permeates the book of Galatians. R. B. Hays writes:

> Paul holds forth the vision of a community of faith in which all are one in Christ (2:11–21; 3:26–29). This is not merely a matter of an isolated slogan in Gal 3:28; it is a central theme of the letter as a whole. Jews and Gentiles are no longer divided because Christ's death brought us together. Therefore, all manifestations of racial and ethnic divisiveness are betrayals of 'the truth of the gospel.' Galatians is one of the canon's most powerful witnesses against a cultural imperialism that excludes anyone from fellowship on the basis of criteria not rooted in the gospel.
>
> (2000: 195–196).

Galatians 3 and 4 unite to form the crux, or the most decisive section, of Paul's argument in Galatians (Betz 1979: 128–129; Longenecker 1990: 97–98, 184–187). Central to Paul's argument in these chapters is the promise to Abraham.[4] In Galatians 3:8–9 Paul quotes Genesis 12:3, writing:

---

[3] Barclay (1996: 209–210) makes a similar observation. Paul, he notes, was indeed arguing theologically. However, the theology that he was presenting had deep social and cultural implications. In fact, Barclay argues that the reason Paul engaged with Jewish customs such as circumcision, dietary laws, and observance of special days was precisely because these elements defined the social/cultural boundary markers between the Jews and the Gentiles. Paul wanted to 'enable an alternative form of community which could bridge ethnic and cultural divisions' (1996: 209–210).

[4] The word 'promise' occurs in 3:14, 16, 17, 18, 19, 21, 22, 29; 4:23, 28.

The Scripture foresaw that God would justify the Gentiles [*ethnē*] by faith, and announced the gospel in advance to Abraham: 'All nations [*ethnē*] will be blessed through you.' So those who have faith are blessed along with Abraham, the man of faith.

Paul uses Abraham and the promise in a similar fashion in Romans 4. His argument in Galatians differs slightly from that in Romans, but Paul's theology regarding Abraham in Romans fits 'seamlessly' into Galatians 3, indicating that 'we are not dealing with an *ad hoc* excursus but with the biblical unfolding of the heart of Paul's theology' (Ebeling 1985: 165).[5]

One of the main points that Paul is stressing in Galatians 3:8 is that the inclusion and blessing of the nations/Gentiles was not an afterthought, but was 'in the mind and purpose of God when God gave his covenant to Abraham' (Longenecker 1990: 115). The word (*proeuēngelisato*) that Paul uses here means 'to proclaim the gospel (good news) in advance'. It refers not just to speaking and preaching, but also to proclamation with full authority and power (Friedrich 1964: 720, 737). The *gospel* is a highly significant term for Paul and the *proclamation of the gospel* is likewise fraught with theological importance. In Galatians, Paul's rebuke of his opponents focuses on the definition of the gospel, summarized in 1:11–12. The following autobiographical section, 1:13 – 2:11, elaborates on this. Indeed, the term 'gospel' is frequent in the first two chapters (1:6, 7, 8, 9, 11, 16, 23; 2:2, 5, 7, 14), but practically disappears in the later chapters. Hansen argues (convincingly) that Paul's definition of the gospel in Galatians 1 and 2 continues in Galatians 3 in terms of *promise*, implying that for Paul the Old Testament Abrahamic *promise* was practically synonymous with the New Testament *gospel* (1989: 98). Dunn (1993: 165) concurs, writing that this 'underlines the fact that Paul saw the gospel of Jesus Christ simply as the working out of that first promise'.

This equation of gospel and Abrahamic promise is significant for our study of race because we have found the Abrahamic promise running like a scarlet thread throughout the Scriptures, surfacing especially when the biblical authors are stressing the universality of God's plan, his call, or his people.

---

[5] For a thorough discussion of the differing nuances in Paul's theology of Abraham in Romans compared with that in Galatians see Berger (1966: 87–88).

In Galatians 3:14 Paul summarizes the argument of 3:6–13, stating:

> He redeemed us in order that the blessing given to Abraham might come to the Gentiles through Christ Jesus, so that by faith we might receive the promise of the Spirit.

The new aspect of this verse is the identification of the promise made to Abraham with the promise of the Spirit (Betz 1979: 152–153; Mussner 1988: 235; Hansen 1994b: 96). At the beginning of Paul's argument in Galatians 3, he reminded the Gentile audience that they received the Spirit by faith and not by law (3:1–4). Now in 3:14 Paul states that this event was in fact a fulfilment of the ancient promise to Abraham. Robert Hays writes, 'The spirit which the Galatians have received is not just a self-authenticating religious experience; rather, the experience is significant for Paul's argument because he interprets it, in light of scripture, as the fulfillment of God's promise to Abraham' (1983: 212).

The connection here in Galatians between the Spirit and the promise to Abraham is interesting because the importance of the Spirit has surfaced several times in this study. Here in Galatians the indwelling of the Spirit is an authentication of one's acceptance into the people of God. We have also noted the importance of the Spirit in the book of Acts in enabling people like Philip to cross over ethnic barriers and reach people who are different from themselves, both culturally and ethnically. In addition, Ephesians 4:3–6 states that the Spirit is a critical element in producing the reality of unity in the Church among diverse peoples.

Paul draws out the conclusion of Galatians 3 in 3:26–29:

> You are all sons of God through faith in Christ Jesus, for all of you who were baptized into Christ have clothed yourselves with Christ. There is neither Jew nor Greek, slave nor free, male nor female, for you are all one in Christ Jesus. If you belong to Christ, then you are Abraham's seed, and heirs according to the promise.

When Paul states that 'there is neither Jew nor Greek, slave nor free, male nor female,' he strikes at three of the major barrier-forming divisions in human society. George (1994: 284) notes that the three pairs represent 'the fundamental cleavages of human existence: ethnicity, economic capacity, and sexuality.'[6] Dunn states that the 'language implies a radically reshaped social world as viewed from a Christian perspective' (1993: 207).

Dunn also observes that Paul does not obliterate the differences. Greeks are still Greeks. Slaves are still slaves. Females are still female. What are obliterated are the barriers formed by these differences and the relative value and status among the people of God based on these differences (1993: 207–208). Hove notes that Paul's focus here is not so much on total 'equality' as it is on unity. Paul is emphasizing the unity that all people have in Christ. The three couplets, Hove argues, are merisms. They are meant to communicate universality. 'There is no distinction in God's people; no race, nation, class, or gender has favored status with God' (1999: 71–76, 86, 91). Likewise, Witherington writes, 'the body of Christ is an egalitarian body with universal scope where social, sexual, and ethnic differences do not determine entrance or status and are not the basis of unity and cohesion of the group' (1998b: 276). This was radical theology for Paul's day because it flew in the face of all traditional cultural norms. It continues to be radical theology today because it conflicts with many of our cultural norms as well. The question for us today is whether we will follow our culture or follow the teachings of Paul on this issue.

As a word of clarification, the stress in this chapter on the social implications of Paul's statements in Galatians should not be taken as an endorsement or affirmation of the 'New Perspective' on Paul.[7] As mentioned above, Paul's contention with the Judaizers was driven by theological concerns that had social implications. That is, he did not criticize the works of the law simply because they were Jewish identity markers. He criticized the works of the law because they stood in contrast to faith. As mentioned above, the theme of justification has social implications for the people of God (and not vice versa).

---

[6] Witherington states not only that this verse strikes at common notions within Judaism, but also that it may strike at common religious and social notions of the Greco-Roman world as well. Thus Witherington quotes a Greco-Roman expression of gratitude that pre-dates the book of Galatians: 'that I was born a human being and not a beast, next a man and not a woman, thirdly, a Greek and not a barbarian' (*Vit. Phil.* 1.33).

Witherington also cites the beginning of a Jewish prayer: 'Blessed be He that He did not make me a Gentile; blessed be He that He did not make me a slave (or ignorant peasant); blessed be He that He did not make me a woman.' This saying appears in several sources; Witherington suggests that one of them is likely to date ultimately to the first century (1998b: 270–271). See also the discussion by George (1994: 285–286).

[7] For a critique on the so-called 'New Perspective' on Paul, see Schreiner (1993) and Pate (2000: 408–428).

R. B. Hays stresses the issue of identity that emerges from this passage. He notes that there are some groups within the Church that seek to define identity on the basis of race or national origin. He suggests that 'such movements are the contemporary analogies of the "circumcision party" within the early church, against which Paul so passionately fought'. R. B. Hays (2000: 274) then turns the tables on us and challenges his Christian readers:

> Paul's passionate rejection of this kind of ethnic/religious 'identity politics' should lead us to reflect carefully on the ground of our own identity. To what extent is our sense of who we are grounded in the gospel of Christ, and to what extent is it determined by other factors?

For many Christians in North America today, the obvious application of Paul's teaching on Jews and Gentiles in Galatians is in regard to the division of the Church into Black and White (R. B. Hays 2000: 278; McKnight 1995: 161–166). R. B. Hays writes, 'in our time, then, our task is analogous to the one that Paul faced. Most of our churches do not face pressure for Gentiles to be circumcised, but we do confront numerous divisions and hostilities between different racial and ethnic groups' (2000: 278).[8] Yet this text also has relevance for believers all around the world in locations where ethnic tensions and ethnic prejudices from within the culture are pressuring Christians to embrace the same ethnic prejudices within the Church. Justification gives all believers equal status before God and unites them together as one people of God.

Colossians: Neither Barbarian nor Scythian

In Colossians 3:1–4 Paul reminds the readers that not only have they died with Christ; they have been raised with him as well. Bruce writes:

---

[8] McKnight addresses the White Church, noting that many Whites simply do not believe that there is a problem with racism or racial divisions in the church. 'Nothing could be further from the truth,' he declares (1995: 163). Furthermore, McKnight notes that the White Church often has a wide discrepancy between what its members say and what they do. Thus they sing about Jesus loving all the little children of the world (red and yellow, black and white), but their practice reflects the belief that Jesus really only loves the White ones (1995: 166). McKnight (163) concludes that one of the main implications of Galatians is that 'God does not mean for there to be black churches, white churches, and Hispanic churches,' but that God intends for all of us to be united together as the one people of God.

'his [Christ's] interests, in fact have become theirs . . . their mind, their attitude, their ambition, their whole outlook must be characterized by their living bond with the ascended Christ' (1984: 131). Then, in Colossians 3:5–11, Paul transitions to practical application. Now that you are in Christ, Paul argues, live like the new men and women that you are. Paul commands that they 'put off' the old life. In 3:8 he lists some of the 'old life' actions that they must put away: wrath, anger, malice, slander, foul language. Then in 3:11, the concluding verse for this section (3:5–11), Paul writes:

Here there is no Greek or Jew, circumcised or uncircumcised, barbarian, Scythian, slave or free, but Christ is all, and is in all.

The similarity between this verse and Galatians 3:28 is obvious. However, as O'Brien (1982: 193) notes, the teaching of Galatians 3:28 is not only repeated but also expanded. The manner of the expansion is important. In our analysis of Galatians 3:28 we noted that Paul was addressing the specific issue of Jews and Gentiles being united in Christ. We applied that verse to today's racial issue in the Church by way of analogy. Although I feel confident that this was a valid (and obvious) application for that biblical teaching, the process of deriving principles from the text and finding analogous situations in today's setting for application can often be less than certain. However, in Colossians 3:11, it is Paul who broadens the theological lesson from just 'Jew and Gentile' into the wider total social–cultural– racial sphere.

Indeed, remember our discussion in Chapter 7 regarding the concept of racial identity in the first-century Greco-Roman world. The three categories that most urban people used for ethnic identification were Greeks, Jews, and Barbarians. Recall that 'Barbarians' were simply those who did not speak Greek or did not live according to the Greco-Roman cultural norms. So Paul's inclusion of 'Barbarians' in his statement of Christian unity indicates that even in the first-century setting the Church was to abolish the prejudiced racial or cultural boundaries that their culture had adopted and the insider–outsider or us–them mentality that was common.

Paul's addition of the term 'Scythian' underlines this. The term 'Scythian' was applied to tribes living in the Black Sea area. Among the educated urban elite of the Greco-Roman world, who saw all people in terms of either Greek or Barbarian, the term 'Scythian' came to epitomize all the negative elements of the Barbarian

(O'Brien 1982: 193).[9] Indeed, Bruce (1984: 150) states that the term actually 'intensifies' the concept of 'barbarian.'

So Paul is challenging the prevailing, commonly held, racially prejudiced view of the Greco-Roman world, and telling the Christians that such divisive barriers should not (or do not) exist in the new people of God. Within the 'new humanity' of the Church, 'the old barriers that divided people from one another – racial, religious, cultural, and social – are abolished' (O'Brien 1982: 192). Paul underlines that in Christ there can be no barriers between human beings; in fact, distinctions are irrelevant in Christ (Wright 1986: 139–140).

The application of this text to today's racially divided Church is even more obvious than that of Galatians 3:28. Wright applies it in this manner (1986: 139–141). Lincoln (2000: 646) suggests the same application, writing:

> What are the contemporary equivalents of the categories listed in 3:11 that ought not to be obstacles to unity and reconciled relationships within the church? . . . Depending on our particular social location, we will also know how far there is to go in the church's being any different from our society's marginalization of particular ethnic groups, whether they be African Americans, Hispanic Americans, or Native Americans.

The context of Colossians 3:11 is also important. Paul writes this verse as the concluding comment on verses 5 to 10. In that section Paul is describing the things from the old life that the new believers are to 'put off'; that is, discard or abolish. Thus the call for destroying barriers is presented in the context of exhorting believers to leave their old ways of the world and move to the new ways of Christ. Racial prejudices and divisions belong to the old man, the worldly culture that we inherited in the flesh. As we become the new humanity, these attitudes – along with anger, rage, slander, and the rest – must be abandoned. Wright summarizes this clearly: 'Nobody must allow prejudices from their pre-Christian days to distort the new humanity which God has created in and through the New Man' (1986: 141).

---

[9] To illustrate the attitude towards Scythians, O'Brien (1982: 193) cites Josephus: 'they are little better than wild beasts' (*Against Apion* 2.269). He also notes that Scythians were occasionally the objects of fun in Greek comedy because of their uncouth ways of speech. See also the citations by Bruce (1984: 150n).

Ephesians: Unity in the Church

Perhaps no other book stresses unity in the Church as much as Ephesians does. O'Brien states that 'cosmic reconciliation and unity in Christ are the central message of Paul's Letter to the Ephesians' (1999: 58). Likewise, Lincoln (1990: xciv) writes: 'Ephesians is supremely concerned about the unity of the Church'. The centrepiece of Paul's[10] argument concerning unity is found in Ephesians 2:11–22. Having dealt with the salvation of the individual in 2:1–10, Paul now 'unveils a new aspect of the work of Christ: the reconciliation of people not only to God but also to one another. Salvation is more than believers receiving forgiveness of their sins . . . Salvation means union with one another' (Best 1998: 235). Both O'Brien (1999: 182) and Martin (1989: 176–179) stress the combination of *vertical* reconciliation (with God) and *horizontal* reconciliation (with one another, especially those of different groups). Snodgrass underscores the point that one *cannot* have only the vertical dimension. In fact, he argues, Ephesians 2:11–22 merges together Christology, soteriology, ecclesiology, and ethics (1996: 146).

As we noted in our discussion of Galatians and Colossians, believers in Christ are now seen as part of his body and part of a new society, a new race of men and women. Ephesians 2:14–16, containing the essence of Paul's argument in Ephesians 2, proclaims the same theological reality:

> For he himself is our peace, who has made the two one and has destroyed the barrier, the dividing wall of hostility, by abolishing in his flesh the law with its commandments and regulations. His purpose was to create in himself one new man out of the two, thus making peace, and in this one body to reconcile both of them to God through the cross, by which he put to death their hostility.

Thus Paul proclaims not only that the cross produced an organic unity among the various groups in the Church, but that it also eliminated the points of hostility between the groups and reconciled them to one another. The 'disparate segments of the first-century world are

---

[10] The controversy over Pauline authorship of Ephesians is outside the scope of this book. I would suggest that those who take the book seriously as authoritative Scripture, but non-Pauline, will frequently arrive at similar theological conclusions to those who maintain Pauline authorship, especially regarding the issue of race.

now called to a harmonious amity within the fellowship of the Christian church' (Martin 1989: 176).

As we found in Galatians and Colossians, this text has theological application that extends beyond the first-century Jew–Gentile situation. Even Best, for example, notes that 'it clearly has a much wider reference in relation to division between groups of people all of whom are Christian' (1998: 235). In the North American Church setting, this text finds major application in addressing the problem of racial division. Snodgrass (1996: 150–151), Sharp (2002: 261–270), and Stott (1979: 111–112) all apply the theology of this text specifically to the racial issue in the Church, especially since the text deals so clearly with reconciliation between hostile groups. Snodgrass (1996: 150–151) writes:

> Nowhere is this theology more important for modern Christians than in dealing with *racial hostility*. Christians of other races are part of us, and divisions cannot be allowed to continue. The racial barrier is like a festering wound in the body of Christ . . . Sunday is often the most segregated day of the week, for Christians worship along racial lines . . . The perversion of both active and passive racism must be challenged and stopped . . . Racism will have to be treated on two levels, both as a general societal problem and specifically within the body of Christ. Racism in any form is prohibited by the equality of all people before God and by his unrestricted love. But the theology of the body of Christ deals with the issue at another level. The point is not merely that all Christians are *equal*; rather, the point is that all Christians have been *joined*, which has far more significance and impact.

Stott (1979: 111–112) likewise emphasizes the importance of this application for the health of the Church. He writes:

> It is simply impossible, with any shred of Christian integrity, to go on proclaiming that Jesus by his cross has abolished the old divisions and created a single new humanity of love, while at the same time we are contradicting our message by tolerating racial or social or other barriers within our church fellowship . . . We need to get the failures of the church on our conscience, to feel the offence to Christ . . . to weep over the credibility gap between the church's talk and the church's walk, to repent of our readiness to excuse and even condone

our failures, and to determine to do something about it. I wonder if anything is more urgent today, for the honour of Christ and for the spread of the gospel, than that the church should be, and should be seen to be, what by God's purpose and Christ's achievement it already is – a single new humanity, a model of human community, a family of reconciled brothers and sisters who love their Father and love each other, the evident dwelling place of God by his Spirit. Only then will the world believe in Christ as peacemaker. Only then will God receive the glory due his name.

Paul and the nations

Most contemporary scholars, whatever their field, tend to view the Table of Nations in Genesis 10 as an archaic enigma. Throughout the history of modern biblical studies Genesis 10 has not been considered as a crucial text, or one that exerted much influence on the rest of Scripture. J. Scott (1995), on the other hand, has recently challenged this view, arguing that for Paul and his Jewish contemporaries, Genesis 10 provided the basis for their geographical view of the world. Scott (1995: 5–56) demonstrates (convincingly) that Genesis 10 exerted a strong influence on the rest of the Old Testament (particularly eschatological texts such as Ezekiel 38 – 39, Daniel 11, and Isaiah 66:18–20, as well as late history such as 1 Chronicles 1:1 – 2:2) and then continued to influence the geographical view of the world in other Jewish literature (Jubilees, Qumran Genesis Apocryphon, Qumran War Scroll, Sibylline Oracles, Josephus, Ps.-Philo, Rabbinic Judaism).

J. Scott then argues that Paul appropriated the Old Testament and Jewish understanding of the geographical world as understood through the lens of Genesis 10. Thus when Paul uses the term *ethnē* he generally has 'nations' in mind rather than individual Gentiles (1995: 57–134). In addition, Scott notes that Paul's use of the Abrahamic promise reveals an awareness of Genesis and the relationship between the Abrahamic promise and the Table of Nations (1995: 129). Finally, Scott presents the idea that the Table of Nations in Genesis 10 lies behind Paul's missionary strategy, particularly as Paul outlines it in Romans 15 (1995: 136–147).[11]

---

[11] R. Riesner (1998: 245–253) argues that Paul's missionary strategy of Romans 15 is based instead on Isaiah 66:18–21. J. Scott and R. Riesner are not extremely far apart, for, as Scott (1995:146) points out, Isaiah 66:18–21 is based on the Table of Nations tradition.

J. Scott's thesis is fairly radical; it has not yet been embraced by mainstream New Testament scholarship. While his evidence from the extra-biblical Jewish literature is strong, his argument that Paul likewise maintained this view is not as conclusive. However, if Scott *is* correct – and he does amass a large amount of evidence – then Genesis 10 is more influential in the New Testament than has been imagined in the past. Likewise the connection between Genesis 10 and the Abrahamic promise of Genesis 12 – 22 becomes an important theological connection. The 'blessing on all the families' (12:3) and the 'blessing on all the nations' (18:18) refer to all the scattered people of the world as described symbolically in Genesis 10. This thinking and this connection thus would have exerted a strong influence throughout the New Testament everywhere the promise of Abraham or 'the nations' was discussed.

Revelation: From every tribe, language, people, and nation

The book of Revelation is truly 'the climax of prophecy', as the title of Richard Bauckham's (1993) book on Revelation suggests. Part of the picture that John presents in the Apocalypse is the portrayal of the true people of God as multi-ethnic and multicultural, coming from all of the nations of the earth. In fact, Bauckham states that the theme dealing with 'the conversion of the nations' is actually 'at the centre of the prophetic message of Revelation' (1993: 239).

In the preceding section we noted that J. Scott (1995: 5–56) demonstrates how influential Genesis 10 was throughout the Old Testament and throughout the Jewish literature of the Intertestamental Period. If Revelation is stressing the conversion of the nations (as Bauckham suggests), and if John is heavily reliant on Old Testament sources for most of his imagery and terminology (as Beale 1999: 76–99 suggests), then it would not be surprising to see allusions back to Genesis 10 in Revelation.

In general, commentaries on Revelation stress the importance of the books of Daniel and Ezekiel to John's thought and imagery. Occasionally the book of Isaiah is added to those Old Testament sources that John draws from. Rarely is Genesis mentioned, and when it is the reference is not usually connected to any organized use of Genesis by John but only a haphazard reference. However, the major themes of Genesis are certainly part of Revelation. Genesis 1 – 11 presents the initial blessing of God in the garden, followed by

193

the rebellion and sin of mankind, followed by separation and scatter-ing. The Abrahamic narratives (Genesis 12 – 22) then present the divine solution to this problem: redemption through the Abrahamic promise. I would suggest that John includes these themes in Revelation as well.

While certainly Daniel and Ezekiel are prominent influences on John in Revelation, it is perhaps helpful to note the allusions to Genesis as well. For example, the reference in Revelation 20:8 to the 'four corners of the earth – Gog and Magog' connects to Ezekiel 38 – 39, but also to Genesis 10:2, where Magog is first mentioned (J. Scott 1995: 216–217). The last two chapters of Revelation are par-ticularly interlaced with clear allusions to Genesis 1 – 12. The major commentators note a few of these connections, but they do not, in general, explore the implications of these connections. Thus Beale (1999: 1047) notes that the statement in Revelation 21:3 ('I will be your God . . .') is rooted in the Abrahamic promise. Beale also states that the 'river' of 22:1 reaches back to the rivers in Genesis 2:10, although he stresses the connection to Ezekiel as primary. Likewise, Mounce (1998: 379) suggests that the scene in Revelation 22 invites the reader to recall the Garden of Eden.

Yet certainly the 'allusions' or connections run deeper than this. John's terminology in Revelation 21 – 22 is drawn *extensively* from the early chapters of Genesis. Consider the following terminology, occur-ring both in Revelation 21 – 22 and in Genesis: heavens and earth (21:1); sea (21:1); he . . . will be their God (21:3);[12] there will be no more death (21:4);[13] I am . . . the beginning (21:6); the tree of life (22:2); no longer will there be any curse (22:3); there will be no more night . . . they will not need . . . the light of the sun (22:5); and the right to the tree of life (22:14, 19).[14]

The purpose of drawing out these parallels is simply to make the point that John does connect his theology with the book of Genesis, and thus to strengthen the thesis that John picks up the theme of Genesis 10 – 12 as well. As mentioned above, Genesis 10 and 11 show the sin and rebellion of humankind, and the resulting scattering

---

[12] As mentioned above, this phrase first occurs as part of the extended promise/covenant to Abraham (Gen. 17:8).

[13] The entry of death into the world is a major theme of Genesis 2 – 9.

[14] In Gen. 3:21–24 God makes garments of skins for Adam and Eve, and then ban-ishes them from the Garden, specifically keeping them from the tree of life. In Revelation 22:14, God's people wash their robes, and enter the city, so that they may have access to the tree of life.

across the earth and separation from God, while Genesis 12:1–3 then presents the answer, redemption through the Abrahamic promise.

In Genesis 10 the population of the world was defined and described by a fourfold formula: according to families, languages, lands, and nations (10:20, 31, NRSV; 10:5 uses the same terms, but in different order). In the Septuagint, the terms for each are *phylē* (family), *glōssa* (language), *chōra* (territory), and *ethnē* (nation). As mentioned in Chapter 3, the Abrahamic promise connects back to this division. Genesis 12:3 states that in Abraham 'all the families [*phylē*] of the earth will be blessed' (the first element in the Genesis 10 fourfold formula) and Genesis 18:18 states that in Abraham 'all nations [*ethnē*] on earth will be blessed' (the last element in the four-fold formula).

Bauckham suggests that the theme of 'the conversion of the nations' is first introduced in Revelation 1:7 by the phrase 'all the peoples [*phylē*] of the earth', which is 'an allusion to the promise to Abraham in Genesis 12:3' (1993: 318–321). Revelation 1:7 combines elements of Daniel 7 and Zechariah 12 (and perhaps Matthew 24:30), so the text is complex. Bauckham, however, is probably correct in noting the Abrahamic promise connection. Commentators are divided on their understanding of this verse. Bauckham (1993: 318–321) and Beale (1999: 197) view the ones who are mourning in 1:7 as repentant Gentiles. Beale understands them to be the fulfilment of Zechariah 12; Bauckham connects them to the Abrahamic promise as well. On the other hand, several commentators view these 'mourners' as unbelievers,[15] so we are left with a certain degree of uncertainty regarding this text.

In Revelation 5:9, however, there is no doubt that the text is speaking of those who have been redeemed. The verse states:

> And they sang a new song:
> 'You are worthy to take the scroll
>   and to open its seals,
> because you were slain,
>   and with your blood you purchased men for God
> from every tribe [*phylē*] and language [*glōssa*]
>   and people [*laos*] and nation [*ethnē*].'

---

[15] For example, see Mounce (1998: 51) and Aune (1997: 59). Keener (2000: 73) and Beasley-Murray (1978: 58–59) both note uncertainty as to whether the mourning of this people indicates repentance or just fear. Beasley-Murray leans towards repentance; Keener leans towards fear.

Bauckham is correct in noting that this text draws from both Daniel 7 and Genesis 10 (1993: 327). He states that John, with his frequent usage of number symbolism, would not have missed the symbolism of Genesis 10: that seventy nations from three sons clearly is symbolic of all the nations of the earth.

Most commentators, on the other hand, connect the fourfold formula (tribe, language, people, and nation) of Revelation 5:9 back to Daniel 7:14, with no mention of Genesis 10. However, in the MT (Hebrew text) of Daniel 7:14 the order of the terms is different (people, nation, language). Furthermore, and perhaps more importantly, the Septuagint (Greek translation) of Daniel 7:14 only mentions two elements, nations (*ethnē*) and families (*genē*, a completely different term), hardly a good match for Revelation 5:9. In the Septuagint, Genesis 10:20 and 10:31, however, match three of the four terms exactly, and in the exact same order. The one term that has been changed is the term for territory (*chōra*, LXX). If John is relying on the Septuagint in Genesis 10 then he has appropriately dropped the term for physical territory (*chōra*) and substituted another term for people (*laos*), in accordance with the main point he is making with the fourfold formula.

Thus it is probable that John is combining aspects of Genesis into his development of Daniel and Ezekiel. The consummation of God's plan for human history includes a reversal of the judgmental aspects of Genesis for those who trust in Christ. The curse is removed; they return to the garden to enjoy fellowship with God; and the scattered ones (every tribe, language, people, and nation), once separated from God, are now brought together under the reign of the Lamb, finding God's blessing as promised to Abraham.

Regardless of which OT text John draws from in Revelation 5:9, the intended picture is clear. The fourfold formula stresses the ethnic and cultural diversity of the people gathered around the throne of God. Bauckham (1993: 336) writes, 'Thus John indicates that the ultimate purpose of the Lamb's conquest is to win all the nations of the world, designated by the four-fold phrase, for his kingdom.' Swete (1977: 81) states that what are purchased by the death of the Lamb are 'representatives of every nationality, without distinction of race or geographical or political distribution'. Keener (2000: 195) concludes that 'God desired a multicultural body of Christ from the very start'.

The fourfold formula (tribe, language, people, and nation) occurs throughout Revelation, playing an important role in the book. It occurs seven times (5:9, 7:9, 10:11, 11:9, 13:7, 14:6, 17:15), and the sequence order of the four terms is different each time.[16] Bauckham (1993: 326) writes, 'In Revelation, four is the number of the world, seven is the number of completeness. The sevenfold use of this four-fold phrase indicates that reference is being made to all the nations of the world. In the symbolic world of Revelation, there could hardly be a more emphatic indication of universalism'.[17]

The fourfold formula is cited again by John in Revelation 7:9:

> After this I looked and there before me was a great multitude that no one could count, from every nation [*ethnē*], tribe [*phylē*], people [*laos*] and language [*glōssa*], standing before the throne and in front of the Lamb. They were wearing white robes and were holding palm branches in their hands.

These people are identified a few verses later, in Revelation 7:13–14:

> Then one of the elders asked me, 'These in white robes – who are they, and where did they come from?'
> I answered, 'Sir, you know.'
> And he said, 'These are they who have come out of the great tribulation; they have washed their robes and made them white in the blood of the Lamb.'

Revelation 7:9 repeats the same fourfold entities of 5:9, but alters the order, placing the term 'nation' [*ethnē*] first instead of 'tribe' or 'family' [*phylē*]. The probable reason for this is to draw a distinction between the use of 'tribe' [*phylē*] here in 7:9, where the term refers to the 'tribes' of the world, and 'tribe' [*phylē*] in 7:4–8, where the term refers to the 'tribes' of Israel. By placing 'nations' first in 7:9, John indicates that he is clearly not referring to physical, literal Israel in that verse.[18]

---

[16] Bauckham (1993: 327–337) tackles the complex problem of trying to discover the purpose behind the variation in the sequence. While Bauckham is not entirely convincing, he appears to be on the right track, and few, if any, others have attempted to explain the phenomenon.

[17] Bauckham (1993: 336) suggests a connection between this fourfold reference to nations that occurs seven times and the sevenfold reference to the Spirit that occurs four times. 'It is to all the nations of the world that the seven spirits are sent out, in order, through the prophetic witness of the church, to win the nations to the worship of the true God'.

[18] The actual connection between 7:1–8 and 7:9–17 is disputed. Some writers maintain that these are two different groups of people, Jews in 7:1–8 and Gentiles (perhaps including Jews) in 7:9–17. Others argue that there is only one group, and that John is employing symbolism and expansion of vision.

The majority of commentators view this verse as a fulfilment of – or at least an allusion to – the Abrahamic promises of Genesis (Bauckham 1993: 224–225; Beale 1999: 429–430; Beasley-Murray 1978: 144–145; Swete 1977: 99; Mounce 1998: 162; Aune 1998: 466–467). However, as mentioned above, they tend to overlook the connection between the Abrahamic promises and the preceding chapters of Genesis 10 – 11. The fourfold formula clearly recalls the division of the world's peoples in Genesis 10, while the rest of the verse, including the stress on 'every nation' and the mention of the uncountable number of people, connects with the Abrahamic promises: that is, the answer to Genesis 10.

These two references (Rev. 5:9 and 7:9) are the only two of the seven fourfold formula references that refer to the redeemed people of God connected to the promises of Abraham. The other five references simply refer to the nations and peoples of the world, in the same fashion as found in Genesis 10. Generally these other references are negative.

However, it may be significant to recall that in Genesis 10 the scattered, separated people of the world are defined according to family/tribe, language, territory, and nation. In the Abraham narratives that follow, similar to an *inclusio*, the text picks up on the first and then the last element of the formula, stating first that 'all the *families/tribes* of the earth will be blessed in Abraham' (12:3) and then that 'all the *nations* of the earth will be blessed in Abraham' (18:18). In Revelation 5 – 7 the same connected pattern is suggested, with *tribes/families* coming first in 5:9 and *nations* coming first in 7:9.

God's people are seen again in Revelation 21 – 22, at the culmination of the Lamb's victory. In John's vision of the New Jerusalem he states that God will be the light for the city and that 'the nations will walk by its light'. Likewise, in 22:2, the leaves from the 'tree of life' provide healing for 'the nations'. Beale (1999: 1107) connects this reference back to 'the nations' of 5:9, noting that this particular blessing is for all the peoples of the world who have believed in the gospel. Bauckham (1993: 318) writes that the vision of the New Jerusalem 'brings to fulfillment the theme of the conversion of the nations'.

In drawing theological conclusions regarding Revelation and the issue of race, it is important that we do not get bogged down in the controversial details of this complex book. I have suggested that Revelation picks up the themes of Genesis 1 – 12 and brings to a climax and consummation the entire course of biblical history. However, even if my suggested connection is questionable, the clear fact remains that the people of God in the book of Revelation are portrayed as being from all the different peoples of the earth. They are multi-ethnic, multicultural, and multilingual. This conclusion fits seamlessly into the theme that we have been tracing throughout Scripture. God's intention is for his people to be multi-ethnic and multicultural, but yet united in their fellowship and their worship of him.

The vision of God's people that John sees suggests that around the throne of God one will find Nigerians, Cubans, Turks, Chinese, Brazilians, Swedes, Afghans, Mexicans, and a host of other peoples from hundreds of different tribes speaking hundreds of different languages. The ethnic races of the world will be mixed together and brought together in worship of God. We in the Church today need to ask ourselves the question as to why our earthly churches differ so much in composition from the congregations depicted in Revelation. If White churches in North American continue to maintain their ethnic exclusion of other races, particularly Black Americans, are they not clearly moving in a direction that is contrary to the portrayal that John gives us?

It is critical that Christians today visualize the true 'body of Christ' and 'the people of God' correctly. This group is *not* a predominantly White congregation! Christians who gather around the throne of God will rub shoulders with people of all races. How can we justify supporting and/or maintaining a system here in our local churches that works to divide and separate us? The ultimate people of God, as portrayed in Revelation, are multi-ethnic, in fulfilment of God's original intention. We in the Church today need to work toward that ideal as well.

Conclusions

Our study of Paul and of the Apocalypse reveals that the inclusion of all the nations of the earth into the people of God was not an afterthought by God, or a shift in his thinking, but rather was part of his eternal plan from the beginning. Thus the mission of Paul to the nations was the fulfilment of the Abrahamic promise as a redemptive solution to Genesis 3 – 11.

Furthermore, our study underlines that the individuals from all tribes, languages, peoples, and nations who believe are all justified in the same manner and are thus equal co-heirs of the kingdom and equal members of the body of Christ. However disparate we may be culturally, we are nonetheless joined together in organic unity by the Spirit. The cross of Christ demolished all barriers between people and God, reconciling people who believe, both to God and to each other. This horizontal reconciliation applies in particular to those Christians who differ from each other and between whom there exists traditional culture-driven hostility. Finally, the ultimate climactic view of Christ's triumphant kingdom portrays people of all races gathered together around the throne worshipping the Lamb together.

The New Testament teaching of Paul and Revelation has direct application to the racial division in the Church today. All believers, regardless of ethnicity, are equally a part of the body of Christ, and it is important for all believers to think in this way and to come to grips with the theological implications of this reality. Furthermore, God desires unity and reconciliation between his children. This desire of our Master is not an obscure doctrine hinted at on the fringes of Scripture, but rather a central theme that is stressed continuously throughout the New Testament. Individual prejudices and cultural–societal structures that divide Christians into groups based on skin colour or other ethnic distinctions are contrary to the teaching of the New Testament. Indeed, Sharp (2002: 251–258) simply calls it 'sin'. The New Testament teaches equality of all believers in regard to status and value, but it also teaches that the believer's *identity* should be based on Christ and not on culturally driven differentiations such as skin colour. Finally, the New Testament teaches reconciliation between Blacks and Whites and an end to the hostility between racial groups in the Church. In place of hostility, the Church is to celebrate unity in Christ through fellowship and worship.

Chapter Ten

Conclusions and applications

This chapter attempts to synthesize the theological conclusions from this study and to suggest appropriate applications for the Church today.

Synthesizing conclusions

The main synthesizing conclusions from this study can be summarized by the following seven statements.

The biblical world was multi-ethnic, and Blacks were involved in God's unfolding plan of redemption from the beginning

Both the Old Testament world and the New Testament world were multi-ethnic, and the ethnicity of the characters that lived out the biblical story was not – and did not resemble – that of White Anglo-Americans. Most of the characters in the Bible were Semitic, but the story constantly includes individuals and groups from a wide spectrum of ethnicity. Furthermore, the book of Genesis makes it clear that all peoples and nations have the same origin and are united by a common humanity.

Within the context of the Black–White racial problem in the United States, it is significant to note that Black Africans from Cush/Ethiopia play an important role throughout Scripture. Black Cushites were active players in the geopolitics and economics of the Ancient Near East. The Cushites controlled Egypt for a short while, and allied themselves with Judah against the Assyrians. The Black African Ebed-Melech played a crucial role in Judah's theological history, saving the prophet Jeremiah and symbolizing the inclusion of future Gentiles who come to God by faith. Likewise, the first non-Jewish believer in the New Testament was a Black African, and a leader of the early Church in Antioch was likewise probably Black. Thus it is clear that the argument, put forward by some contemporary opponents of the gospel, that the Judeo-Christian tradition only came to Africa through European-instituted slavery in the seventeenth, eighteenth, and nineteenth centuries is completely erroneous. Black Africans appear early in Genesis and continue to appear throughout the biblical story. Without a doubt, the picture in Revelation that describes God's people as deriving from every tribe, language, people, and nation includes millions of Black believers. Indeed, the incredible explosive expansion of Christianity across Africa that has occurred in the post-colonial period, combined with the millions of Black believers in the USA and in other non-African countries, provides a suggestive glimpse of just how much 'colour' there will be around the throne of God at the climax of history.

Also, it is important that White Christians guard against projecting a 'White' world back into the Bible. There is a tendency in many White Churches to assume that the Bible basically tells a story about White people and that the other races are simply added on as part of our gracious missionary enterprise. Pastors and teachers (and film directors) across North America need to correct this misconception and inform their people that neither Abraham, David, nor Paul had blond hair and blue eyes.

All people are created in the image of God, and therefore all races and ethnic groups have the same status and unique value that results from the image of God

One of the tragic legacies of Western civilization is the idea of White racial superiority. Consciously and subconsciously, both by individuals and by social structures, both in obvious and in subtle forms, this thinking continues in the West, not only in the secular world but in the Church as well. It is critical that the Church proclaim loudly and clearly that such thinking is explicitly contradicted by Scripture, which teaches that all peoples are equal. This truth is applicable for Christians around the world in situations where one ethnic group believes that it is superior to another.

Genesis 10 and the Abrahamic promise combine to form a theme that runs throughout Scripture, constantly pointing to the global and multi-ethnic elements inherent in the overarching plan of God

The book of Genesis is a critical starting point for biblical theology. In this study we have discovered that the main themes emerging out of Genesis continue to surface across the pages of Scripture, highlighting some basic biblical premises about racial issues. Genesis 3 – 11 portrays the sin and rebellion of the human race against God. This sin resulted in the scattering and separation described in Genesis 10, where people were scattered and separated both from God and from each other. They were scattered according to tribe/family, language, territory, and nation. However, in the Abraham narratives of Genesis 12 – 22 God promised that through Abraham all the tribes/families of the world and all the nations of the world would find blessing. This theme blossoms and flowers in the prophetic literature and then finds ultimate fulfilment in Christ. Paul connects the gift of the Spirit with the blessing of Abraham. He also underlines the fact that, as indicated by the Abrahamic promise, the inclusion of all peoples of all ethnic groups into the people of God was part of God's overarching plan from the beginning. The unity of all the peoples of the earth through faith in Christ is not an afterthought, but has always been part of the main plan and purpose of Christ.

Racial intermarriage is sanctioned by Scripture

I suspect that this conclusion will be the one that is the most difficult for some White readers to come to grips with (although it should be noted that in some regions of the United States interracial marriages are becoming more and more accepted). Nonetheless, it is critical that we proclaim clearly and without any ambiguity that the Scriptures approve of interracial marriages between believers. Moses married a Black woman and God gave his total approval. The text is not ambiguous. Paul's proclamation of organic unity and total equality in the Church likewise destroys the barrier of racial intermarriage prohibition. This truth is important for the Church, because the ban by Whites on interracial marriages – especially those between Blacks and Whites – lies at the very heart of racism. To forbid one's children to marry people of another race, based not on their relationship with Christ, but solely on their skin colour, implies the heresy of racial superiority. When White Christians forbid their children to marry Black believers they make a mockery of Paul's theology of unity in Christ. Regardless of what White Christians may say about racial equality, the interracial marriage prohibition proclaims *by action* that their primary identity is not their relationship to Christ, but rather their relationship with their White culture: that is, the world. Likewise, to speak of racial reconciliation while continuing to prohibit racial intermarriage is extremely hypocritical. This issue lies at the crux of racial division.

White Christians in the United States will make little progress toward racial reconciliation if they continue to deny this biblical truth. Scripture sanctions interracial marriages between believers. This truth likewise has worldwide application, and should be embraced by Christians everywhere, especially in those regions of the world where ethnic tensions within the Church exist. The Church today needs to proclaim this loudly and clearly, both in its teaching and in its actions.

The gospel demands that we carry compassion and the message of Christ across ethnic lines

The ethnic-based tension between Jews and Samaritans in the first century is analogous to the ethnic-based tensions between Blacks and Whites in North America today. Thus the theology presented in Luke-Acts by its numerous episodes concerning Samaritans is apropos for us. The story of the Good Samaritan and the story of Philip's missionary action in Samaria combine to stress the need for believers to cross all major ethnic barriers with the acted-out message of 'love your neighbour' and the truth of the gospel. Furthermore, the Good Samaritan story emphasizes the need truly to act out the theology of 'love your neighbour' and not just to talk about it theoretically. Certainly there has been much progress in recent years in White congregations regarding their thinking or their theology regarding race; for many, however, it is the accompanying action that lags behind. Maybe our heart is touched, but like the priest in the parable, all too often we cross over to the other side of the road and try not to get involved. The gospel challenges us to do otherwise.

The New Testament demands active unity in the Church, a unity that explicitly joins differing ethnic groups together because of their common identity in Christ

The New Testament proclaims that in Christ believers form a new humanity. The old barrier of hostility and division between ethnic groups has been demolished by the Cross, and now all peoples of all groups are to be one in Christ. Our primary identity as humans is to be based on our union with Christ, and no longer based on traditional human sociological connections. Christians of other races are not just equal to us; they are joined to us. We are both part of the same body, united by the presence of the Holy Spirit that dwells within us both. We are also fellow heirs, brothers and sisters of the same family. While there may be practical and sociological reasons for creating and maintaining Churches that are ethnic specific (Black Churches, Hispanic Churches, White Churches, Korean Churches, etc.), this division into ethnically based worshipping communities is contrary to the imperatives of Paul. Furthermore, the exclusion from full participation in a worshipping community of someone of another race reflects such a disobedient attitude that it can only be classified as sin. The continued maintenance of racially divided Churches in the United States points only to the fact that a large majority of Christians in that country are probably identifying themselves more with their racial background, with all its cultural baggage, than they do with Christ and the gospel.

The picture of God's people at the climax of history portrays a multi-ethnic congregation from every tribe, language, people, and nation, all gathered together in worship around God's throne

The visions of John in the book of Revelation give us a glimpse of the people of God at the consummation of history. The image he portrays is based on the fourfold formula of Genesis 10 (every tribe, language, people, and nation). The fourfold formula stresses the ethnic diversity of the people of God who worship him around the throne. This multi-ethnic image, where people of all races and ethnic groups are shoulder to shoulder worshipping God, portrays exactly the same unity of believers that Paul calls for in his epistles. It is a picture of the reality that will exist in the climactic kingdom of Christ, and, as such, provides a model for us to strive toward. John sees the kingdom of Christ as a multi-ethnic congregation. Blacks, Whites, and all other races will be mixed together, united through the redemption of the Lamb and in their worship of God. For the Church to oppose such a reality in the life of the Christian community here and now is to oppose the direction toward which the Kingdom is designed to move. God's plan is clear: he wants his people to be united across ethnic lines. When Christians oppose this, either actively through prejudice, or passively, by quietly supporting the status quo, they are truly in opposition to God's plan for his Church. How much better it would be for the Church if we would but grasp the image of the people of God in Revelation and realize that the Church is made up of people from every nationality and race in the world. When Christians think of the concept 'the people of God' they need to visualize what John described: people of every tribe and every language and every people and every nation, all gathered around the throne, worshipping the Lamb together.

Final thoughts

Our culture is strong and powerful. A 'critical mass' of active White Church membership that can overcome the pull of tradition and culture in the United States and make real progress in this area has not yet emerged. Yet the gospel continues to call us to put off the 'old man' and to be transformed in the renewing of our minds; to be reformed into a new humanity where racial equality is actualized. Earlier generations have failed miserably to obey the imperatives of Scripture that have been discussed above, denying both the theology and the practice of racial equality. My own generation, the Baby Boomers, has had the truth presented to it more clearly and more powerfully than the earlier generations did. Most of us *know* the theological truth of racial equality, yet we waver and remain tentative. We know the theological truth about race, but we still have strong ties to the old ways of our culture and we are reluctant to venture out in trust into new sociological areas, where all races are equal in practice and not just in theory.

My hope lies in the next generation of Christians, aptly called 'Generation X'. If parents, teachers, and pastors can proclaim this truth to the rising generation in a clear manner, I am optimistic that *they* can sever the ties with the 'old man' from our culture and make some real progress toward the vision of Christian unity that the Scriptures present. This generation is much more open to change, especially in regard to ethnic issues. It also has the zeal and the passion that will be required to effect any change in this area. What it needs is leadership: pastors, teachers, parents, and peers; people who will teach, challenge, rebuke, encourage, dream, and weep until the Church actualizes the unity that lies on the heart of our Lord.

Ultimately, of course, the Kingdom of Christ marches onward, with or without us. The White Church in the West does not define Christianity; indeed, the centre of Christianity is rapidly shifting away from the Western world. In this book I have made both an exegetical and an emotional appeal to the White Christians in the United States to embrace a theology and a practice of racial equality and unity that is based on Scripture. Yet whether *we* respond with obedience or with disobedience, Christ's Kingdom will move forward toward his goal and toward the vision that John shows us in the Apocalypse, where those who gather around the Lamb to sing a new song will be from every tribe and language and people and nation.

Bibliography

Achtemeier, E. (1986), *Nahum–Malachi*, Interpretation, Atlanta: John Knox.

Adamo, D. T. (1989), 'The African Wife of Moses: An Examination of Numbers 12:1–9', *ATJ* 18:230–237.

——— (1998), *Africa and Africans in the Old Testament*, San Francisco: Christian Universities Press.

Adams, W. Y. (1970), *Nubia: Corridor to Africa*, Princeton: Princeton University.

Ahlström, G. W. (1986), *Who Were the Israelites?*, Winona Lake, Ind.: Eisenbrauns.

Albenda, P. (1982), 'Observations on Egyptians in Assyrian Art', *BES* 4:5–32.

Aldred, C. (1951), *New Kingdom Art in Ancient Egypt During the Eighteenth Dynasty: 1590–1315 BC*, London: Alec Tiranti.

Al-Nubi, S. I. (1997), 'Soldiers', in S. Donadoni (ed.), *The Egyptians*, Chicago: University of Chicago.

Andersen, F. I., and D. N. Freedman (1989), *Amos*, AB, New York: Doubleday.

Anderson, A. A. (1989), *2 Samuel*, WBC, Dallas: Word.

Anderson, J. G. C. (1971), 'The Eastern Frontier under Augustus', *CAH* 10:242–283.

Anderson, R. T. (1992), 'Samaritans', *ABD* V:940–947.

Anderson, R. W. (1995), 'Zephaniah ben Cushi and Cush of Benjamin: Traces of Cushite Presence in Syria-Palestine', in S. W. Holloway and L. K. Handy (eds.), *The Pitcher is Broken: Memorial Essays for Gösta W. Ahlström*, JSOTSS 190, Sheffield: Sheffield.

Aune, D. E. (1997), *Revelation 1 – 5*, WBC, Dallas: Word.

——— (1998), *Revelation 6 – 16*, WBC, Nashville: Thomas Nelson.

Baines, J. (1996), 'Contextualizing Egyptian Representations of Society and Ethnicity', in J. S. Cooper and G. M. Schwartz (eds.), *The Study of the Ancient Near East in the Twenty-first Century*, Winona Lake, Ind.: Eisenbrauns.

Baker, D. W. (1992), 'Cushan', *ABD* 1:1220.

Barclay, J. M. G. (1996), 'Neither Jew nor Greek: Multiculturalism and the New Perspective on Paul', in M. G. Brett (ed.), *Ethnicity and the Bible*, Leiden: E. J. Brill.

Barker, K. L., and W. Bailey (1998), *Micah, Nahum, Habakkuk, Zephaniah*, NAC, Nashville: Broadman & Holman.

Barrett, C. K. (1994), *The Acts of the Apostles*, ICC, Edinburgh: T. & T. Clark.

Bauckham, R. (1993), *The Climax of Prophecy: Studies in the Book of Revelation*, Edinburgh: T. & T. Clark.

Beale, G. K. (1999), *The Book of Revelation*, NIGTC, Grand Rapids and Carlisle: Eerdmans and Paternoster.

Beasley-Murray, G. R. (1978), *Revelation*, NCB, Grand Rapids and London: Eerdmans and Marshall, Morgan & Scott.

——— (1987), *John*, WBC, Waco: Word.

Beegle, D. M. (1992), 'Moses', *ABD* 4:917.

Bennett, R. A. (1971), 'Africa and the Biblical Period', *HTR* 64:483–500.

——— (1996), 'Zephaniah', in L. E. Keck (ed.), *The New Interpreter's Bible*, Vol. 7, Nashville: Abingdon.

Bentzen, A. (1952), *Introduction to the Old Testament*, Vol. 1, Copenhagen: G. E. C. Gad.

Bergen, R. D. (1996), '*1, 2 Samuel*', NAC, Nashville: Broadman.

Berger, K. (1966), 'Abraham in den paulinischen Hauptbriefen', *MTZ* 17:47–89.

Berkouwer, G. C. (1962), *Man: The Image of God*, Grand Rapids: Eerdmans.

Berlin, A. (1994), *Zephaniah*, AB, New York: Doubleday.

——— (1995), 'Zephaniah's Oracle against the Nations', in A. B. Beck et al. (eds.), *Fortunate the Eyes that See*, Grand Rapids: Eerdmans.

Berridge, J. M. (1992), 'Jehudi', *ABD* 3:674.

Best, E. (1998), *A Critical and Exegetical Commentary on Ephesians*, ICC, Edinburgh: T. & T. Clark.

Betz, H. D. (1979), *Galatians*, Hermeneia, Philadelphia: Fortress.

Bickerman, E. J. (1988), *The Jews in the Greek Age*, Cambridge, Mass.: Harvard University.

Birch, B. C., et al. (1999), *A Theological Introduction to the Old Testament*, Nashville: Abingdon.

Blenkinsopp, J. (1988), 'Second Isaiah – Prophet of Universalism', *JSOT* 41:83–103.

—— (1996), *A History of Prophecy in Israel*, Louisville: Westminster John Knox.

Block, D. I. (1997), *The Book of Ezekiel: Chapters 1–24*, NICOT, Grand Rapids: Eerdmans.

Blomberg, C. L. (1992), *Matthew*, NAC, Nashville: Broadman.

Bock, D. L. (1994), *Luke, Volume 1: 1:1 – 9:50*, BECNT, Grand Rapids: Baker.

——(1996), *Luke, Volume 2: 9:51 – 24:53*, BECNT, Grand Rapids: Baker.

Booij, T. (1987), 'Some Observations on Psalm LXXXVII', *VT* 37.01:16–25.

Borgen, P. (1992), 'Philo and the Jews in Alexandria', in P. Bilde et al. (eds.), *Ethnicity in Hellenistic Egypt*, Aarhus, Denmark: Aarhus University.

Borghouts, J. F. (2000), 'Witchcraft, Magic, and Divination in Ancient Egypt', in J. M. Sasson (ed.), *Civilizations of the Ancient Near East*, Peabody, Mass.: Hendrickson, 1775–1785.

Bowman, A. K. (1986), *Egypt after the Pharaohs 332 BC–AD 642: From Alexander to the Arab Conquest*, Berkeley: University of California.

Bradley, L. R. (1971), 'The Curse of Canaan and the American Negro', *CTM* 42:100–110.

Breasted, J. H. (1906), *Ancient Records of Egypt: Historical Documents*, Chicago: University of Chicago.

Brenner, A. (1982), *Color Terms in the Old Testament*, JSOTSS 21, Sheffield: Sheffield.

Bresciani, E. (1997), 'Foreigners', in S. Donadoni (ed.), *The Egyptians*, Chicago: University of Chicago.

Brett, M. (1981), 'Classical North Africa', in R. Oliver and M. Crowder (eds.), *The Cambridge Encyclopedia of Africa*, Cambridge: Cambridge University.

Brett, M., and E. Fentress (1996), *The Berbers*, Oxford, UK and Cambridge, Mass.: Blackwell.

Brett, M. G. (1996), 'Interpreting Ethnicity: Method, Hermeneutics, Ethics', in M. G. Brett (ed.), *Ethnicity and the Bible*, Leiden: E. J. Brill.

Bright, J. (1981), *A History of Israel*, Philadelphia: Westminster.

Brown, R. E. (1993), *The Birth of the Messiah: A Commentary on the Infancy Narratives in the Gospels of Matthew and Luke*, New York: Doubleday.

Bruce, F. F. (1984), *The Epistles to the Colossians, to Philemon, and to the Ephesians*, NICOT, Grand Rapids: Eerdmans.

—— (1988), *The Book of Acts*, NICNT, Grand Rapids: Eerdmans.

—— (1992a), 'Laodicea', *ABD* IV:229–231.

—— (1992b), 'Phrygia', *ABD* V:365–368.

Brueggemann, W. (1982), *Genesis*, Interpretation, Atlanta: John Knox.

—— (1990), *First and Second Samuel*, Interpretation, Louisville: John Knox.

—— (1991), *To Build, to Plant: Jeremiah 26 – 52*, ITC, Grand Rapids and Edinburgh: Eerdmans and Handsel.

—— (1994), 'The Book of Exodus', in L. E. Keck (ed.), *The New Interpreter's Bible*, Vol. 1, Nashville: Abingdon.

—— (1997), *Theology of the Old Testament*, Minneapolis: Fortress.

—— (1998), '"Exodus" in the Plural (Amos 9:7)', in W. Brueggemann and G. W. Stroup (eds.), *Many Voices, One God: Being Faithful in a Pluralistic World*, Louisville: Westminster John Knox.

Bryan, B. M. (1991), *The Reign of Thutmose IV*, Baltimore: Johns Hopkins.

Bryce, T. (1998), *The Kingdom of the Hittites*, Oxford: Oxford University.

Budd, P. J. (1984), *Numbers*, WBC, Waco: Word.

Budge, E. A. W. (1902), *A History of Egypt*, Vol. II, *Egypt under the Great Pyramid Builders*, London: Kegan Paul, Trench, Trübner.

—— (1968), *A History of Egypt*, Vol. III, *Egypt under the Amenemhats and Hyksos*, Oosterhout, Netherlands: Anthropological Publications.

Bugner, L. (ed.) (1976), *The Image of the Black in Western Art*, Vol. 1, *From the Pharaohs to the Fall of the Roman Empire*, New York: William Morrow.

Bullard, R. G. (2001), 'The Berbers of the Maghreb and Ancient Carthage', in E. Yamauchi (ed.), *Africa and Africans in Antiquity*, East Lansing, Mich.: Michigan State University.

Burrow, D. (1808), *Involuntary, Unmerited, Perpetual, Absolute, Hereditary Slavery, Examined: on the Principles of Nature, Reason, Justice, Policy, and Scripture*, Lexington, Ky.: n.p.

Burstein, S. M. (1995), *Graeco-Africana: Studies in the History of Greek Relations with Egypt and Nubia*, New Rochelle, NY: A. D. Caratzas.

—— (1997), *Ancient African Civilizations: Kush and Axum*, Princeton, NJ: Markus Wiener.

—— (2001), 'The Kingdom of Meroe', in E. Yamauchi (ed.), *Africa and Africans in Antiquity*, East Lansing, Mich.: Michigan State University.

Butler, T. (1983), *Joshua*, WBC, Waco: Word.

Caird, G. B. (1953), 'II Samuel', in G. A. Buttrick (ed.), *The Interpreter's Bible*, Nashville: Abingdon.

Carmichael, J. (1967), *The Shaping of the Arabs: A Study in Ethnic Identity*, New York: Macmillan.

Carroll R., M. D. (1992), *Contexts for Amos: Prophetic Poetics in Latin American Perspectives*, Sheffield: Sheffield.

—— (2000), 'Blessing the Nations: Toward a Biblical Theology of Mission from Genesis', *BBR* 10.1.

—— (ed.) (2000), *Rethinking Contexts, Rereading Texts: Contributions from the Social Sciences to Biblical Interpretation*, Sheffield: Sheffield.

Carroll, R. P. (1986), *The Book of Jeremiah*, OTL, Philadelphia: Westminster.

Carson, D. A. (1991), *The Gospel According to John*, Leicester and Grand Rapids: Inter-Varsity and Eerdmans.

—— (2002), *Love in Hard Places*, Wheaton: Crossway.

Carter, C. E., and C. L. Meyers (1996), *Community, Identity, and Ideology: Social Science Approaches to the Hebrew Bible*, Winona Lake, Ind.: Eisenbrauns.

Casson, L. (1959), *The Ancient Mariners: Seafarers and Sea Fighters of the Mediterranean in Ancient Times*, New York: Macmillan.

Cassuto, U. (1978), *From Adam to Noah*, Jerusalem: Magnes Press.

Černý, J. (1954), 'Consanguineous Marriages in Pharaonic Egypt', *JEA* 40:23–29.

Chalcraft, D. J. (ed.) (1997), *Social-Scientific Old Testament Criticism*, Sheffield: Sheffield.

Childs, B. S. (1974), *The Book of Exodus*, OTL, Philadelphia: Westminster.

—— (1985), *Old Testament Theology in a Canonical Context*, Philadelphia: Fortress.

—— (2001), *Isaiah*, OTL, Philadelphia: Westminster John Knox.

Christensen, D. L. (1984), 'Zephaniah 2:4–15: A Theological Basis for Josiah's Program of Political Expansion', *CBQ* 46:669–682.

Clements, R. E. (1988), *Jeremiah*, Interpretation, Atlanta: John Knox.

—— (ed.) (1989), *The World of Ancient Israel: Sociological, Anthropological, and Political Perspectives*, Cambridge: Cambridge University.

———— (1996), 'A Light to the Nations: A Central Theme in the Book of Isaiah', in J. W. Watts and P. R. House (eds.), *Forming Prophetic Literature*, JSOTSS 235, Sheffield: Sheffield.

Cogan, M. (2000), *I Kings*, AB, Garden City, NJ: Doubleday.

Cogan, M., and H. Tadmor (1988), *II Kings*, AB, Garden City, NJ: Doubleday.

Cohen, S. J. D. (1983), 'From the Bible to the Talmud: The Prohibition of Intermarriage', *HAR* 7:23–39.

———— (1987), *From the Maccabees to the Mishnah*, in W. A. Meeks (ed.), Library of Early Christianity, Vol. 7, Philadelphia: Westminster.

Conroy, C. (1978), *Absalom! Absalom! Narrative and Language in 2 Sam 13–20*, AnBib 81, Rome: Pontifical Biblical Institute.

Conzelmann, H. (1987), *Acts of the Apostles*, Hermeneia, Philadelphia: Fortress.

Copher, C. P. (1989), 'Three Thousand Years of Biblical Interpretation with Reference to Black Peoples', in G. Wilmore (ed.), *African American Religious Studies*, Durham, NC: Duke University.

Craffert, P. F. (1996), 'On New Testament Interpretation and Ethnocentrism', in M. G. Brett (ed.), *Ethnicity and the Bible*, Leiden: E. J. Brill.

Cragie, P. (1976), *The Book of Deuteronomy*, NICOT, Grand Rapids: Eerdmans.

Cross, F. M. (1973), *Canaanite Myth and Hebrew Epic*, Harvard: Harvard University.

Crown, A. D. (ed.) (1989), *The Samaritans*, Tübingen: J. C. B. Mohr.

Crüsemann, F. (1996), 'Human Solidarity and Ethnic Identity', in M. G. Brett, *Ethnicity and the Bible*, Leiden: E. J. Brill.

Culpepper, R. A. (1995), 'The Gospel of Luke', in L. E. Keck (ed.), *The New Interpreter's Bible*, Nashville: Abingdon.

Cunliffe, B. (1997), *The Ancient Celts*, Oxford: Oxford University.

Currid, J. D. (1997), *Ancient Egypt and the Old Testament*, Grand Rapids: Baker.

Dalley, S. (1985), 'Foreign Chariotry and Cavalry in the Armies of Tiglath-Pileser III and Sargon II', *Iraq* 47:31–38.

Dalley, S., and J. N. Postgate (1984), *The Tablets from Fort Shalmeneser*, Cuneiform Texts from Nimrud, Vol. III, London: British School of Archaeology in Iraq.

Davidson, R. (1998), *The Vitality of Worship: A Commentary on the Book of Psalms*, Grand Rapids and Edinburgh: Eerdmans and Handsel.

Davies, G. F. (1999), *Ezra & Nehemiah*, Berit Olam, Collegeville, Minn.: Liturgical Press.

Davies, P. R. (1992), *In Search of Ancient Israel*, JSOT 148, Sheffield: Sheffield.

Davies, W. D., and D. C. Allison (1988), *The Gospel According to Saint Matthew*, Vol. 1, ICC, Edinburgh: T. & T. Clark.

Deddo, G. (1997), 'Persons in Racial Reconciliation: The Contributions of a Trinitarian Theological Anthropology', in D. L. Okholm (ed.), *The Gospel in Black and White*, Downers Grove, Ill.: InterVarsity.

Delcor, M. (1978), 'Les Kéréthim et les Crétois', *VT* 28:409–422.

Deutsch, R., and M. Heltzer (1994), *Forty New Ancient West Semitic Inscriptions*, Tel Aviv: Archaeological Center Publications.

Dillard, R. B. (1987), *2 Chronicles*, WBC, Waco: Word.

Dorrien, G. (1998), *The Remaking of Evangelical Theology*, Louisville: Westminster John Knox.

Dothan, T. (1992), 'Philistines', *ABD* V:326–333.

——— (2000), 'The "Sea Peoples" and the Philistines of Ancient Palestine', in J. M. Sasson (ed.), *Civilizations of the Ancient Near East*, Peabody, Mass.: Hendrickson, 1267–1279.

Dunham, D. (1946), 'Notes on the History of Kush 850 BC–AD 350', *AJA* 50:380–390.

Dunn, J. D. G. (1993), *The Epistle to the Galatians*, BkNTC, Peabody, Mass.: Hendrickson.

——— (1998), *The Theology of Paul the Apostle*, Grand Rapids: Eerdmans.

Durham, J. I. (1987), *Exodus*, WBC, Waco: Word.

Duvall, J. S., and J. D. Hays (2001), *Grasping God's Word: A Hands-on Approach to Reading, Interpreting, and Applying the Bible*, Grand Rapids: Zondervan.

Ebeling, G. (1985), *The Truth of the Gospel: An Exposition of Galatians*, Philadelphia: Fortress.

Eggebrecht, A. (1984), *Das Alte Agypten: 3000 Jahre Geschichte und Kultur des Pharaonenreiches*, Munich: C. Bertelsmann.

Ellis, E. E. (1974), *The Gospel of Luke*, NCB, Grand Rapids and London: Eerdmans and Morgan & Scott.

——— (1991), '"The End of the Earth" (Acts 1:8)', *BBR* 1:123–132.

Emerson, M. O., and C. Smith (2000), *Divided by Faith: Evangelical Religion and the Problem of Race in America*, Oxford: Oxford University.

Enns, P. (2000), *Exodus*, NIVAC, Grand Rapids: Zondervan.

213

Epstein, L. (1942), *Marriage Laws in the Bible and Talmud*, Cambridge, Mass.: Harvard.

Erickson, M. J. (1985), *Christian Theology*, Grand Rapids: Baker.

Evans, A. T. (1995), *Let's Get to Know Each Other: What White and Black Christians Need to Know About Each Other*, Nashville: Thomas Nelson.

Evans, C. A. (1990), *Luke*, NIBC, Peabody, Mass.: Hendrickson.

Evans, M. J. (2000), *1 and 2 Samuel*, NIBC, Peabody, Mass.: Hendrickson.

Exell, J. S., and T. H. Leale (1892), *Homiletic Commentary on the Book of Genesis*, in *The Preacher's Complete Homiletic Commentary*, New York: Funk & Wagnalls, repr. Baker, 1980.

Felder, C. H. (1989), *Troubling Biblical Waters: Race, Class, and Family*, Maryknoll, NY: Orbis.

——— (1991), *Stony the Road We Trod: African American Biblical Interpretation*, Minneapolis: Fortress.

Fensham, F. C. (1982), *The Books of Ezra and Nehemiah*, NICOT, Grand Rapids: Eerdmans.

Ferguson, E. (1993), *Backgrounds of Early Christianity*, Grand Rapids: Eerdmans.

Ferguson, J. (1969a), 'Classical Contacts with West Africa', in L. A. Thompson and J. Ferguson (eds.), *Africa in Classical Antiquity*, Ibadan, Nigeria: Ibadan University.

——— (1969b), 'Aspects of Early Christianity in North Africa', in L. A. Thompson and J. Ferguson (eds.), *Africa in Classical Antiquity*, Ibadan, Nigeria: Ibadan University.

Fields, B. L. (2001), *Introducing Black Theology: 3 Crucial Questions for the Evangelical Church*, 3 Crucial Questions Series, G. Osborne, ed., Grand Rapids: Baker.

Finegan, J. (1959), *Light From the Ancient Past: the Archaeological Background of Judaism and Christianity*, Princeton: Princeton University.

Floyd, M. H. (2000), *Minor Prophets, Part 2*, FOTL, Grand Rapids: Eerdmans.

Ford, J. M. (1984), *My Enemy is My Guest: Jesus and Violence in Luke*, Maryknoll, NY: Orbis.

Fowler, B. H. (1994), *Love Lyrics of Ancient Egypt*, Chapel Hill, NC: University of North Carolina.

Fox, M. V. (1997), 'Cairo Love Songs', in W. W. Hallo and K. L. Younger (eds.), *The Context of Scripture*, Leiden: E. J. Brill, 1.50.

Fox, N. S. (2000), *In the Service of the King: Officialdom in Ancient Israel and Judah*, Cincinnati: Hebrew Union College.

Freedman, D. N., and B. E. Willoughby (1999), '*ibrî*', *TDOT* X:430–445.

Fretheim, T. E. (1991), *Exodus*, Interpretation, Louisville: John Knox.

—— (1994), 'Genesis', in L. E. Keck (ed.), *The New Interpreter's Bible*, Vol. 1, Nashville: Abingdon.

Friedrich, G. (1964), '*euangelion*', *TDNT* II:707–737.

Gardiner, A. (1961), *Egypt of the Pharaohs: An Introduction*, Oxford: Clarendon.

Gelb, I. J. (1980), *Computer-aided Analysis of Amorite*, Chicago: University of Chicago.

Gelston, A. (1992), 'Universalism in Second Isaiah', *JTS* 43: 377–398.

George, T. (1994), *Galatians*, NAC, Nashville: Broadman.

George, T., and R. Smith (eds.) (2000), *A Mighty Long Journey: Reflections on Racial Reconciliation*, Nashville: Broadman & Holman.

Ghaki, M. (1987), 'The Berbers of the Pre-Roman Period', in A. Khader and D. Soren (eds.), *Carthage: A Mosaic of Ancient Tunisia*, New York: W. W. Norton.

Ginzberg, L. (1956), *Legends of the Bible*, Philadelphia: JPS.

Glazier-McDonald, B. (1987), 'Intermarriage, Divorce, and the *BAT-'ĒL NĒKĀR*: Insights into Mal 2:10–16', *JBL* 106.4: 603–611.

Gnirs, A. M. (2001), 'Military: An Overview', in D. B. Redford (ed.), *The Oxford Encyclopedia of Ancient Egypt*, Oxford: Oxford University, 2:400–406.

Goldingay, J. (2001), *Isaiah*, NIBC, Peabody, Mass.: Hendrickson.

Gordan, A. (2001), 'Foreigners', in D. B. Redford (ed.), *The Oxford Encyclopedia of Ancient Egypt*, Oxford: Oxford University, 1:544–548.

Gottwald, N. K. (1964), *All the Kingdoms of the Earth*, New York: Harper & Row.

Gowan, D. E. (1996), 'Amos', in L. E. Keck (ed.), *The New Interpreter's Bible*, Vol. 7, Nashville: Abingdon.

—— (1998), *Theology of the Prophetic Books*, Louisville: Westminster John Knox.

Grant, M. (1992), *A Social History of Greece and Rome*, New York: Charles Scribner's Sons.

Gray, G. B. (1912), *Numbers*, ICC, Edinburgh: T. & T. Clark.

―――― (1969), 'The Foundation and Extension of the Persian Empire', *CAH*, Vol. 4, 1–25.

Green, J. B. (1997), *The Gospel of Luke*, NICNT, Grand Rapids: Eerdmans.

Greenberg, M. (1961), 'Hab/piru and Hebrews', in B. Mazar (ed.), *The World History of the Jewish People*, Vol. II, *Patriarchs*, Israel: Jewish History Publications.

Greenfield, J. (1967), 'Some Treaty Terminology in the Bible', in *Fourth World Congress of Jewish Studies*, Vol. 1.

Gregoire, H. (1810), *An Enquiry Concerning the Intellectual and Moral Faculties and Literature of Negroes*, repr. College Park, Md.: McGrath, 1967.

Grenz, S. (2000), *Theology for the Community of God*, Grand Rapids and Vancouver: Eerdmans and Regent College.

Grogan, G. W. (1986), 'Isaiah', in F. E. Gaebelein (ed.), *The Expositor's Bible Commentary*, Grand Rapids: Zondervan.

Grudem, W. (1994), *Systematic Theology: An Introduction to Biblical Doctrine*, Leicester and Grand Rapids: Inter-Varsity and Zondervan.

Haak, R. D. (1995), 'Cush in Zephaniah', in S. W. Holloway and L. K. Handy (eds.), *The Pitcher is Broken: Memorial Essays for Gösta W. Ahlström*, JSOTSS 190, Sheffield: Sheffield.

Haenchen, E. (1971), *The Acts of the Apostles: A Commentary*, Oxford: Basil Blackwell.

Hagner, D. A. (1993), *Matthew 1 – 13*, WBC, Dallas: Word.

Hall, H. R. (1969), 'Egypt to the Coming of Alexander', *CAH*, Vol. 6, 137–166.

―――― (1970), 'The Restoration of Egypt', *CAH*, Vol. 3, 289–315.

Hall, J. M. (1997), *Ethnic Identity in Greek Antiquity*, Cambridge: Cambridge University.

Hall, R. G. (1992), 'Circumcision', *ABD* I:1025–1026.

Hallo, W. W. (1960), 'From Qarqar to Carchemish: Assyria and Israel in the Light of New Discoveries', *BA* 23:34–68.

Hamilton, V. P. (1990), *Genesis 1 – 17*, NICOT, Grand Rapids: Eerdmans.

―――― (1995), *Genesis 18 – 50*, NICOT, Grand Rapids: Eerdmans.

Hansen, G. W. (1989), *Abraham in Galatians: Epistolary and Rhetorical Contexts*, JSNTSS 29, Sheffield: Sheffield Academic Press.

―――― (1994a), 'Galatia', in D. W. J. Gill and C. Gempf (eds.), *The Book of Acts in its First Century Setting*, Vol. 2, *The Book of Acts in its Graeco-Roman Setting*, Grand Rapids and Carlisle: Eerdmans and Paternoster.

—— (1994b), *Galatians*, IVPNTC, Downers Grove, Ill.: InterVarsity.

Harper, W. R. (1905), *Amos and Hosea*, ICC, Edinburgh: T. & T. Clark.

Hassan, F. (2000), 'Egypt in the Prehistory of Northeast Africa', in J. M. Sasson (ed.), *Civilizations of the Ancient Near East*, Peabody, Mass.: Hendrickson.

Haycock, B. G. (1972), 'Landmarks in Cushite History', *JEA* 53:230–237.

Hayes, C. (1999), 'Intermarriage and Impurity in Ancient Jewish Sources', *HTR* 92:3–36.

Hayes, W. C. (1973), 'Egypt: Internal Affairs From Tuthmosis I to the Death of Amenophis III', *CAH*, Vol. 2, 313–416.

Hays, J. D. (1996a), 'The Cushites: A Black Nation in Ancient History', *BibSac* 153:270–280.

—— (1996b), 'The Cushites: A Black Nation in the Bible', *BibSac* 153:396–409.

—— (1998), 'From the Land of the Bow: Black Soldiers in the Ancient Near East', *BR* 14:28–33, 50–51.

—— (2000), 'Moses: The Private Man Behind the Public Figure', *BR* 16:16–26, 60–62.

Hays, R. (1983), *The Faith of Jesus Christ: An Investigation of the Narrative Substructure of Galatians 3:1 – 4:11*, SBL Dissertation Series 56, Chico, Cal.: Scholars Press.

Hays, R. B. (1996), *The Moral Vision of the New Testament: Community, Cross, New Creation; A Contemporary Introduction to New Testament Ethics*, New York: Harper San Francisco.

—— (2000), 'The Letter to the Galatians', in L. E. Keck (ed.), *The New Interpreter's Bible*, Vol. 11, Nashville: Abingdon.

Hengel, M. (1980), *Jews, Greeks, and Barbarians*, Philadelphia: Fortress.

—— (1989), *The Zealots: Investigations into the Jewish Freedom Movement in the Period from Herod I until 70 AD*, Edinburgh: T. & T. Clark.

Hess, R. S. (1994), 'The Genealogies of Genesis 1 – 11 and Comparative Literature', in R. S. Hess and D. T. Tsumura (eds.), *I Studied Inscriptions from before the Flood: Ancient Near Eastern, Literary, and Linguistic Approaches to Genesis 1 – 11*, Winona Lake, Ind.: Eisenbrauns.

Hodge, C. T. (2001), 'Afroasiatic', in E. M. Yamauchi (ed.), *Africa and Africans in Antiquity*, East Lansing, Mich.: Michigan State University.

Hoerth, A. J., G. M. Mattingly, and E. M. Yamauchi (1994), *Peoples of the Old Testament World*, Grand Rapids: Baker.

Hoffman, M. A. (1979), *Egypt Before the Pharaohs: The Prehistoric Foundations of Egyptian Civilization*, New York: Alfred A. Knoph.

Hoffmeier, J. K. (1996), *Israel in Egypt*, Oxford: Oxford.

Hoffner, H. A. (1973), 'The Hittites and Hurrians', in D. J. Wiseman (ed.), *Peoples of Old Testament Times*, Oxford: Clarendon.

———— (1994), 'Hittites', in A. J. Hoerth et al. (eds.), *Peoples of the Old Testament World*, Cambridge and Grand Rapids: Lutterworth and Baker.

Holladay, W. L. (1989), *Jeremiah 2*, Hermeneia, Minneapolis: Fortress.

Holter, K. (2000), *Yahweh in Africa*, New York: Peter Lang.

Honor, L. G. (1926), *Sennacherib's Invasion of Palestine: A Critical Source Study*, New York: Columbia University.

Hostetter, E. C. (1992), 'Putiel', *ABD* V:561.

House, P. R. (1998), *Old Testament Theology*, Downers Grove, Ill.: InterVarsity.

Hove, R. (1999), *Equality in Christ? Galatians 3:28 and the Gender Dispute*, Wheaton, Ill.: Crossway.

Howard, M. (1994), 'Philistines', in A. J. Hoerth et al. (eds.), *Peoples of the Old Testament World*, Cambridge and Grand Rapids: Lutterworth and Baker.

Howe, S. (1998), *Afrocentrism: Mythical Pasts and Imagined Homes*, London: Verso.

Huehnergard, J. (1992), 'Languages (Introductory)', *ABD* IV: 155–170.

Hultgren, A. J. (2000), *The Parables of Jesus: A Commentary*, Grand Rapids: Eerdmans.

Irvine, K. (1970), *The Rise of the Colored Races*, New York: Norton.

Isaac, E. (1992), 'Ham (Person)', *ABD* III:31–32.

Isichei, E. (1995), *A History of Christianity in Africa: From Antiquity to the Present*, Grand Rapids: Eerdmans.

James, T. G. H. (1973), 'Egypt: From the Expulsion of the Hyksos to Amenophis I', *CAH*, Vol. II, Part 1.

———— (1988), *Ancient Egypt: The Land and its Legacy*, Austin: University of Austin.

Jameson, S. (1968), 'Chronology of the Campaign of Aelius Gallus and C. Petronius', *JRS* 58:71–84.

Janowski, B. (1983), 'Psalm CVI 28–31 und die Interzession des Pinchas', *VT* 33:237–247.

Janzen, W. (1994), *Old Testament Ethics: A Paradigmatic Approach*, Louisville: Westminster John Knox.

Jeffers, J. S. (1999), *The Greco-Roman World of the New Testament Era*, Downers Grove, Ill.: InterVarsity.

Jenni, E. (1997), '*hôy*', in E. Jenni and C. Westermann (eds.), *Theological Lexicon of the Old Testament*, Peabody, Mass.: Hendrickson, 1:357–358.

Jeremias, J. (1958), *Jesus' Promise to the Nations*, Studies in Biblical Theology 24, Naperville, Ill.: Alec R. Allenson.

———— (1969), *Jerusalem in the Time of Jesus: An Investigation into Economic and Social Conditions during the New Testament Period*, Philadelphia: Fortress.

Johnson, L. T. (1991), *The Gospel of Luke*, Sacra Pagina, Collegeville, Minn.: Liturgical Press.

———— (1992), *The Acts of the Apostles*, Sacra Pagina, Collegeville, Minn.: Liturgical Press.

Johnston, G. H. (1997), '*sārîs*', *NIDOTTE* 3:288–295.

Jónsson, G. A. (1988), *The Image of God: Genesis 1:26–28 in a Century of Old Testament Research*, Coniectanea Biblica, Old Testament Series 26, Lund: Almquist & Wiksell.

Kaiser, W. C. (2000), *Mission in the Old Testament: Israel as a Light to the Nations*, Grand Rapids: Baker.

Keener, C. S. (1999), *A Commentary on the Gospel of Matthew*, Grand Rapids: Eerdmans.

———— (2000), *Revelation*, NIVAC, Grand Rapids: Zondervan.

Keener, C. S., and G. Usry (1997), *Defending Black Faith: Answers to Tough Questions about African-American Christianity*, Downers Grove, Ill.: InterVarsity.

Keesmaat, S. C. (2000), 'Strange Neighbors and Risky Care', in R. N. Longenecker (ed.), *The Challenge of Jesus' Parables*, Grand Rapids: Eerdmans.

Keil, C. F., and F. Delitzsch (1986 reprint), *Commentary on the Old Testament*, 10 volumes, Grand Rapids: Eerdmans.

Kirkpatrick, A. A. (1890), *The Second Book of Samuel*, CB, Cambridge: Cambridge University.

Kistemaker, S. J. (1990), *Exposition of the Acts of the Apostles*, BNTC, Grand Rapids: Baker.

Kitchen, K. A. (1973a), 'Philistines', in D. J. Wiseman (ed.), *Peoples of Old Testament Times*, Oxford: Clarendon.

———— (1973b), *The Third Intermediate Period in Egypt (1100–650 BC)*, Warminster, England: Aris & Phillips.

———— (2001), 'Sheshonq I', in D. B. Redford (ed.), *The Oxford Encyclopedia of Ancient Egypt*, Oxford: Oxford University, 3:280–281.

Klein, R. W. (1999), 'The Books of Ezra and Nehemiah', in L. E. Keck (ed.), *The New Interpreter's Bible*, Vol. 3, Nashville: Abingdon.

Knauf, E. A. (1992), 'Zerah', *ABD* VI:1080–1081.

Knoppers, G. N. (1994), 'Sex, Religion, and Politics: The Deuteronomist on Intermarriage', *HAR* 14:121–141.

Köstenberger, A. J. (1998), *The Missions of Jesus and the Disciples according to the Fourth Gospel*, Grand Rapids: Eerdmans.

Köstenberger, A. J., and P. T. O'Brien (2001), *Salvation to the Ends of the Earth: A Biblical Theology of Mission*, NSBT, Downers Grove, Ill. and Leicester: InterVarsity and Apollos.

Kraus, H.-J. (1989), *Psalms 60 – 150*, Minneapolis: Augsburg.

Kwapong, A. A. (1969), 'Citizenship and Democracy in Fourth-century Cyrene', in L. A. Thompson and J. Ferguson (eds.), *Africa in Classical Antiquity*, Ibadan, Nigeria: Ibadan University.

LaGrand, J. (1999), *The Earliest Christian Mission to 'All Nations' in the Light of Matthew's Gospel*, Grand Rapids: Eerdmans.

Lang, B. (1998), '*nkr*', *TDOT* IX:423–431.

Larkin, W. J. (1995), *Acts*, IVPNTC, Downers Grove, Ill. and Leicester, England: InterVarsity.

Leahy, A. (2000), 'Ethnic Diversity in Ancient Egypt', in J. M. Sasson (ed.), *Civilizations of the Ancient Near East*, Peabody, Mass.: Hendrickson [orig. pub. 1995, Macmillan].

———— (2001), 'Libya', in D. B. Redford (ed.), *The Oxford Encyclopedia of Ancient Egypt*, Oxford: Oxford University, 2:290–293.

Lemaire, A. (1995), 'Name of Israel's Last King Surfaces in a Private Collection', *BAR* 21:49–52.

Lemche, N. P. (1991), *The Canaanites and Their Land: The Tradition of the Canaanites*, JSOTSS 110, Sheffield: Sheffield.

———— (1998), *The Israelites in History and Tradition*, London and Louisville: SPCK and Westminster.

Leon, H. J. (1960), *The Jews of Ancient Rome*, Peabody, Mass.: Hendrickson.

Levine, B. (1993), *Numbers 1 – 20*, AB 4, New York: Doubleday.

Levine, L. I. (1992), 'Jewish War (66–73 CE)', *ABD* III:839–845.

Levinskaya, I. (1996), *The Book of Acts in its Diaspora Setting*, Vol. 5 in B. W. Winter (ed.), *The Book of Acts in its First Century Setting*, Grand Rapids and Carlisle: Eerdmans and Paternoster.

Lewis, B. (1990), *Race and Slavery in the Middle East*, New York: Oxford University.

Lewis, J. (1968), *A Study of the Interpretation of Noah and the Flood in Jewish and Christian Literature*, Leiden: E. J. Brill.

Limburg, J. (1988), *Hosea–Micah*, Interpretation, Atlanta: John Knox.

Lincoln, A. T. (1990), *Ephesians*, WBC, Dallas: Word.

—— (2000), 'The Letter to the Colossians', in L. E. Keck (ed.), *The New Interpreter's Bible*, Vol. 11, Nashville: Abingdon.

Longenecker, R. N. (1990), *Galatians*, WBC, Dallas: Word.

Macqueen, J. G. (2000), 'The History of Anatolia and of the Hittite Empire: An Overview', in J. M. Sasson (ed.), *Civilizations of the Ancient Near East*, Peabody, Mass.: Hendrickson.

Marshall, I. H. (1978), *The Gospel of Luke: A Commentary on the Greek Text*, NIGTC, Grand Rapids: Eerdmans.

Martin, R. P. (1989), *Reconciliation: A Study of Paul's Theology*, Grand Rapids: Zondervan.

Martin-Achard, R. (1997), '*gûr*', in E. Jenni and C. Westermann (eds.), *Theological Lexicon of the Old Testament*, Peabody, Mass.: Hendrickson.

Maston, T. B. (1959), *The Bible and Race*, Nashville: Broadman.

Matthews, K. A. (1996), *Genesis 1 – 11:26*, NAC, Nashville: Broadman.

Matthews, V. H. (1991), *Manners and Customs*, Peabody, Mass.: Hendrickson.

Mauch, T. M. (1962), 'Phinehas', *IDB* 3:799–780.

Mays, J. L. (1969), *Amos*, OTL, Philadelphia: Westminster.

—— (1994), *Psalms*, Interpretation, Louisville: John Knox.

McCann, J. C. (1996), 'Psalms', in L. E. Keck (ed), *The New Interpreter's Bible*, Vol. 4, Nashville: Abingdon.

McCarter, P. K. (1984), *II Samuel*, AB, Garden City, NY: Doubleday.

McComiskey, T. E. (1985), 'Amos', in F. E. Gaebelein (ed.), *The Expositor's Bible Commentary*, Grand Rapids: Zondervan.

McGrath, A. E. (1997), *Christian Theology: An Introduction*, Oxford: Blackwell.

McKenzie, S. L. (1997), *All God's Children: A Biblical Critique of Racism*, Louisville: Westminster John Knox.

McKissic, W. D. (1990), *Beyond Roots: In Search of Blacks in the Bible*, Wenonah, NJ: Renaissance Publications.

McKnight, S. (1995), *Galatians*, NIVAC, Grand Rapids: Zondervan.

McNutt, P. (1999), *Reconstructing the Society of Ancient Israel*, Louisville: Westminster John Knox.

Melugin, R. F. (1997), 'Israel and the Nations in Isaiah 40 – 55', in H. T. C. Sun and K. L. Eades (eds.), *Problems in Biblical Theology*, Grand Rapids: Eerdmans.

Mendels, D. (1992), *The Rise and Fall of Jewish Nationalism: Jewish and Christian Ethnicity in Ancient Palestine*, Grand Rapids: Eerdmans.

Mendenhall, G. (1992), 'Amorites', *ABD* I:199–202.

Mitchell, S. (1993), *Anatolia: Land, Men, and Gods in Asia Minor*, Vol. 1, *The Celts and the Impact of Roman Rule*, Oxford: Clarendon.

Moberg, D. O. (1972), *The Great Reversal: Evangelism versus Social Concern*, Philadelphia: J. B. Lippincott.

Montet, P. (1968), *Egypt and the Bible*, Philadelphia: Fortress.

Moore, T. S. (1997), 'To the Ends of the Earth: The Geographic and Ethnic Universalism of Acts 1:8 in Light of Isaianic Influence on Luke', *JETS* 40:389–399.

Moran, W. L. (1992), *The Amarna Letters*, Baltimore: Johns Hopkins.

Morris, G. (1994), 'Convention and Character in the Joseph Narrative', *Proceedings EGL & MWBS* 14:69–85.

Morris, L. (1971), *The Gospel According to John*, NICOT, Grand Rapids: Eerdmans.

Motyer, J. A. (1993), *The Prophecy of Isaiah*, Downers Grove, Ill.: InterVarsity.

Mounce, R. H. (1998), *The Book of Revelation*, NICNT, Grand Rapids: Eerdmans.

Müller, W. W. (1992), 'Seba', *ABD* V:1064.

Mussner, F. (1988), *Der Galaterbrief*, HTKNT, Freiburg: Herder.

Myers, J. M. (1965), *II Chronicles*, AB, Garden City, NJ: Doubleday.

Na'aman, N. (1986), 'Habiru and Hebrews: The Transfer of a Social Term to the Literary Sphere', *JNES* 45:271–288.

——— (1990), 'The Historical Background to the Conquest of Samaria (720 BC)', *Bib* 71:206–225.

——— (1992), 'Amarna Letters', *ABD* I:174–181.

Nolland, J. (1993), *Luke 9:21 – 18:34*, WBC, Dallas: Word.

North, C. R. (1964), *The Second Isaiah: Introduction, Translation and Commentary to Chapters XL – LV*, Oxford: Clarendon.

Noth, M. (1968), *Numbers: A Commentary*, OTL, Philadelphia: Westminster.

O'Brien, P. T. (1982), *Colossians, Philemon*, WBC, Waco: Word.

——— (1999), *The Letter to the Ephesians*, PNTC, Grand Rapids and Leicester: Eerdmans and Apollos.

O'Connor, D. (1993), *Ancient Nubia: Egypt's Rival in Africa*, Philadelphia: University of Pennsylvania.

Okholm, D. L. (ed.) (1997), *The Gospel in Black and White: Theological Resources for Racial Reconciliation*, Downers Grove, Ill.: InterVarsity.

Oppenheim, A. L. (1977), *Ancient Mesopotamia: Portrait of a Dead Civilization*, Chicago: University of Chicago.

Oswalt, J. N. (1986), *The Book of Isaiah Chapters 1 – 39*, NICOT, Grand Rapids: Eerdmans.

——— (1991), 'The Mission of Israel to the Nations', in W. V. Crockett and J. G. Sigonountos (eds.), *Through No Fault of Their Own: The Fate of Those Who Have Never Heard*, Grand Rapids: Baker.

——— (1998), *The Book of Isaiah Chapters 40 – 66*, NICOT, Grand Rapids: Eerdmans.

Pate, C. M. (2000), *The Reverse of the Curse: Paul, Wisdom, and the Law*, WUNT 114, Tübingen: Mohr Siebeck.

Patterson, R. D. (1980), 'saris', in R. Laird Harris et al., *Theological Wordbook of the Old Testament*, Chicago: Moody Press.

——— (1991), *Nahum, Habakkuk, and Zephaniah*, WEC, Chicago: Moody.

Pernigotti, S. (1997), 'Priest', in S. Donadoni (ed.), *The Egyptians*, Chicago: University of Chicago.

Peterson, E. H. (1999), *First and Second Samuel*, WstBC, Louisville: Westminster John Knox.

Picard, G. C., and C. Picard (1968), *The Life and Death of Carthage*, New York: Taplinger.

Pink, A. W. (1922), *Gleanings in Genesis*, Chicago: Moody, repr. 1950.

Polhill, J. B. (1992), *Acts*, NAC, Nashville: Broadman.

Porten, B., and A. Yardeni (1993), 'Literature, Accounts, Lists', in *Textbook of Aramaic Documents from Ancient Egypt*, Vol. III, Jerusalem: Hebrew University.

Potter, R. C. (1997), 'Race, Theological Discourse and the Continuing American Dilemma', in D. L. Okholm (ed.), *The Gospel in Black and White: Theological Resources for Racial Reconciliation*, Downers Grove, Ill.: InterVarsity.

Power, K. (1999), 'Family, Relatives', in A. D. Fitzgerald (ed.), *Augustine Through the Ages: An Encyclopedia*, Grand Rapids: Eerdmans.

Priest, J. (1853), *Bible Defense of Slavery*, Glasgow, Ky.: W. S. Brown.

Pritchard, J. B. (ed.) (1969), *Ancient Near Eastern Texts*, Princeton, NJ: Princeton University.

Propp, W. H. C. (1999), *Exodus 1 – 18*, AB, New York: Doubleday.

Quirke, S., and J. Spencer (1992), *The British Museum Book of Ancient Egypt*, London: British Museum.

Rahlfs, A. (1979), *Septuaginta*, Stuttgart: Deutsche Bibelgesellschaft.

Reade, J. E. (1976), 'Sargon's Campaigns of 720, 716, and 715 BC: Evidence from the Sculptures', *JNES* 35:99–102.

——— (1983), *Assyrian Sculpture*, London: British Museum.

Redford, D. B. (1992), *Egypt, Canaan, and Israel in Ancient Times*, Princeton, NJ: Princeton University.

Reisner, G. A. (1922), 'The Pyramids of Meroë and the Candaces of Ethiopia', *Sudan Notes and Records* 5:173–196.

——— (1923), 'The Meroitic Kingdom of Ethiopia: A Chronological Outline', *JEA* 9:67–73.

Rhoads, D. M. (1976), *Israel in Revolution: 6–74 CE*, Philadelphia: Fortress.

Rice, G. (1975), 'Two Black Contemporaries of Jeremiah', *JRT* 32:95–109.

——— (1978), 'Was Amos a Racist?' *JRT* 35:35–44.

——— (1979), 'The African Roots of the Prophet Zephaniah', *JRT* 36:21–31.

Riches, J. (1996), 'Cultural Bias in Biblical Scholarship', in M. G. Brett (ed.), *Ethnicity and the Bible*, Leiden: E. J. Brill.

Ricks, S. D. (1992), 'Sheba, Queen of', *ABD* V:1170–1171.

Riesner, R. (1998), *Paul's Early Period: Chronology, Mission Strategy, Theology*, Grand Rapids: Eerdmans.

Ritner, R. R. (2001), 'Magic', in D. B. Redford (ed.), *The Oxford Encyclopedia of Ancient Egypt*, Oxford: Oxford University, 2:321–336.

Rivers, R. (1889), Untitled article in *Central Methodist*, 19 January.

Robbins, G. (1993), *Women in Ancient Egypt*, Cambridge, Mass.: Harvard University.

Roberts, J. J. M. (1991), *Nahum, Habakkuk, and Zephaniah*, OTL, Louisville: Westminster John Knox.

Robertson, O. P. (1990), *The Books of Nahum, Habakkuk, and Zephaniah*, NICOT, Grand Rapids: Eerdmans.

——— (1998), 'Current Critical Questions Concerning the "Curse of Ham" (Gen 9:20–27)', *JETS* 41:177–188.

Rogerson, J. W. (1989), 'Anthropology and the Old Testament', in R. E. Clements (ed.), *The World of Ancient Israel: Sociological, Anthropological, and Political Perspectives*, Cambridge: Cambridge University.

Ross, A. P. (1988), *Creation and Blessing*, Grand Rapids: Baker.

——— (1991), 'Proverbs', in F. E. Gaebelein (ed.), *Expositor's Bible Commentary*, Grand Rapids: Zondervan.

Runnalls, D. (1983), 'Moses' Egyptian Campaign', *JSJPHRP* 14:135–156.

Russmann, E. R. (2001), 'Egypt and the Kushites: Dynasty XXV', in E. M. Yamauchi (ed.), *Africa and Africans in Antiquity*, East Lansing, Mich.: Michigan State University.

Sailhamer, J. (1990), 'Genesis', in F. E. Gaebelein (ed.), *The Expositor's Bible Commentary*, Grand Rapids: Zondervan.

Sarna, N. M. (1989), *Genesis*, The JPS Commentary, Philadelphia/ Jerusalem: JPS.

Schneider, J. (1964), '*eunouchos*', *TDNT* II:765–768.

Schreiner, T. R. (1993), *The Law and its Fulfillment: A Pauline Theology of the Law*, Grand Rapids: Baker.

Schulte, H. (1988), 'Baruch und Ebedmelech – Persönliche Heilsorakel im Jeremiabuche', *BZ* 32:257–265.

Schultz, R. (1997), '*špṭ*', *NIDOTTE* 4:213–220.

Scott, B. B. (1989), *Hear Then the Parable: A Commentary on the Parables of Jesus*, Minneapolis: Fortress.

Scott, J. M. (1994), 'Luke's Geographical Horizon', in D. W. J. Gill and C. Gempf (eds.), *The Book of Acts in its First Century Setting*, Vol. 2, *The Book of Acts in its Graeco-Roman Setting*, Grand Rapids and Carlisle: Eerdmans and Paternoster.

——— (1995), *Paul and the Nations: The Old Testament and Jewish Background of Paul's Mission to the Nations with Special Reference to the Destination of Galatians*, WUNT 84, Tübingen: J. C. B. Mohr (Paul Siebeck).

Seitz, C. R. (1983), 'The Prophet Moses and the Canonical Shape of Jeremiah', *ZAW* 101:3–27.

——— (1993), *Isaiah 1 – 39*, Interpretation, Louisville: John Knox.

Sharp, D. R. (2002), *No Partiality: The Idolatry of Race and the New Humanity*, Downers Grove, Ill.: InterVarsity.

Shinnie, P. L. (1967), *Meroe: A Civilization of Sudan*, New York: F. A. Praeger.

Simons, J. (1994), 'The "Table of Nations" (Genesis 10): Its General Structure and Meaning', in R. S. Hess and D. T. Tsumura (eds.), *I Studied Inscriptions from before the Flood: Ancient Near Eastern, Literary, and Linguistic Approaches to Genesis 1 – 11*, Winona Lake, Ind.: Eisenbrauns.

Smallwood, E. M. (1969), 'The Jews in Egypt and Cyrenaica during the Ptolemaic and Roman periods', in L. A. Thompson and J. Ferguson (eds.), *Africa in Classical Antiquity*, Ibadan, Nigeria: Ibadan University.

Smith, H. P. (1899), *The Books of Samuel*, ICC, Edinburgh: T. & T. Clark.

Smith, H. S. (1972), *In His Image, But . . . : Racism in Southern Religion, 1780–1910*, Durham, NC: Duke University.

Smith, J. M. P. (1911), *Micah, Zephaniah, and Nahum*, ICC, Edinburgh: T. & T. Clark.

Smith, R. L. (1972), 'Amos', BBC, Nashville: Broadman.

——— (1984), *Micah–Malachi*, WBC, Waco: Word.

Snodgrass, K. (1996), *Ephesians*, NIVAC, Grand Rapids: Zondervan.

Snowden, F. M. (1970), *Blacks in Antiquity: Ethiopians in the Greco-Roman Experience*, Cambridge, Mass.: Harvard University.

——— (1983), *Before Color Prejudice: The Ancient View of Blacks*, Cambridge, Mass.: Harvard University.

——— (2001), 'Attitudes towards Blacks in the Greek and Roman World: Misinterpretations of the Evidence', in E. Yamauchi (ed.), *Africa and Africans in Antiquity*, East Lansing, Mich.: Michigan State University.

Spalinger, A. (1973), 'The Year 712 BC and its Implications for Egyptian History', *JARCE* 10:95–101.

Spencer, J. R. (1992), 'Phinehas', *ABD* V:346–347.

Stein, R. H. (1992), *Luke*, NAC, Nashville: Broadman.

Stern, E. (1971), 'Phinehas', *EncJud* 13:466.

Stott, J. (1979), *The Message of the Ephesians: God's New Society*, BST, Leicester and Downers Grove, Ill.: InterVarsity.

——— (1990), *The Spirit, the Church, and the World: The Message of Acts*, Downers Grove, Ill.: InterVarsity.

——— (1999), *Human Rights and Human Wrongs: Major Issues for a New Century*, Grand Rapids: Baker.

Strouhal, E. (1992), *Life of the Ancient Egyptians*, Norman, Okla.: University of Oklahoma.

Stulman, L. (1995), 'Insiders and Outsiders in the Book of Jeremiah: Shifts in Symbolic Arrangements', *JSOT* 66:65–85.

Sweeney, M. A. (1996), *Isaiah 1 – 39*, FOTL, Grand Rapids: Eerdmans.

Swete, H. B. (1977), *Commentary on Revelation*, Grand Rapids: Kregel.

Tallquist, K. (1914), 'Kusaia'; *Assyrian Personal Names*, Acta Societatis Scientiarum Fennicae XLIII, No. 1, Helsingfors: n.p.

Tannehill, R. C. (1986), *The Narrative Unity of Luke-Acts*, Vol. 1, *The Gospel According to Luke*, Philadelphia: Fortress.

—— (1990), *The Narrative Unity of Luke-Acts*, Vol. 2, *The Acts of the Apostles*, Minneapolis: Fortress.

Tate, M. E. (1990), *Psalms 51 – 100*, WBC, Dallas: Word.

Taylor, J. H. (1991), *Egypt and Nubia*, London: British Museum.

Thompson, J. A. (1980), *The Book of Jeremiah*, NICOT, Grand Rapids: Eerdmans.

Thompson, L. A. (1969), 'Eastern Africa and the Graeco-Roman World', in L. A. Thompson and J. Ferguson (eds.), *Africa in Classical Antiquity*, Ibadan, Nigeria: Ibadan University.

—— (1989), *Romans and Blacks*, Norman, Okla.: University of Oklahoma.

Throntveit, M. A. (1992), *Ezra-Nehemiah*, Interpretation, Louisville: John Knox.

Török, L. (1997), *The Kingdom of Kush: Handbook of the Napatan–Meroitic Civilization*, Leiden: E. J. Brill.

Trigger, B. (1965), *History and Settlement in Lower Nubia*, New Haven: Yale.

—— (1976), *Nubia Under the Pharaohs*, Boulder, Co.: Westview.

—— (1978), 'Nubian, Negro, Black, or Nilotic?' in S. Wenig (ed.), *Africa in Antiquity: The Arts of Ancient Nubia and the Sudan*, Vol. 1, *The Essays*, Brooklyn: The Brooklyn Museum.

Tuell, S. S. (2001), *First and Second Chronicles*, Interpretation, Louisville: John Knox.

Ullendorf, E. (1974), 'The Queen of Sheba in Ethiopian Tradition', in J. B. Pritchard (ed.), *Solomon and Sheba*, London: Phaidon.

Usry, G., and C. S. Keener (1996), *Black Man's Religion: Can Christianity be Afrocentric?* Downers Grove, Ill.: InterVarsity.

Van Beek, G. W. (1974), 'The Land of Sheba', in J. B. Pritchard (ed.), *Solomon and Sheba*, London: Phaidon.

Van Winkle, D. W. (1985), 'The Relationship of the Nations to Yahweh and to Israel in Isaiah XL – LV', *VT* 35:446–458.

VanGemeren, W. A. (1991), 'Psalms', in F. E. Gaebelein (ed.), *The Expositor's Bible Commentary*, Grand Rapids: Zondervan.

Von Rad, G. (1961), *Genesis*, OTL, Philadelphia: Westminster.

—— (1966), *Deuteronomy*, OTL, Philadelphia: Westminster.

Von Soden, W. (1994), *The Ancient Orient: An Introduction to the Study of the Ancient Near East*, Grand Rapids: Eerdmans.

Waltke, B. K. (2001), *Genesis*, Grand Rapids: Zondervan.

Waltke, B. K., and M. O'Connor (1990), *An Introduction to Biblical Hebrew*, Winona Lake, Ind.: Eisenbrauns.

Walton, J. H., V. H. Matthews, and M. W. Chavalas (2000), *The IVP Bible Background Commentary: Old Testament*, Downers Grove, Ill.: InterVarsity.

Ward, J. M. (1962), 'Jehudi', *IDB* 2:819.

Watts, J. D. W. (1985), *Isaiah 1 – 33*, WBC, Waco: Word.

—— (1987), *Isaiah 34 – 66*, WBC, Waco: Word.

Welsby, D. A. (1998), *The Kingdom of Kush*, Princeton, NJ: Markus Weiner.

Wenham, G. J. (1987), *Genesis 1 – 15*, WBC, Waco: Word.

—— (1994), *Genesis 16 – 50*, WBC, Waco: Word.

—— (2000), *Story as Torah*, Edinburgh: T. & T. Clark.

Wenig, S. (1969), *The Woman in Egyptian Art*, Leipzig: Leipzig.

Westendorf, W. (1968), *Painting, Sculpture, and Architecture of Ancient Egypt*, New York: H. N. Abrams.

Westermann, C. (1969), *Isaiah 40 – 66*, OTL, Philadelphia: Westminster.

—— (1984), *Genesis 1 – 11: A Commentary*, Minneapolis: Augsburg.

—— (1985), *Genesis 12 – 36: A Commentary*, Minneapolis: Augsburg.

—— (1986), *Genesis 37 – 50: A Commentary*, Minneapolis: Augsburg.

—— (1991), *Prophetic Oracles of Salvation in the Old Testament*, Louisville: Westminster John Knox.

Wevers, J. W. (1993), *Notes on the Greek Text of Genesis*, SBLSCS 35, Atlanta: Scholars Press.

Whiston, W. (trans.) (1960), *Josephus: Complete Works*, Grand Rapids: Kregel.

White, D. (2001), 'An Archaeological Survey of the Cyrenaican and Marmarican Regions of Northeast Africa', in E. Yamauchi (ed.), *Africa and Africans in Antiquity*, East Lansing, Mich.: Michigan State University.

Whittaker, C. R. (1994), *Frontiers of the Roman Empire: A Social and Economic Study*, Baltimore: Johns Hopkins University.

Wilfong, T. (2001), 'Marriage and Divorce', in D. Redford (ed.), *The Oxford Encyclopedia of Ancient Egypt*, Oxford: Oxford University.

Williams, B. (1992), 'Egypt, History (Neolithic)', *ABD* 2:331–342.

Williams, R. J. (1973), 'The Egyptians', in D. J. Wiseman (ed.), *Peoples of Old Testament Times*, Oxford: Clarendon.

Williamson, H. G. M. (1985), *Ezra, Nehemiah*, WBC, Waco: Word.

—— (1992), 'Samaritans', in J. B. Green et al. (eds.), *Dictionary of Jesus and the Gospels*, Downers Grove, Ill.: InterVarsity.

Wilson, J. A. (1951), *The Culture of Ancient Egypt*, Chicago: University of Chicago.

Wilson, J. V. K. (1972), *The Nimrud Wine Lists*, London: British School of Archaeology in Iraq.

Wilson, R. R. (1992), 'Genealogy, Genealogies', *ABD* 2:929–932.

—— (1994), 'The Old Testament Genealogies in Recent Research', in R. S. Hess and D. T. Tsumura (eds.), *I Studied Inscriptions from before the Flood: Ancient Near Eastern, Literary, and Linguistic Approaches to Genesis 1 – 11*, Winona Lake, Ind.: Eisenbrauns.

Wilson, S. (1973), *The Gentiles and the Gentile Mission in Luke-Acts*, Cambridge: Cambridge University.

Wiseman, D. J. (ed.) (1973), *Peoples of Old Testament Times*, Oxford: Clarendon.

Witherington, B. (1994), *Jesus the Sage: The Pilgrimage of Wisdom*, Minneapolis: Fortress.

—— (1995), *John's Wisdom: A Commentary on the Fourth Gospel*, Louisville: Westminster John Knox.

—— (1998a), *The Acts of the Apostles: A Socio-Rhetorical Commentary*, Grand Rapids and Carlisle: Eerdmans and Paternoster.

—— (1998b), *Grace in Galatia: A Commentary on Paul's Letter to the Galatians*, Grand Rapids: Eerdmans.

Wolf, H. M. (1985), *Interpreting Isaiah*, Grand Rapids: Zondervan.

Woodward, K. L. (2001), 'The Changing Face of the Church', *Newsweek*, 6 April.

Worth, R. H. (1999a), *The Seven Cities of the Apocalypse and Greco-Asian Culture*, New York: Paulist.

—— (1999b), *The Seven Cities of the Apocalypse and Roman Culture*, New York: Paulist.

Wright, N. T. (1986), *Colossians and Philemon*, TNTC, Leicester: Inter-Varsity.

Yamauchi, E. (1992), 'The Archaeology of Biblical Africa: Cyrene in Libya', *Archaeology in the Biblical World* 2:6–18.

—— (2001a), 'The Romans and Meroe in Nubia', in S. Matteo (ed.), *ItaliAfrica: Bridging Continents and Cultures*, Stony Brook, New York: Forum Italicum.

——— (ed.) (2001b), *Africa and Africans in Antiquity*, East Lansing, Mich.: Michigan State University.

——— (forthcoming), *Africa and the Bible*, Grand Rapids: Baker.

Young, B. H. (1998), *The Parables: Jewish Tradition and Christian Interpretation*, Peabody, Mass.: Hendrickson.

Yurco, F. J. (2001), 'Egypt and Nubia: Old, Middle, and New Kingdom Eras', in E. M. Yamauchi (ed.), *Africa and Africans in Antiquity*, East Lansing, Mich.: Michigan State University.

Zevit, Z. (1969), 'The Use of *ʿbd* as a Diplomatic Term in Jeremiah', *JBL* 88:74–77.

Index of modern authors

Index of Scripture references

INDEX OF SCRIPTURE REFERENCES

INDEX OF SCRIPTURE REFERENCES

Index of ancient sources